RUNNING RISKS

Angella Issajenko

as told to
Martin O'Malley and Karen O'Reilly

Macmillan of Canada
A Division of Canada Publishing Corporation
Toronto, Ontario, Canada

Canadian Cataloguing in Publication Data

Issajenko, Angella, date.
Running risks

ISBN 0-7715-9120-9

1. Issajenko, Angella, 1958- . 2. Runners (Sports) – Canada – Biography. I. O'Malley, Martin. II. O'Reilly, Karen, 1952- . III. Title.

GV1061.15.177A3 1990 796.42'092 C90-094453-6

1 2 3 4 5 FP 94 93 92 91 90

Cover design by Don Fernley

Front cover photo by Claus Andersen, Allsport
Back cover photo courtesy of CanaPress
Authors' photo by Linda Kooluris Dobbs

Macmillan of Canada
A Division of Canada Publishing Corporation
Toronto, Ontario, Canada

Printed in Canada

Contents

Run slowly, slowly, horses of the night:
The stars move still, time runs, the clock will strike,
The Devil will come, and Faustus must be damned.
– Christopher Marlowe

1
Time Bomb

Monday, March 13, 1989
It was still dark when I got up at five o'clock in the morning. The house was quiet. My husband, Tony, was asleep in another room. Sasha, my three-year-old daughter, who had taken to sleeping with me, barely stirred when I climbed out of bed. I stood in the dark for a while, looking down at Sasha's tiny face, then I looked out the window at the bare black branches of the maple trees against the streetlights and a cold, gray sky.

I felt strong, that old adrenaline surge. It's a powerful feeling; I was aware of the muscles in my legs, my back, my arms. When I sat at the antique makeup table, I traced the lace edge of my nightgown in the oval mirror. My fingers were cold.

In all the years I had spent traveling through Europe and Asia and South America and North America for international track and field events, I had never fussed as much over the way I looked as I did that morning I first appeared at the Dubin Inquiry in Toronto. It was headed by Mr. Justice Charles Leonard Dubin and was officially titled the Commission of Inquiry into The Use of Drugs and Banned Practices Intended to Increase Athletic Performance. And it was happening because Ben Johnson got caught at the 1988 Olympic Games in Seoul, South Korea.

Good old Ben — BJ we called him. He had won the gold medal. He had set another world record, 9.79 seconds in the men's 100-metre race. He had beaten Carl Lewis, the U.S. sprinter. That made Ben the fastest man alive. He had the world at his feet. A newspaper headline in the Toronto *Sun* in September had said it all: "Ben Did

It His Way." Then he got caught. Found out by pee in a bottle. Ben was disqualified, stripped of his gold medal, disgraced. The newspaper headlines changed to "Canada's Shame" and "Johnson Loses It All." The inquiry was called later that fall.

I became involved because Ben and I were teammates; we belonged to the Mazda Optimist Track and Field Club, and we were the elite of Canadian amateur athletes. We had trained together under the same coach, Charlie Francis, since I joined the club in January 1978, when it was known as the Scarborough Optimist Track and Field Club. Over the years, Charlie and I had become friends – best friends.

My claim to fame, after nearly ten years of hard work, was that I was a six-time world record holder in the women's indoor 60-metres; I held the current world record in the women's indoor 50-metres; I was ranked fourth in the world in the 100-metres. I had broken fifty Canadian records; I was Canadian Champion twenty-four times; I was twice named female athlete of the year, and I had been appointed to the Order of Canada.

When Charlie Francis said that he suspected sabotage in Seoul, that someone had messed with Ben's test, I believed him. How could I not? I'm not saying I didn't know Ben had been taking anabolic steroids. I certainly did know – I had shot the stuff into his bottom many times. Steroids have to be injected in the gluteus muscles, the "glutes" – and it's not something you do to yourself. The Mazda athletes who used steroids helped one another, though Ben never did it for anyone else. Maybe he didn't like handling needles.

When Charlie said he thought someone might have put something in Ben's beer before his test, or someone might have sunk steroids into Ben's skin through massage before the test, I knew it could be true. There are ointments so strong, you can dab them on your skin and taste them on your tongue within seconds. Members of our team had been taking anabolic steroids and other drugs for years. We knew how long they took to clear out of the system, so we knew when to stop taking them before we had to attend meets and submit to doping tests. I couldn't understand how Ben had blown it so badly. He knew about these clearance times as well as any of us.

To me, in the aftermath of Seoul, solid proof that sabotage was behind Ben's fall from glory lay in the simple fact that he had been caught for a drug that he wasn't taking. Ben's urine test showed positive for the anabolic steroid stanozolol. The team physician, Dr. Jamie Astaphan, had had us on a doping program since the spring of 1986 that included various ratios of human growth hormone, vitamin B-12, diuretics, and an anabolic steroid he called estragol that he said he got from an East German athlete.

As far as we knew, none of us had been on stanozolol since at least early 1986. It was impossible to believe that it could have showed up in Ben's sample.

I backed up Charlie, and I backed up Ben: it had to be sabotage. And then, one night in early October 1988, after Seoul, I saw Ben on television. It looked as though he was casting around, looking for someone to blame. I knew he'd been under a great deal of pressure from the media. He'd been hounded. He looked frightened. But I couldn't believe my ears when he denied ever taking drugs, when he implied that Charlie and Dr. Astaphan had been slipping steroids into him without his knowledge. Ben said he'd "never knowingly" taken drugs.

Never knowingly? I remember how Ben would joke – he was often a very funny guy – about how these steroids enhanced his sex life. All the guys knew that with steroids they could get, and maintain, such heroic erections that they could satisfy a harem.

After the debacle in Seoul, Ben kept being portrayed as naive, even retarded, but the fact was that when he was at his peak he virtually ran the track and field team himself. He could be pushy, obnoxious, and unbelievably arrogant. At airports around the world, I recall he came to expect flights would be held just for him, as if he were Mick Jagger. Just before Seoul, he had closed another promotion deal for himself, this one worth $250,000. When Charlie suggested that a portion of the earnings at one of our races – $300 each – should go to junior members of the team, Ben's negotiating position was, "Fuck 'em."

When Ben got caught in Seoul, I wondered if his arrogance had managed finally to convince him that he was invincible, that they wouldn't dare touch the fastest man on the planet.

We kept hearing rumors that prominent U.S. track stars were failing tests but that the powers-that-be wouldn't do anything about it. Ben considered himself better than the U.S. stars, and he was, so he must have thought he was above the rules, too. So it hit me, when he said "never knowingly." My husband and I watched all this on television in our living room in Toronto. We looked at each other, blinking. We were dumbfounded.

And then I blew.

My rage at Ben's insinuation may have been unreasonable, but I thought if anybody had reason to hang Charlie out to dry, it sure as hell wasn't Ben. Ben was *so* poor when he started training back in 1978. I remember him and his family at the beginning. They all lived in this little flat until his mother was able to get into an Ontario government housing project. He was so poor that he would come to a lot of the training camps without a penny in his pocket. I don't know how he expected to eat – most of the camps lasted two weeks. Charlie paid for his meals, paid for his vitamins, paid for almost everything there. And when Ben got his first car, when he had a little money and bought a Trans-Am, Charlie co-signed for it. I couldn't believe that Ben would turn on someone who would give him the last shirt on his back if Ben needed it.

And I was incensed at the image of Ben that was coming across in the media. To this day, I don't know whether Ben consciously decided to project himself as an idiot, barely able to remember his own name, or if his lawyers advised him to do so. It might have had something to do with an early story in the papers that appeared just after Ben lost his medal. Dick Pound, the International Olympic Committee executive vice-president, was quoted as saying that Ben possessed "child-like" innocence and that he was the "unwitting victim of his manipulating entourage."

Give me a break! None of these people knew Ben. They had met him on a couple of occasions at the Olympics, had a little small talk. You don't base an opinion of someone on a couple of minutes of small talk at banquets here and there.

After seeing Ben on television, I raged around the house for a while. Then Jean Sonmor of the Toronto *Sun* called. She couldn't have called at a better time. She got a great story. She wanted to know how we were doing after the Olympics, and I told her, but good.

It had gone so badly for me at the 1988 Games that I really didn't want to talk about it. I didn't even make the semifinals in the women's 100-metres. I'm not sure how the business about Ben came up – whether she brought it up or I did – but I decided the lying had to stop. Somebody had to tell these people that Ben was lying, that he was not a brainless idiot manipulated by some rotten coach and some equally rotten doctor. I told Sonmor that I would tell the truth, that if I had to go and testify at an inquiry I did not intend to perjure myself. I told her that Ben knew he'd been taking steroids and that he knew he'd been doing it for years. I told her I didn't think it was fair of him to blame anybody else.

I did not give much thought to what would happen down the road as a result of my outburst. That same day, I called Al Sokol, a reporter at *The Toronto Star*. I knew him quite well, and I was hoping he would write a story about the threatening telephone calls my family had been getting. The West Indian community in Toronto was on my tail again – as a black woman married to a white man, I am seen as a traitor. Sokol came over to the house, and the next thing I knew, he called someone at the *Star* and they offered to buy the story for $10,000, plus syndication rights. This was actually the second offer I had received, though nothing ever came of the first one, for $400,000, from a London tabloid.

In any case, I balked. I guess I was confused at the idea of putting a price on the story. I'd just get on my high horse and shout about all the bullshit to whomever happened to be in my way. The next morning – it was October 8, 1988 – Sokol called back to say the deal was off because I'd blurted the story to another reporter and it was already in the *Sun*.

I asked him, "What story?" Then I remembered Sonmor's call.

I walked down the street, looking for a *Sun* box. When I found one, I crouched down and looked at the front page behind the wire mesh. I could read, "Teammate Lashes Out at Johnson." Under that it said, "Issajenko Vows to Tell All to Steroids Inquiry." I felt a fist in my stomach. I dropped in my quarter, grabbed the paper and flipped to the sports section.

The headline was big enough to make you think we had landed on the moon again: "TIME BOMB."

Sonmor's story began: "Angella Taylor Issajenko lashed out at Ben Johnson yesterday in a passionate defense of national sprint coach Charlie Francis.

"The *Sun* interview is the first fissure in the wall of denials the elite Mazda athletes have presented the world since Johnson was stripped of his Olympic medal two weeks ago."

I stood on the sidewalk, holding the paper against the autumn wind. My name kept jumping out at me. The story covered the entire page, with an old photograph of Charlie stretching my left foot back on some track.

I kept reading:

"An emotional Issajenko repeatedly implied that Johnson knew exactly what he was doing and that steroids had been part of the program for a long time."

Holy Moly!

The "TIME BOMB" headline came from that long telephone conversation with Sonmor the day before, when I told her, "I can't wait for the fucking probe." (The *Sun* had politely used "f— —ing probe"). "I'm going to tell the people of Canada what I know and it's going to be like a nuclear bomb exploding."

I had felt apprehensive walking down the street to get a copy of the newspaper, but standing there on the sidewalk, reading it, I felt the weight of the lies and deceit begin to lift from my shoulders. I took a deep breath, straightened my spine, and looked up at the clouds. The shit was about to hit the fan. I knew the story might provoke more death threats. But the lying was over, at last.

I read on, this time my own words:

" 'This s— —'s been going on for a long time – long before there was a penny in it. It's got nothing to do with money. . . .' "

And, " 'I have no idea what Ben's doing or thinking or even *if* he's thinking for himself. Why would he leave Charlie and Jamie holding the bag? He says he's never knowingly taken steroids, but if he didn't do it then somebody did it to him and that's a f— —ing criminal offence. That's assault, man!' "

The Angella Issajenko I liked best was the one who said (in a separate boxed story in a bottom corner of the page), " 'What's the big deal? It was just a footrace. It was a 100-metre dash over in 9.79 seconds. That's all it was.' "

I walked home, cut out the story, and dropped it in a cardboard box – my clippings file.

Looking back, I would say that I regret only one thing in my tirade. It's true that the use of anabolic steroids had been going on for a long time, long before there was a penny in it. But I'm not so sure anymore that it had nothing to do with money.

All the fussing with my wardrobe on my first day before the Dubin Inquiry helped keep me calm.

On the weekend, I had gone to my favorite dress shop, Lipton's in the Eaton Centre, and used my credit card to buy a couple of outrageous outfits. One was a houndstooth dress with a wide white collar and a belt. It actually made the newspaper headlines the next day. The other was a gray two-piece loose-cut suit, very elegant. I went shopping for this big event thinking I'd be on the stand for two days. It turned out I was on longer, so I had to spin out my wardrobe with an older outfit to last the full three days.

Some people have accused me of being vain, and perhaps I am. A lot of them had a field day with me when I got my nose fixed. I think everybody thought I was trying to look white, or less black.

The truth is, I never really thought there was anything wrong with my nose. I got it done in 1985, when I was pregnant. Tony decided he didn't like his nose. He kept complaining about this nose of his, so he decided to get it done. Impulsively, I decided, hell, I'm going to get mine done, too.

(The cosmetic surgeon decided that if I was going to wear my nose a little pointier, then I would need a chin implant to balance it off. Sometimes, when I see an old picture, I'm not sure it was worth it. I guess it was just a fun thing to do, something Tony and I did together. Getting my nose fixed took my mind off my expanding belly for a while; call it therapy.)

I think I must have driven Tony crazy that morning. He was still half asleep when I started trying on the dresses, first one, then the other. Which one to wear?

I probably woke up our tenants downstairs, the way I crashed around. And every time I turned around, one of the cats was in the way. We have a fat orange tabby and a black and white longhair, and it was just meow, meow, meow. Every little noise seems so loud at that hour of day.

Tony finally opened one eye and pointed at the houndstooth dress. "That one," he whispered, then fell back to sleep.

I curled my hair, did what I could with it. I knew I had to be prepared in my mind when I left the house. I wanted that magic combination of concentration and adrenaline, the way I felt in the starting blocks, before the gun.

What kept going through my mind that morning was that I wanted to look good when I appeared on the stand. For years, Charlie had drilled into us that we should look good – not necessarily in the sense of what we were wearing, but in projecting a fine image. The writer Jack London would have said he wanted us to look like we had our "silk." It would be the first time many of the reporters would see me in anything other than my track wear.

Later, when I watched my longtime teammate Mark McKoy on television, I was appalled when I saw him sitting up there on the stand chewing gum, like a cow chewing its cud. He was sarcastic and rude. He called Charlie an idiot, and it sounded like he mispronounced the name of Carol Anne Letheren, the Canadian *chef de mission* at the Seoul Olympics. She has since become president of the Canadian Olympic Association. I think he called her Leatherhead.

At seven o'clock, I called a taxi. The plan was to meet my lawyers, Gayle Pinheiro and Dennis O'Connor, at the Park Plaza Hotel at Bloor Street and Avenue Road in midtown Toronto, then we would walk over to the inquiry at the hearing room at 1235 Bay Street.

I paid the price for all my fussing and vanity in that short walk. The weather had been cold all week, six below zero, and that day it got up to about zero. I was wearing a fashionable spring trench coat over my houndstooth dress, and my ass was freezing. I had on high heels, which was a disaster because I live in flats and running shoes. I marched on, wobbling, freezing.

Still, I was feeling pretty feisty. I had made up my mind that I wasn't going to let anyone browbeat me, not even Mr. Justice Dubin himself. A month earlier, I had watched the proceedings when they started in Montreal, with the weightlifters. I could see that Dubin kept coming on with this cheating business, scolding and lecturing. At one point, Dubin told Denis Garon, one of the weightlifters, that he had a "pretty nice life for a young man." He listed the perks of being an amateur athlete in this country: travel to other countries, an allowance, a residence, tuition benefits.

Then Dubin told him, "All of this is to try to make you a good citizen of this country, and you don't become a good citizen by setting an example for others by cheating." He kept giving the weightlifters a moral tongue-lashing.

I thought to myself, he'd better not try that stuff on me. I didn't want this man giving me a lesson in morality.

I don't suppose I'll ever be an attraction on the lecture circuit. People want to hear guys like Ben Johnson and Mark McKoy get up there and say things like, "I'm sorry I did drugs. I never should have done what I did."

Well, if you're so sorry, guys, why don't you find a suitable charity and give it all the money you earned? Because the only way these guys achieved what they did was through performance-enhancing drugs. And if they had to do it all over again, and they could get away with it, I'm sure they'd do it. I'd be doing it, too.

I think I made Gayle nervous. She was worried that if Dubin got my dander up, I would probably get upset and shoot my mouth off. She probably was thinking of the "TIME BOMB" headline. What she didn't know was that when I was very young, they used to call me Cayenne Pepper. It was because I had a quick temper. Gayle had reason to be nervous.

I knew that Dubin had absolutely no idea what it takes to be a successful athlete – or, more accurately, what it takes to be a successful Canadian amateur athlete at the international level. What could a judge know about that? I doubt he could even run 100 metres, and I'm not being disrespectful. I have a fair idea of what it takes to become a judge, but few people really know what it takes to become a world-class athlete.

I wanted to tell him. I was determined to let him know. I had already started the process by handing a briefcase full of drugs over to the inquiry back in November 1988.

The briefcase held more than a dozen bottles of what my teammates and I had, until Seoul, called estragol. After Seoul, Jamie changed the story and we were told it was furazabol, an injectable anabolic steroid made in Japan. We were told the trade name for this drug was Miatolon. It is a water-based steroid, something a high-school science class would refer to as a suspension, meaning that when it settled in the bottle, the lower liquid was a chalky, milky-white solution and the upper liquid was almost clear.

I had been on a program of these estragol injections since January 1986 along with Ben Johnson and Tony Sharpe. Others in the Mazda group began taking injections a little later. Charlie Francis had bought the bottles from Jamie when the doctor left Canada to return to St. Kitts in August 1986, and he had left them with me for safekeeping in February 1988. I kept the briefcase under my bed.

On November 22, 1988, Walter Greczko and Gary McQueen, commission investigators, arrived at my house with Gayle Pinheiro to pick it up. Dennis O'Connor had advised me to hand it over, so I did.

During the inquiry, it would come to light that the bottles had been analyzed by the Bureau of Dangerous Drugs Testing Labs and were found to contain not neither estragol nor furazabol, but Winstrol-V, the brand name for stanozolol.

That was a surprise.

As we walked to the inquiry, pushing into that wind, I remembered how I hadn't even noticed the cold when I first arrived in Canada, on a January evening in 1975. I had been too excited. I'd never been on an airplane before – I was sixteen years old – and the only thing I knew about Canada was from the Christmas cards I got showing snowmen in top hats with carrot noses. Sometimes the snow on the cards would be sprinkled with magical bits of sparkling paper. I never imagined snow as being cold, just pretty. I arrived at the Toronto airport wearing a light pair of slacks and a matching blouse. My mother stepped forward out of the crowd and offered me a coat. Sure enough, it was snowing, and it *was* pretty. But that was a long time ago.

When we arrived at the commission offices, I went upstairs to blow my nose. It took me a while to warm up, and I wanted to make sure I looked all right, so I spent a little time in front of the mirror, fussing again. Then I had a cup of coffee with Dennis and Gayle and looked around the hearing room. The shades were drawn, so the room looked dull in the fluorescent lighting. The shades and the walls were a neutral gray and there were five or six rows of long tables arranged before Dubin's carved wooden desk. There were several floor and table microphones around the room. We were early, so we took our coffee and sat in another room.

We joked around a bit; I don't really remember what we said. I had been under a lot of pressure myself in the past few months, ever since Seoul. Some woman had been harassing Tony and me with telephone calls. We could tell by her accent that she was West Indian. She kept saying, "Shut your fucking mouth." By telling the truth, or threatening to, I was hurting Ben's defence.

Other people in the West Indian community were furious with me, too. They wanted to believe everything Ben said because it's all part of this black-white business. They thought I should automatically side with Ben because I'm black. I encounter this often in Toronto: I provoke anger merely by being married to a white man.

Tony is very Russian, very blond, and very white. He is also distractingly gorgeous. I stopped going out to bars with him years ago because the women are all over him. They walk up and just sit there steaming. It's like they're in heat. The guys on the team used to call him the Magnet, the way he attracts these hungry admirers. Most of the women ended up calling Tony's mother and his grandmother because they were the only Issajenkos listed in the telephone book.

It was the same with the death threats. Tony's mom and grandmother kept getting those calls, too. One woman did sound dangerous. She threatened to keep calling and even dared to suggest that I had better take my daughter, Sasha, and leave town. I called the police, and we eventually found out who she was. Maybe that scared her. She went into the police station to apologize, and I decided not to press charges.

Just before ten o'clock, when I had to go on the stand, we walked back into the hearing room. It was packed. I recognized some of the lawyers from watching the sessions when Charlie had been on television. There was Robert P. Armstrong, counsel for the commission. And Ben Johnson's two lawyers; Jamie Astaphan's two lawyers; Charlie's lawyer; Thomas C. Barber, lawyer for the Sport Medicine Council of Canada; two lawyers for the Government of Canada; Julian Porter, lawyer for the College of Physicians and Surgeons of Ontario; a lawyer for Sport Canada; Roger Bourque for the Canadian Track and Field Association; and two lawyers for the Canadian Olympic Association. Bishop Dolegiewicz and David Steen, two Olympic athletes, had lawyers present, and there was a lawyer for Waldemar Matuszewski, who worked as a physiotherapist for the Mazda team.

I knew nearly every reporter in the room. The cameramen were over to one side, and all the reporters seemed to be wearing suits. I don't know why that struck me as unusual, except that the reporters who cover track and field usually dress as casually as the athletes. In the inquiry room, in their suits, they looked much more serious and somber, the way some people look when they dress up for a funeral.

Some of the reporters shouted questions. Gillian Findlay of the CBC asked me if I was going to dispute what Charlie had said, and suddenly the immensity of the situation hit me. This was not just another media event. I guess nobody noticed because I tried so hard to hide it. As I looked around the room, my eyes were filling with tears. I kept thinking, what have I got myself into?

The room itself was ordinary, rather like a boarding lounge at an airport, but all these people, all these — suits.

When the time came, I walked to the front and was sworn in. ". . . promise to tell the truth, the whole truth, and nothing but the truth?"

"I do."

You bet.

I took my place on the stand behind the microphone, settled into the chair, and placed the photocopied and annotated excerpts from my diary on the desk in front of me. (I was dismayed the next day to read that one of the reporters in the room dubbed it "the drug diary.")

Robert Armstrong, the lawyer for the commission, stood at a lectern at the front of the gallery a few feet away from me, shuffling through his papers. He is a youngish-looking man in his early fifties, dark-haired. That day he was conservative and broad-shouldered in a dark suit with a white handkerchief in his breastpocket — the very picture of a partner with Tory Tory DesLauriers & Binnington, cuff links and all. He spoke with a slight drawl during the inquiry — "Did'ja remember *that*, Ms Issajenko?" — and the only time over the next three days that he showed any impatience with the long and sometimes complicated proceedings was when he took a sip of water, or removed his glasses to hang them from his fingertips over the lectern. I became fascinated by his long fingers and expressive hands. If we got into a sensitive area of questioning, he'd lightly adjust the knot in his tie and treat us to a bit of droll humor. I wasn't afraid of any question he would ask me. I wanted him to ask the tough questions. It was like that morning on the street, reading the "TIME BOMB" story in the *Sun*. I wanted the lying to stop.

Armstrong leaned into his microphone and asked, "Ms Issajenko, first of all, I'm going to ask you some questions about your background and then some questions about your athletic career.

To get it right on the record, you were born on September 28, 1958, in Jamaica – is that right?"

"That's correct," I said.

"And I understand for the next sixteen years or a little more you lived in Jamaica and attended school in Jamaica."

"Yes, I did."

The houndstooth dress had a large white collar, which framed my face and made me feel very black in front of this white audience of suits.

2

In the Island

I was born in 1958 in St. Andrew, Jamaica, though I have no memory of the place. There was a hospital there. My mother took me as a baby to live with her mother, Vasthie, in the rural area outside Mandeville, a hamlet in the central Parish of Manchester.

Like a lot of Jamaican kids, I had no idea who my father was — I still don't to this day — but it was never a worry. I try to explain to Canadians how things are in the island, but I don't think they believe me. It's not like in Canada, where people have problems when they can't find their mother or father, or they develop neuroses if their parents give up on them.

Marriage is not a big deal in Jamaica, not as big as it is here. Maybe it is because of generations of slavery — marriage, after all, represents some kind of profound hope. When my mother went to live in Kingston and my grandmother went away to England, they left me to live with my maternal great-grandparents.

I was christened Angella Marie Taylor, Taylor being my father's surname. As long as I lived in Jamaica I was Marie Taylor. Years later, when I enrolled at school in Canada, I filled out a form with my full name, and everyone began to call me Angella. I didn't fight it. Canada was a new life, so why not start with a new name?

In Jamaica, I was Marie Taylor, the great-granddaughter of Jacob Bent, a retired fisherman, and his wife, May. My mother's name was Olive Bird, but I rarely saw her. Once in a while, she'd arrive from Kingston. On birthdays and some holidays, she'd send me a little "CARE" package.

All those growing-up years, I considered my real mother to be my grandmother Vasthie, who had gone to England, though I didn't really know her, either. I had pictures of her. Maybe it was because I developed a bond with her before she left, when I was two. My mother was her only child. I am an only child too. Jamaicans tend to trace their history through their mothers more than through their fathers. I suppose this also reflects how they feel about marriage.

I was brought up sharply on the issue of marriage many years later, in Canada, when I became pregnant with my first daughter, Sasha. I was one of the top female athletes in the country and I had been appointed to the Order of Canada, but a major sponsor cancelled my promotional appearance because I was pregnant, and not yet married. (If there is one thing I have learned from amateur athletics, it's to play by the rules. Not the rules in the official handbooks – other, unpublished rules. Tony and I were married shortly after.)

Grandmother Vasthie, who ultimately did marry in England and change her surname to Harris, stayed in constant contact with me when I was growing up in Jamaica. She wrote letters, always asking after me, checking to see how I was doing. It was Grandmother Vasthie who later insisted that I move to Canada.

Once a year, at Christmas, Grandmother Vasthie sent me a huge parcel. Sometimes, it would contain a great big doll with fringed eyelashes. I would ask for something, anything, and she would send it. Sometimes I'd get ten dresses at once, or six pairs of shoes. And soaps, powders, and hairbows. The dresses were outrageous, some with big crinolines, others styled like pinafores. I used to get all dressed up for school, because where else was I going to go? The only places I went were school and church on Sundays. I once got a part as an angel in a school play, wings and all, and I'm sure it was because I owned a perfect white dress.

It was different with the shoes. I would leave the house in the morning, dressed for school with my fancy shoes on. Some were black patent leather, some were red leather or white leather sandals with a delicate pattern of holes in the vamp and a little ankle strap with a buckle. I would take them off down the road so I could run barefoot in the chalky dust with the rest of the kids.

I started out in what they called infant school. These were private classes run by a local woman on the wide front veranda of her big house. At recess, we'd play in the leafy plum tree outside. There weren't many kids in the school, maybe ten, because you had to pay to attend. My grandmother sent the money. So, rather than feeling disadvantaged, I felt supremely advantaged in my early years because of dear Grandmother Vasthie. She was like God to me, a faraway God in England.

We had to climb up a steep hill to get to the infant school. We learned our ABCs, our 1-2-3s, and we started to read and write, all on that cool, shaded veranda. Every morning, and at every noon break, we had to say prayers. I had a couple of little friends and just before saying "Amen" before going home for lunch, we'd dash out and run straight down the hill ahead of everyone else. We were always in trouble when we came back.

We had chalk and books, and there were benches and a blackboard on the veranda. When I compare it to what my daughter is learning in kindergarten, I can see it was quite advanced. The teacher was strict. If she gave a lesson and we couldn't do it, she spanked us. Two plus two equals five, and – whack! By the time I got to public school, I was far ahead of the other kids in grade one.

Mandeville is at the crossroads of two surfaced highways, just west of a railway line. Nearby is a ridge of land that rises to about three thousand feet above sea level, the Don Figueroa Mountains. The main road through town starts out about forty miles east, in Kingston, where it is called Washington Boulevard. It ends in the neighboring Parish of St. Elizabeth, to the west, where it becomes Bamboo Avenue.

There are sugar plantations all over the island, but the major resource industry is the manufacture of alumina. Jamaica is the third-largest producer of alumina in the world. The country's economy will boom if they ever get these new aluminum air-powered cars on the market. The principal ore in aluminum is bauxite, a powdery rock. I grew up knowing the odor and the soft grit of bauxite because Mandeville sat between two major bauxite pits. Mandeville is also a major citrus-growing area. There were so many grapefruits and lemons that they couldn't all be harvested. They would ripen and plop to the ground and rot. I think of this every time I have to pay sixty-nine cents for a grapefruit in Toronto.

We lived thirteen miles outside Mandeville, in the countryside. When I was growing up, in the 1960s, the roads were dirt, and they had just started running the wires for electricity. We had no electricity in our home. Hour upon hour on weekends I listened to a battery-powered radio. My favorite program was the Dick Clark dance show. There were only two radio stations to choose from, both of which played a lot of 1950s stuff – Brook Benton, Fats Domino, Nat King Cole, Patti Page, Buddy Holly. They played a lot of music you could slow dance to, dreamy stuff. I listened mostly on my own; the others in the family had things to do.

We led simple lives. We used kerosene lamps at night, those lovely lamps with a Tiffany shade on top. They cast a warm glow you don't get with incandescent light bulbs.

Without electricity, we had no refrigeration. During the holidays, or on special occasions, a man would drive up in a truck with huge blocks of ice. We'd dig a massive hole in the ground and fill it with sawdust and then put the blocks of ice in there. Ice melts very slowly when it is covered with sawdust, so we could keep things cool for a long time. We used to eat a lot of salted codfish, just like the Brits. We collected rainwater in a deep cistern covered with a wire screen at the back of the house.

We never thought of ourselves as poor or disadvantaged. I didn't know what poor meant in Jamaica. In Canada, people think you're poor if you don't have a television set or a car. We didn't want for much in Jamaica. We didn't have to buy many things. We planted most of our food, and we didn't even have buildings for the animals. At night, you'd bring them close to the house in case someone might steal them. Our chickens roosted in the tangerine tree.

Our house was a lot like the others in the area, quite small, set on an acre or two of land. It had two bedrooms and was made of concrete blocks, with a tin roof. It gets really hot in Jamaica, but I never suffered from the heat the way I do in Toronto, where the humidity is bad all summer. In Jamaica, there was always a fresh breeze, with the smell of the sea in it. We had glass louvers on the windows and you could wind them open with a crank at the bottom of the frame. At the front of the house was a straw-roofed veranda. It was shaded by the leaves of ivy that covered one side of the house and climbed over this straw roof. The house sat back from the road and up on a small hill, so with the ivy and the porch, it was hidden. It felt secluded.

I used to read on the front porch in the shade of the leaves. I liked fairy tales and nursery rhymes. We got most of our books from a mobile library that arrived once a week. The van would pull up at the grade school and we would exchange books. Later I got to like the Brontë sisters' books, especially *Jane Eyre*. I read it over and over. I fantasized that someday I would marry a man just like Mr.

Rochester. I pictured him as tall and handsome. (Years later, I saw Orson Welles play Mr. Rochester in a movie and it sort of ruined the image.)

Great-grandmother May had a garden at the side of the house. She grew Joseph's-coat flowers, named after Joseph and his coat of many colors. They are beautiful, with a dark blue flower and many, many colors in the leaves. She also grew Easter lilies. In the middle of the garden, she had a tangerine tree, which she assured me was mine. It gave us tons of fruit. A big guava tree at the bottom of the hill gave us fruit for jams and jellies. And we had what we called a pear tree. In Jamaica, we called avocados pears.

We ate a lot of green bananas, which we boiled. And yams, sweet potatoes, and all sorts of vegetables and cabbages. There is a spinach in the island that we liked, I think it was called calalu. At breakfast, we had eggs, bread, and tea. Sometimes we bought curried chicken and rice for lunch at school. At home, we ate in the kitchen, or outside on the veranda. Great-grandfather Jacob ate alone at the table. I brought him his dinner, but he always ate alone.

At the foot of the hill our house was on, there was a small lime pit – in Jamaica, they mix lime and water to create a kind of mortar – and whenever it rained, the pit would fill with water and someone was always falling into it.

Great-grandmother May wore her hair in two braids wound up and under a scarf. She never went without her scarf, like most of the women in the area. She smoked a pipe. She had a friend who would come over and the two of them would sit on the veranda yapping and smoking their pipes. My Grandmother Vasthie would send pipes from England. We grew our own tobacco – just regular tobacco; I don't *think* it was ganja – and we would lay it in the sun to dry. Those two women would sit there, tamping down the tobacco, yapping. I recall that May was always in an apron, for cooking and cleaning. She was very dark-skinned, almost ebony like my mother.

My great-grandfather was almost fair in comparison. Jacob was light-skinned, with freckles on his nose. He didn't do a lot of smiling, but I remember I used to follow him everywhere. I was like his shadow. He had a big vegetable garden and all kinds of animals running around – chickens, goats, pigs. The highlight of my day was when I would rush home from school so I could go with him to bring the cow in from the field.

I preferred the company of my great-grandfather, perhaps just because we did so many things together. If he was doing something around the house or replanting vegetables, I'd do it with him. We'd sit together and he would tell me stories. Sometimes, he'd let me milk the cow in the morning. We'd milk it and run back with the milk to the kitchen to boil it before drinking it. One day, we had gone to get the cow in and we were away off in the bush. He pointed out one tree, a great tree that had a long branch going off in one direction. Jacob told me someone in the neighborhood had hanged himself from that branch. Maybe he was trying to frighten me, to discourage me from wandering too far from home in the bush. The story stuck in my mind. People in the island are very superstitious, and they believe in ghosts. I believed in ghosts.

There were four of us in that little house. Besides me and my great-grandparents, there was Enid. Enid was their youngest child, born in 1942. She was my great-aunt, sixteen years older than me, but she had the mind of a five-year-old. The story I heard was that Enid was born that way because when Great-grandmother May was pregnant with Enid she was told that her husband, Jacob, had died at sea. It wasn't true, but the news so upset May that Enid ended up retarded. Enid probably had a mild case of Down's syndrome. Great-grandmother May was forty-two when she had Enid.

Enid was plump, and dwarfish I think, at just over four feet tall. She had long hair and big eyes, kind of cute in her way. She could not comprehend much, though she could identify the letters of the alphabet. If you showed her a word, like City, she could spell it out – "C-I-T-Y" – but it wouldn't mean anything to her. She could write her name. Enid stayed home most of the time, though she loved to go to church. Sometimes, she would run away, and if we couldn't find her, we would go to the church and find her sitting alone in a pew. It was my responsibility to get her dressed and comb her hair and take her to church on Sundays.

Maybe this is why I became such a loner. Enid was my mother's age, and she and I were playmates. We would play hide and seek, and skip rope, and climb trees. And run.

For some reason, I was afraid of lizards. I don't know why, because I knew they were afraid of me, but if I saw a lizard in an orange tree or a tangerine tree, I'd get Enid to kill it before I went up there. She wasn't afraid of them; I think she liked them. There were green ones, up to six inches long, and white ones with black eyes. She'd throw a stone and hit it and. . . *yuck!* It splattered.

Sometimes I'd get impatient with Enid because she did not grasp things easily and I'd be mean to her, hit her. The Cayenne Pepper in me. I regret those moments because Enid was my best friend. I loved her.

In those early days, when Enid and I went to church, it was the Church of God. This was an evangelical Protestant denomination that stressed personal conversion, sanctification, the imminent return of Jesus Christ, baptism by immersion, and speaking in tongues. My great-grandparents never went, not that I can remember. It was an emotional gathering. People would shout "*Ayyy*-man!" And the preacher would go on like those evangelists you see on TV, like Jimmy Swaggart. You know the way they talk, how the voices go up and down and the way they shout and weep and wail. The church was plain – no decorations – and there was an altar at the front where people would go and confess their sins.

The preacher's favorite sermon was designed to keep you aware of the here-one-minute, gone-the-next proximity of Hell.

"You might be walkin' *home*," he'd shout. "Walkin' *home* from this meetin' here and, *bang!* – outta nowhere – comes a car, hits you, *kills* you! And where you gonna go if you not up to speed with God Almighty?" Straight to Hell, of course. He worked on people's fears. Before heading home, the congregation would rush up to him, collapse on their knees, and confess. It was all rather odd because there were only two old cars in the entire community. A person would have to be blind and deaf not to know when one of them got rolling.

Even I would go up and confess something. I'd kneel and tell him I had cursed or broken a dish or smacked Enid. I did it because I was terrified of going to Hell on my way home. All this was very funny to the younger crowd. It was wild, watching the grown-ups shouting and rolling around on the ground. They'd all be dressed in their Sunday best. Some wore fancy hats or, more often, a lace veil so their heads would be covered. I wore a lace veil.

There was another religion in the neighborhood, too. Apocalopamania, I think it was called. Sometimes, out of curiosity, Enid and I went to their meetings. They were usually held outside, in a vacant field beside the grocery store. Years later, I watched a documentary on television on religious ceremonies in a village in

Haiti, and those meetings were similar. There would be a lot of drumming and shouting – "Hallelujah! Hallelujah!" – and they'd be rolling and writhing on the ground, speaking in tongues – *Lulululululuuuu.* Too much. To this day, I am wary, confused maybe, about organized religion.

The most influential belief in the island when I was young was obeah, a form of religion that uses sorcery. It is practiced, or was practiced, in parts of the West Indies, South America, the southern United States, and Africa. (Obeah is a West African word.) It is a kind of voodoo, which is a mixture of African cult worship and elements borrowed from Catholicism. Followers of obeah believe you can visit someone's grave, maybe a dead relative's grave, and ask them to harm someone living, and it will happen. They say you can "work obeah" on your enemies. The leaders of obeah call themselves faith healers, though they mostly promise to hurt rather than heal. People pay them to work an obeah curse. Who knows how many "accidents" are the result of some faith healer making sure his obeah worked?

Many years after my great-grandfather died, a man in the neighborhood was on his deathbed. He was trying to absolve himself of sins by confession, and he said that he had had my grandfather killed with obeah. It turned out he was the man who took over my great-grandfather's fishing boats and gear. So, who knows?

A few years ago, Ben Johnson visited his father in Falmouth, Jamaica, and came back to Canada with the story that there was some woman trying to kill him with obeah. Ben had this ring, a silver ring with two x marks on it. He said a man had given it to him and as long as he wore it nothing would happen to him. At our training camp in Guadeloupe, several of us were lounging by the swimming pool when Ben dropped the ring and it fell to the bottom of the pool. Ben was in a panic. He had all the guys diving, trying to find it at the bottom of the pool, until finally Rob Gray, one of Ben's teammates, retrieved it. They all believed somebody can harm you with obeah.

By the time I was sixteen, I had been through the Church of God thing, then the Seventh-Day Adventists, then the Roman Catholics. Everyone had a different day to go to church, or a different way of going to church, and if you didn't abide by it you'd go straight to Hell. After a time I didn't care anymore. And the television evangelists were the worst of the lot. They're such creeps, with their cheap suits and pompadours and their gimme, gimme attitude. The Canadian rock singer, Ronnie Hawkins, has it all figured out: "Believe in God?" he says, "Man, I believe in God like nobody else. It's the fucking ground crew I don't trust."

In Jamaica, one of my jobs was to polish the floors. We had square linoleum tiles in the kitchen and wooden plank floors in the rest of the house. I washed the floors first, then put polish on the wood floors and rubbed them hard with the inner husk of a coconut. It makes a good polishing brush. You could break your leg walking on one of those polished floors when I was finished.

Another chore was to bring our goat out each morning and tie her up to graze. I'd bring her back in at night. I had only one goat, and the idea was to sell her kids to make money, for cash flow. But every time my goat had babies, they died. Finally, one night, she died too. All night we heard her out there crying. I think somebody poisoned her.

I decided to try my luck with a black pig. I got it as a baby, but pigs get big quickly. We had a pigsty made of wood, and my job was to throw water in there – pigs love to roll around in water and mud. It cools them. Great-grandfather Jacob had several pigs by then. I also had to feed the pigs, but I just couldn't go near them. They'd get awfully miserable sometimes. I'd stand back a way and throw the water and the food at them.

Great-grandfather Jacob was retired, but he kept his fishing route on the Caribbean Sea, to the south of the island. Another man – the one who confessed that he worked obeah on Jacob – was running it for him. Every couple of weeks, Great-grandmother May would get up really early, before dawn, and saddle her donkey with hampers, two straw sacks that dropped on either side of the animal, held by a leather strap with padding underneath so it wouldn't chafe. Then she'd walk to the coast. It was a long walk. She didn't return until six or seven at night. The two hampers would be filled with fish, which we smoked or packed in salt.

It was a lovely time. Life was a simple rhythm of getting up in the morning, going to school, coming home. Once a year, there was a local picnic with reggae music playing all day long and ice cream cones. People in the islands just lived from day to day with nothing to bother them, nothing but those bloody ghosts.

Another of my jobs was to go to the grocery store and buy Great-grandfather Jacob his white rum. Jacob liked overproof rum. He drank a lot of it when I was a little girl. Anyone can buy it in the island, even five-year-olds. There was no sign at the front of the store that indicated it sold liquor, but everyone knew. It was a tiny building, no bigger than the houses, with cool, tiled floors. Great-grandmother May was strict about my coming home right after school and not talking to boys along the way, but she had no objection to my going to the local rum shop in the evening to get Jacob his overproof white rum.

To this day, if I am taking alcohol at all, it has to be one of those cute little drinks with rum in it. Or, since I met Tony, vodka. I'll also drink straight white rum. That's how Great-grandfather Jacob took it. He had a friend – I knew him only as Dee – who lived across the street. The two of them would go out to the bars and drink it up. But by the time I was old enough to be aware of what was happening, Great-grandfather Jacob had almost stopped drinking.

I never saw Jacob drunk, but he and Dee must have tied it on some nights, long past my bedtime. One evening, Dee came over to get him and they ended up in the bars until they staggered home, both of them. When he got home, Jacob tried to pee, but couldn't. His urinary tract was blocked. He had to be taken to the hospital, where the doctor said he would stay for a week. He was supposed to come home the following Friday.

He died Thursday night.

Someone took down the ivy on the veranda after Jacob's funeral.

The wake was at our home, with the tables set for feasting outside at the front of the house. I sat on the veranda, shaded by the big leaves. There are not many funeral homes in the Jamaican countryside, so they brought my great-grandfather's body home. People in the island are buried within two days because it is so hot. But first, the body is kept at home so people can come by and pay their respects. They strip the body, then take the mattress off a bed and pack the springs with ice. The body is laid out on the ice on newspapers, beneath a sheet. They used the room Enid and I shared. They chose the single bed in the corner, my bed.

The night they took my great-grandfather off the ice and put him in his coffin and buried him, they put the mattress back on my bed and I slept on it. I wasn't afraid. Then someone took down the ivy, and my world began to change.

I started to attend public school and took parts in some of the plays. These days, I can't carry a tune, but I could sing very well when I was a girl. Maybe it's because of the steroids. My voice has become a little deeper.

One teacher wrote a part for me and made me the villain. I was a gossip-monger, and I was supposed to tell my best friend something I should never have told her. I think that's the way the teacher saw me, a bit of a hellion, because of my temper. I still have a terrible temper. I wasn't really a fighter, but I liked to start fights. I'd push two people together to get them fighting. The principal spanked me for that a number of times.

School was a long, flat, one-story building with big windows that pushed out from the bottom to allow in the breeze. There were concrete floors and individual seats with desks in the middle of the classrooms. The brighter kids sat at long benches along the sides. There was no support, or protection, for your back. If you were talking in class, the principal snuck up behind and whacked you hard on your back. I was one of the brighter kids and always got good marks. A lot of whacks, too. One morning the principal caught me whispering and, with a clenched fist, *whammed* me on the back. I had never been hit so hard in my life.

Great-grandmother May never took much interest in my schoolwork in those three or four years after Jacob died. She never asked how I was getting along. She never went to any of the plays, but most of the parents were like that. Only a handful of parents showed up for those little theatrical events. They were mainly concerned that you got home on time, that you didn't go out at night, and that you didn't talk to boys. Most parents were more interested in teaching the girls to cook, clean, sew, and wash.

I was a tomboy in public school. If one of the boys liked you, they'd write love letters, or give you candies, but I can't remember much about that. The girls all wore starched, pleated skirts with bloomers attached. We called them skorts. I liked to play baseball, skort and all, because I could really hit the ball, but I wasn't very good at the other parts of the game. I tried high-jumping.

Mostly, I liked to run. I started going into after-school races because of the prizes. Winning meant getting nursery rhyme books and powder puffs. The powder puffs came in pink plastic boxes with transparent tops. The powder is in the box and the puff sits in the bubble on top with a nice pink bow in the middle. I loved those powder puffs.

There was one girl who was faster than I was in public school. Her family was very religious, however, so she didn't enter many races because most track and field day events were on weekends. Maybe her people didn't think it was a very godly thing for her to do. So, starting in about grade five or six, I always won. We ran on grass, in our bare feet.

Track and field is the least expensive sport to get into. All you need is running shoes, and in the island we got by without even them. It's not that unusual, perhaps it's even more in keeping with the spirit of the original Olympic Games. The freeborn men who competed at Olympia in ancient Greece didn't wear anything. They competed in the nude, and women were barred from watching. As recently as 1960, at the Olympic Games in Rome, Abebe Bikila, a black African, won the Olympic marathon running in his bare feet. Only when he won again in 1964, in Tokyo, did he wear running shoes. In the 1970s, Zola Budd was still running in her barefeet.

There was a phase in Jamaica when I wanted to be a stewardess, though I had never even seen one for real. I probably saw pictures of them in magazines. I had never been on an airplane. I didn't know what stewardesses did, but they seemed to be a glamorous lot. I thought maybe they had something to do with flying the airplane and I imagined them landing in all kinds of exotic places.

Great-grandmother May was very stern in those days. As long as Enid and I did our jobs around the house, and came home on time, she would leave us alone. I can't say that I tried hard to please her. I don't know if I really cared. The person I continued to hold in highest regard was Grandmother Vasthie in England. I wrote her many letters, and she always answered them. She encouraged me to do well and complimented me on my successes. If I tried to please anyone, it was always Grandmother Vasthie, my half-imagined mom.

For a long time I was terrified of ghosts. I wasn't unusual. Everyone in the islands is scared to death of ghosts. They're always talking about ghosts and people harming people in scary ways, bad things happening to people. Everybody worries about ghosts.

I would never walk alone at night because the streets were so dark. Ghosts! I'd cover my head at night with the sheet, but sometimes you can see through a white sheet, and I'd see ghosts. One night, I was sure somebody was standing at the foot of the bed. I could see this shape through the sheet. When I got up the next morning, I couldn't speak for fear. I was *sure* it was a ghost.

Late on an afternoon in 1970, when I was just turned twelve, Great-grandmother May took to her bed, complaining of a headache. She went into a coma. One of her sons hitched a ride in one of the local cars to Mandeville and brought a doctor to examine her. The doctor said there was nothing he could do for her because it was a brain hemorrhage. Three days later she died.

When they laid her body out on the ice, on her own bed, I found myself alone in the room, and I remember clearly that I could see this one small part of her upper arm exposed. I poked at it, maybe just because the skin was showing. This time, I *was* afraid. She had asked me to do something for her just before she got sick and I had taken my jolly time doing it. She had got upset with me, and we never really got to talk again because she fell into that coma. I don't even remember what she had been angry about, but we never got a chance to make up. I thought she might come back to haunt me. I was terrified of her ghost.

And, now that she was dead, I didn't know where I was going to live.

As it turned out, I stayed in my great-grandparents' home, with Enid. One of my great-grandmother's daughters, Ciceline, had come back from England and was living across the way — you could see her house from our house — so we went there to eat and then came home to sleep, just the two of us. I was scared to death. It got worse.

For a little while before May died, a local woman named Beryl had come to help around the house. Beryl was my mother's age, in her mid-twenties. I think they were chums when they were younger. My mother came down from Kingston for a couple of days after the funeral and I heard them talking about old times. Beryl would do the washing and some of the cooking and cleaning. After May died, she continued to come to the house for a while.

Beryl had a friend, Gloria. Gloria was older, in her late twenties. She had long, lustrous hair, and her skin was lighter than most. She was pretty. Gloria had three or four children, and she had brought them to live with her mother, three blocks away.

One morning, a neighbor dropped by with terrible news: Gloria had been murdered. There was talk that the murderer was going to come to our house and drown himself in the cistern out back. They warned Enid and me to stay away from Gloria's house. But I was curious. This wasn't a ghost, just a murderer. I decided to go and see what I could see.

Gloria's murderer was a local man named Doc. We called him Dockey. He was a quiet man, very hardworking. He had lived alone in the neighborhood most of his life. I knew him well, like most of the kids.

There was a rumor that some man from England had come to visit on holiday and Dockey suspected he had something going with Gloria. The night she was killed, Gloria dropped by the neighbor's house where this man had been staying. Dockey got jealous, went to the house, dragged Gloria outside, and hacked her to death with a machete. They must have heard her screams, but no one came out to help her.

When I got there, I saw pieces of Gloria's hair in the dirt. I recognized it. There was blood everywhere. And then I saw three fingers, the last three fingers of Gloria's right hand. She must have raised her arms, trying to defend herself. I can see them now, lying in the dirt in the road.

I walked home that morning, but I would never walk by that house again at night. My fear of ghosts got worse. I kept thinking the ghost of Gloria would visit our house. I lived alone with Enid, scared of ghosts, and, for the first time, maybe of men, too.

A few years ago, I heard Dockey was released from jail. He went back to live in the neighborhood. Beryl left shortly after the murder to work for a public health nurse. Enid moved in with Ciceline and I went to live with Hilda Hamilton, another great-aunt.

Now, I was a Seventh-Day Adventist.

3

Lightning in Your Heart

In Jamaica, you pay to go to high school, as you would for college or university, unless you pass the Common Entrance Examinations. If you fail the exams, and if you can't pay, and if you are a girl, your life is pretty well circumscribed and predetermined. You become a maid, or a seamstress, or a cook, and you have babies. And you live and die in the island.

In Jamaica, too, you do not always go to the high school of your choice. You go where the board of education tells you to go. Often, it is a long way from home. Grandmother Vasthie kept writing letters to me from England, urging me to take the exams, and, of course, I did. I never questioned her advice.

One day, at Hilda's house, we looked in the newspaper to find my examination results. In the island, all the marks are published in the newspaper. That's how you — and everyone else — learned if you passed or failed. I was twelve years old. We cleared the dishes from the kitchen table and spread out the paper, smoothing one page at a time.

And there it was: Marie Taylor, PASS. I remember the page it was printed on, where it was on the page, and the tiny smudged letters of my name in a gray mass of agate type. Being accepted into high school made me special. From that day on, I was treated differently.

I was to go to a school called Holmwood Technical that was in Clarendon, just beyond the border of Manchester. It was about twenty miles from home, but it might as well have been on another continent. I knew nothing about Clarendon, nothing about Manchester. Commuting to high school was out of the question; there still were only a few vehicles in the community, and they were for emergencies.

Arrangements were made for me to board at a hostel for girls in Clarendon. A Chinese couple ran the hostel, and they were Catholic, and very strict. As a Seventh-Day Adventist, I had got used to worshipping on Saturdays when I lived with Hilda. At the hostel, Sunday mass was compulsory, and I had to wear a white dress, white socks, and polished black shoes. Only the senior girls were allowed to wear stockings.

I liked it in Clarendon, once I got over missing Enid. I found my amusement wherever I could. The Chinese woman's husband, for example, was the fattest man I had ever seen, a Goodyear Blimp on two legs. The sheer immensity of the man always made me want to laugh, but I couldn't – not in front of him, anyway – because he was in charge of the place. It wouldn't be putting too much of an edge on it to say that he rolled into church every Sunday morning. Came in the door sideways and *squ-ee-eezed* between the pews. We had to struggle to keep from laughing, which made it all the funnier.

I saw my first white person when I went off to high school. It happened the first week after I arrived, one afternoon when I went to a small grocery store. He was a white man, probably a tourist, and he was burnt red and peeling. I don't know why these things struck me as so funny, but I thought he looked like a lobster. Then I noticed the woman he was with. She was white, with long blonde hair tied back in a ponytail. And that's what it looked like, a horse's tail – all soft and silky. I wanted to touch it. I have envied white women for their hair ever since I stood there that brilliant afternoon, holding a bottle of pop, staring at that woman's ponytail.

(I'm always cutting my own hair short, then letting it grow, and some days if I really work at it – curling, blowing, brushing – it looks very nice, not too kinky, and it has a healthy shine. But most mornings it looks like Bill the Cat in the comic strip "Outland," like I stuck my finger in a light socket.)

We had to be back at the hostel right after school. If we were late, we'd get a detention, which meant washing the dishes, or pulling weeds out of the flower garden. The Chinese woman made us do this in our uniforms, and it was hot, sweaty work. Later, we had to wash, starch, and press the uniform. I was easy to discipline; I didn't want to work in that garden and find some lizard without Enid around.

There were four or six girls to a room at the hostel. We slept on bunk beds, and I managed to get a top bunk, where I felt more private. One of the comforts I had was a blue bedspread with frills along the edge that I had brought with me from home. We weren't supposed to bring bedding to the hostel, but the Chinese woman thought it was beautiful, and so she let me keep it.

I was alone most of the time, despite my three roommates. One of them had an older sister at the school, and they hung around together and didn't have much to do with us. Another girl at the school, Carmen, had been one of my only friends at home, but when I got to Clarendon she had already been there a year and she didn't think it was "cool" to hang around with a first-year student.

In Jamaica, the senior students treat new students very badly. It's an island form of hazing. They call the boys grubs and the girls grubesses. I was a grubesse. A new boy called Junior – he was my second cousin – was a grub. After classes one afternoon, some senior guys caught Junior, took him to an empty room, tied his shoelaces together, hoisted him on a stool, and told him to blow out the lightbulb in the ceiling. They stood around, laughing, and Junior got so dizzy he fainted and fell off the stool. Sometimes seniors made you run errands for them, or made you buy lunch for them, but they never gave you enough money so you had to use your own lunch money.

One of the senior girls took a protective interest in me, maybe because her boyfriend's name was Taylor and she thought we were related. I finally got caught, however. One evening a bunch of senior girls found me alone behind the school and they made me open my history book and sing from it. They wouldn't let me go. They stood around and laughed and laughed while I sang about Ferdinand Magellan, platypuses in Tasmania and Ernest Shackleton's expedition to the Antarctic aboard the *Nimrod*.

I was scared, and I hated them. My whole life I've felt real disdain for people like that, cowards who run in packs, and I'm sure it goes back to when I was a grubesse.

I had my lonely times. When I was thirteen, my mother left Jamaica for a country I had never heard of: Canada. I remember in geography they had a huge map of the world at the front of the room – they would draw it down like a shade over the blackboard –

with all the countries in different colors. I saw Canada up near the top, a wide slash of pink, part of the British Empire.

It looked awfully big.

The teachers at the high school encouraged us to get involved in extracurricular activities, mainly sports, and a lot of the kids joined netball teams. It is a British game, patterned after basketball but played with a soccer ball. It is tremendously popular in the Caribbean, where both men and women play it, though in most other places it is considered strictly a women's sport. It was around this time that Jamaica hosted the worldwide Netball Tournament, and a lot of the kids tried to identify with the stars of the national team. I wasn't one of them because I wasn't keen on team sports. I had become a loner.

After classes, I started going out to the track and field events. I gravitated to running, which was unusual for a girl my age then. Many of the girls ran when they were in elementary school, but few of them wanted to run in high school. Probably they wanted to go with the herd, wear makeup, tease their hair, fuss about their clothes, catch the boys' eyes. That keeps a lot of girls from running.

Running really is a pretty ungainly thing to do if you're trying to impress the boys. You grunt and sweat a lot, you fall on your ass, and most girls consider this too big a risk. Eventually I was the only senior girl in the school to run.

We ran barefoot on grass in lanes marked with lime. Sometimes two people would hold a thread across the finish line. One time when I was running they didn't let go of the thread in time and it slashed my neck. It took me a while to get over that; I guess it's like a rider who's thrown off his mount, or a diver who hits the board. I can laugh about it now, that fear of the finish line. Years later, in Canada, my trainer designed a series of exercises for me so I would keep my back from arching at the finish line. He wanted my upper chest to break the tape.

Most of the time, I ran 150-metre sprints. There were no starting blocks, just a standing start. Sometimes they'd fire a gun to start the race, but what I remember most is the grass. The intramural races were held on weekends, and I liked to arrive early on Saturday mornings so I could sit on the grass and watch the phys ed teachers prepare the field, which always involved trimming the grass. The adults were like different people those weekends, more relaxed, calling jokes to one another. There never was a more peaceful time in my life than those mornings when the grass was still wet with dew. The smell of freshly cut grass has an evocative hold on me. It's a childhood fragrance, and just a whiff of it on a summer morning in Toronto carries me back to those Saturdays at the track in the island.

We were still running for powder puffs, occasionally a ribbon or a medal. I once competed in an all-girls final in our district, but I didn't win. I don't remember being disappointed, though I began to like winning.

I have often thought about that feeling, moments before the race, when the starter says, "On your mark . . . ." I find it nearly erotic. It's the adrenaline, sure, but there's more. It's an unbearable mix of fear and excitement, of lightning in your heart, and you can feel it flash to the nerve ends. It's a feeling of – ignition. It is what a champion feels.

In high school, I couldn't even eat before a race. It was as though I was already too intensely alive. It's a distillation, a synthesis, of fierce energy, pure life. No one can touch it, add to it, take away from it. It's a natural high, your body gives it to you, and I can understand why someone might want to shoot it into a vein if they knew that feeling even once.

I dedicated more time to my running, but not for any world-class dreams or lofty aspirations. It just made me feel good, and at school I was beginning to feel that my life was taking shape. I had made it into high school and I was adjusting to the idea of school as home. That's when I considered engineering as a career. I knew that with a profession, the island is a fine place to live, even for a woman. I enrolled in "shops," courses in woodworking and metalworking.

I also had won some cachet among my classmates because my mother was in Canada. I still considered my grandmother in England my real mother, but it was nice to know that Olive Bird could cause a stir. In the island, one automatically assumes that life will be better if you leave. They call it "going abroad." Everyone wants to go abroad.

I've seen this on other Caribbean islands, too, as I did when we trained in Guadeloupe. There, they all wanted to go to New York. And it's not unique to the Caribbean; when I competed in Communist countries, I found everyone wanted to go to America, where the money grows on trees. That's how most Jamaicans see Canada and the United States. I didn't, not then. I felt I had a future in Jamaica. I thought I was on my way.

When I was thirteen, one of the phys ed teachers took an interest in me. I can't remember her name, but she was a black woman, about six feet tall, and she had pale, yellowy skin. We weren't buddies – students kept a respectful distance from teachers – but she used to watch me run those times I competed in the weekend races. She urged me to run in intramural and district meets against other schools. At the end of my second year, I returned home for the summer to live with Hilda and her family and I had been home only about a week when this teacher called me back to Clarendon. She wanted me to run in an all-Jamaica high school championship meet in Kingston.

I had never been to Kingston, the capital of Jamaica. In those days, the fairy tale picture that came into my head for any strange, faraway place I had never been to was the Land of Oz – Dorothy and the yellow brick road.

I boarded one of those old, dusty buses that lumber through the countryside and traveled back to Clarendon to visit my phys ed teacher in the big house she shared with some other teachers. I stayed with them overnight, so we could set out for Kingston early in the morning. I was the only athlete she had chosen from the school. Maybe the others weren't good enough or maybe they weren't interested, but it made me feel special to be the only one she picked to go to Kingston.

We left at daybreak in a car the teacher had borrowed from a friend. Heading down the road, just the two of us, I felt very grown up. And I felt like I was going to the end of the earth. I had never been more than twenty miles from my home.

As we neared Kingston, driving by the curve of the harbor, I saw my first sailing boats. There were fair-weather clouds, but the morning already was hot and steamy. The boats were far off in the distance, bobbing on the water, the sun catching their sails. They looked like swans.

And Kingston! I'd never imagined an Oz like this. The streets were crowded with people, and cars and buses and trucks and wagons. Bicycles clattered by. Policemen blew their whistles. People haggled at the open markets, people of all shapes, sizes, and colors. Some wore suits and ties, some wore turbans, bright saffron robes, or saris. And there were young guys in bushy Afros, thick combs stuck out of the back pockets of their jeans. From the sidewalks and bars I could hear steel-band music, rock, reggae. Even in the car, my feet wanted to dance.

My favorite weather always has been a tropical storm. Storms break the monotony in the countryside. They can be dangerous, for sure, but they're an honest enemy. They howl and lash at you, they push against the windows and bend the trees nearly to the ground, but when they've blown out to sea the air is always fresh and tangy. It feels as though something's been resolved, like something *happened*. Kingston was like a tropical storm that you made yourself, with crowds and music. It felt as if you could have one any time you wanted. That's what it was like in Kingston – something was happening.

I didn't know the world could get that hot. The heat seemed to rise from the streets, as if the city itself was baking. Sweat dripped from my face. I was hungry, but I couldn't think of eating. I was too excited. The teacher had a friend in Kingston and we drove there and lounged around the house before going to the stadium. All the time, I was aware that I was the reason we were there, waiting for my race at the stadium. My race was scheduled for late in the afternoon.

The stadium was enormous, a great bowl of people. It was the national stadium, regularly used for soccer. The high-jumpers and long-jumpers and discus-throwers were doing their grunty things in the field, which was encircled by the running track. The stands were filled to the sky with people, waves of people dressed in all the colors of the spectrum. And there was this constant, raucous murmur, as if you were standing at the edge of the sea. Sometimes I wonder how big that stadium would look to me today.

Funny, but standing there, trying to take everything in, my eyes began to focus on individuals in the mass of people in the stands. There were a lot of women in white T-shirts and blue denim jeans and skirts – I guess it was the style of the day – but what caught my eye were the women wearing lime green. Some of the athletes were even wearing lime green shorts. They just seemed to look more comfortable in lime green. Probably it was because of the heat, but that's when I made the connection between something fashionable and something "cool." I made a mental note to write Grandmother Vasthie in England and ask for a lime green blouse.

My attention wandered to the athletes, many of whom wore shorts made of a shiny, plastic-looking material. They had matching tank tops that they called singlets. The material made them look unnaturally sleek, like something out of a magazine. Some of the girls had fancy elastics with colored plastic balls attached to hold back their hair. Then I noticed the running shoes. They looked strangely exotic, with bright colors and stripes and high sides that covered the ankles. On the track, the athletes wore shoes with spikes.

I walked over to the edge of the track, which didn't look like any track I'd ever seen before. It was incredibly long; I could barely see the far curve. It must have been a standard 400-metre track, but I had never run on anything longer than 150 metres. At school, after crossing the finish line, we just ran off the track and came to a stop in a field of tall grass.

I wasn't going to be running on grass that afternoon. I wasn't sure what I would be running on, but it sure wasn't grass. I had never seen a track like the one at the stadium in Kingston. It was even, brick-colored, hard and mean-looking in the sun. I knelt down and pushed my fingers on the track, and it pushed back. Rubberized! I know now that it must have been either Chevron or Tartan, trade names for a synthetic resin surface that was originally invented for horse racing in the United States.

I couldn't have been the only one in Kingston astounded by the track that day. The first time a Tartan track had been used in the Olympic Games was in 1968 in Mexico. Before that, tracks were made of cinder or clay, or any available dirt. I can't remember how many lanes were marked off that afternoon in Kingston, or even how fast I thought I could run on that springy, rust-colored track; all I kept thinking was that I would stub my toe on it badly. I was going to run in my bare feet, the way I'd run on the grass at home and on the field those Saturday mornings in Clarendon.

For the first time that day, I heard the hollow, disembodied voice of a public-address announcer, and it sounded like every other competitor was named Scott. As it turned out, it was only one person, another woman runner. This girl Scott seemed to be entered in every event. Everyone was cheering for her. And she was winning everything — 100-metres, 200-metres, long jump. She was a big, muscular girl, yet she moved with tremendous grace and power. I was spellbound. When she passed once I was so close to the track that I could hear her breathing – sharp, guttural grunts. I could see the determination in her face, the concentration. She exuded a kind of passionate pain and rapture I had never seen before. But then, I had never seen a woman like her before.

I was then about the same height as I am now, five feet, six inches. I wore my hair in two pigtails, held with elastic bands. No makeup – I was still a grubesse. I wore my school phys ed outfit, one of those heavily starched skorts.

I didn't warm up for my race. I never had before, so why bother now? I just slipped my shoes off and I was ready to go. Then I saw the starting blocks.

I have my own set of blocks today, but back then, my God, they looked like some carpenter's tool. They're a shaft of aluminum, about four feet long, with two angled blocks attached that you can adjust to fit the length of your legs, for your crouch at the start. They have long spikes underneath that fasten to the track, so you can push off, like you're pushing off from a curb.

You need the blocks for a start, yet there's a lot of technique, too, and some runners are just better at it than others. I was never a terrific starter. For most of my career my strength was finishing, accelerating. Ben Johnson, BJ, could explode from the blocks.

There was a movie in the early 1980s called *Personal Best*, about women athletes preparing for the Olympics, and Mariel Hemingway plays a rookie who has never used starting blocks. In the hurdles, when she pushes off for the first time, she falls flat on her face. That's probably what would have happened to me if I'd used the blocks that afternoon.

I was entered in the 150-metre race. All I can remember is the sound of the starting pistol. After that, it was like every other race I've ever run before or since – a complete silence overtakes me. I hear nothing of the spectators, I feel nothing but air beneath my feet, I see nothing but the finish line.

And even that was different on this day in Kingston. It was an official tape, stretched between two poles with no one holding it. The girl in front of me, whose name was Jacqueline Pusey, broke it on her chest.

I came second. I don't remember what the prize was, but I do remember thinking that I was used to winning, and I had lost.

Later, in Canada and in Europe, I ran against Jacqueline Pusey again, even that muscular Scott girl, and I beat them both. What surprised me all those years later, though, was seeing so many familiar faces in Canada from that one afternoon at the national stadium in Kingston. One way or another, I suppose, with or without Grandmother Vasthie, I would have ended up in Canada on some kind of track scholarship. By 1979, I was competing against Jacqueline Pusey to represent the Americas Team at the World Cup.

But that day, I had no idea of a future in running. My teacher and I drove from Kingston to Clarendon that evening and I went back to spend the summer holiday with Ciceline and Hilda, and Enid.Things began to change quickly in my third year at high school. I was preparing for my third form examinations, which are quite demanding. In Jamaica, you fail, pass, or pass with distinction. I wanted to pass with distinction. English literature and grammar were heavily stressed in the third form, and the examinations were sent to England for grading. That was when Grandmother Vasthie sent me a letter directing me to leave school and join my mother in Canada. I was shocked.

I didn't want to go to Canada. I was happy in school in Jamaica. After the upheaval of my great-grandparents' deaths, after moving around from aunt to aunt, I felt I had found security and some sort of direction. My marks at school were excellent, or, at least, good. But I didn't allow myself to get angry, because Grandmother Vasthie wanted me to go. I never questioned her judgment.

What I didn't know was that Grandmother Vasthie had been trying for years to persuade my mother to live with her in England. Olive didn't want to go. However, my grandmother had relatives, distant cousins, in Canada, and she was the one who had convinced Olive to emigrate there. She thought life would be better for us if we escaped Jamaica. Went abroad.

It all happened fast. I don't think it took more than six months. It seemed I had just left Hilda's to return to school after the summer when I had to get a passport picture, then find a justice of the peace to sign it. I didn't go to Kingston to get the final papers, but someone must have, because everything in Jamaica gets done in Kingston. Grandmother Vasthie bought the ticket for the flight to Canada.

My schoolmates envied me, though they tried to hide it. I can't recall anyone warning me that Canada might be cold, or filled with white people. Everyone in the island thinks the good life is somewhere else. For many people from the islands, life is, in fact, not better somewhere else, but when people go away they seldom return, and so the myth persists. People believe what they want to believe.

As an adult, I think about this a lot. I've come to accept that the good life here is largely an illusion. Life goes on at such a fast pace in Canada. People are constantly worrying. In the islands, people live more day to day; they don't worry so much. Here, it's how can I pay the mortgage? How can I support a family? How can I buy a car? How can I heat my house? It costs so much to buy a house here, and if you don't buy a house you feel locked out. If you rent an apartment — if you can find a decent apartment — the rent is outrageous and every year or two they bump it up higher. A lot of islanders come here and find they can't afford to keep up their schooling, which I'm sure they considered the key to the good life. It just seems a treadmill of worry, and it's much worse if you have children. If the good life is a television and a fancy refrigerator and a microwave oven, I guess it's here in Canada, but I'm not so sure. I think you can get sick and die here from worry alone.

It was understood that I would leave high school in Jamaica, which was a very prestigious situation for me, attend high school in Canada, and, as they say in the island, "make something of yourself." Those words echoed in my head: *Make something of yourself.*

On the day after Christmas that year, 1974, they had a big dance in Manchester. They had a gigantic sound system, pounding out reggae. I wore a lilac-colored suede skirt and jacket, which was much too heavy for the warm weather. It was from Grandmother Vasthie, of course, a Christmas gift. I always think of that lilac-colored outfit when it gets cold in Toronto. For years after I arrived, I wished I had taken it with me from Jamaica.

I didn't take much with me. There was no going-away party, just this big, noisy Boxing Day dance that we all went to. The plan was that I would leave for Canada when my passport came through. It arrived early in January.

The day I went to say goodbye to Enid, I didn't cry. I don't think Enid realized that I was leaving and might never come back. It was a little like those terrible weeks when we lived alone, when I was scared to death of the ghosts — the ghost of my unforgiving great-grandmother, those ghostly finger-bits of Gloria's. I suppose any big change in life can bring to mind the ghosts of memories and the ghosts of fears with no name. These days, though, when I'm afraid, it's usually of people who are alive and well.

I never saw Enid again. She still lives in Jamaica in a house Grandmother Vasthie owns. It's all been renovated, and the rent for the house pays for Enid's support. The world is still a playhouse for Enid. I'd like to go back and visit her someday, show her a picture of my children. She'd like that. Enid would be about forty-seven now.

The day I left for Canada, in early 1975, a neighbor in the district gave me a ride to the airport in Kingston. He was the father of Carmen, my childhood friend at high school. He had a big car he used as a taxi, and we stopped to pick up somebody else on the way to the airport. None of my relatives came. Kingston was too far away.

I had never been on an airplane. I'd never even seen an airplane up close. I'm sure I didn't say two words to Carmen's dad, and as we neared the airport I had my nose pressed against the window of the car. Those big silver birds were sitting on the runway, glinting in the sun. The air was full of the sharp, acrid smell of fuel. The grass in the ditches by the airport was parched brown, but the sky was as blue as I had ever seen it. As we walked to the terminal from the parking lot, the noise of jet engines hurt my ears.

Carmen's dad carried my suitcase, and he kept nudging me along, motioning to the doors of the airport. It was like a dream. I couldn't hear anything he said. Then, we were inside the terminal building, where it was carpeted, and suddenly quiet and cool. I had not felt air-conditioning before.

Carmen's dad waited with me in the line to the ticket agent. He wanted to make sure everything was all right. I don't remember seeing him leave. My whole body strained forward to the boarding gate. Someone in a uniform pried my fingers off the handle of my suitcase. I was wearing my little denim outfit, denim slacks with a matching shirt with long sleeves. It was the style of the day, from Grandmother Vasthie of course.

Once I got to my seat in the airplane, I was scared to look around. I have a funny amnesia about the trip to Canada. I can hardly remember anything about it. I don't know who sat on either side of me, but I recall thinking it would be rude to stare over someone's lap to see out the window. I stared straight ahead at the back of the seat in front of me for the whole flight. I did notice the stewardesses, who were all black, and beautiful in smart uniforms. One of them even offered me a soft drink, but I couldn't look straight at her to thank her. I had a lot on my mind.

I hadn't seen my mother since 1972, when she visited me briefly before she left Jamaica. I had a pretty good idea what she would look like, but I wasn't sure; three years is a long time in a teenager's life. I carried a picture of her in my wallet. I took it out once and studied it, this woman called Olive Bird who was my mother. I thought, maybe we would get along famously. I thought she might be something like the big sister I never had.

4

The Pig Palace

As the plane approached Toronto, it looked as though we were flying above the stars. The lights of the city were dazzling, so many lights, and it was snowing. I didn't know it was snowing until we were taxiing along the runway and the white flakes melted on the window at the end of my row.

Inside the terminal, it seemed incredibly crowded and bright. I followed along with the other passengers through the corridors, on moving staircases they called escalators, past glassed-in spaces, until I came to a large, open room where I got in a line leading to a wicket where a customs agent examined my papers. My mother noticed me as soon as I left the wicket.

It would be nice to write about a happy reunion, mother and daughter whooping and hugging, but Olive and I never had that kind of relationship. We didn't hug or kiss like everyone around us. She handed me a coat she was carrying on her arm. She said she was worried about the summer-weight pants I was wearing. Olive is high-strung, excitable. It's hard to say what went wrong between us. I probably never gave her much chance to be a mother, as I always regarded Grandmother Vasthie as my mother.

I don't remember being cold as we walked to the car in the parking garage. And the snow was not at all like the pictures on the Christmas cards Grandmother Vasthie sent, no snowmen or soft, white hills. The snow drifted down from the sky like lace curtains, swirling in the lights outside the terminal.

Olive always worked hard, first in a nursing home, later in a garment factory, and she probably thought I was a lazy good-for-nothing, sprawled in front of the TV at her apartment. I was hypnotized by it. Television induces some kind of a stupor. I'm convinced, now, that the long-term, cumulative effect of indiscriminate television-watching is harmful to the mind. It makes you mentally lazy. These days, I am careful about what I allow my daughter, Sasha, to watch on TV, and I rarely watch it myself. I didn't even bother to watch the Commonwealth Games in New Zealand and our new "clean" track and field team. But those first few months in Canada, I became a television addict. Mostly cop shows – "Barnaby Jones", "The Rockford Files", "Cannon". I even watched Lawrence Welk!

At sixteen, I still had a temper. Once, Grandmother Vasthie came from England for a brief visit, and the tension in the apartment got so bad that my mother threw a Pyrex dish at me. I threw it back at her and then stomped into my room and smashed the mirror over my dresser. For the first time, I used my mother's unmarried status against her. If we had a fight, I'd say the meanest things I could think of. I wanted to hurt her, and I did. Maybe, living in Canada, I was suddenly embarrassed by my family situation because the values here were so different. Teenagers are impressionable. Maybe I felt bitter about not knowing anything about my father. Olive has never spoken to me about him.

Our relationship deteriorated still further when Olive's longtime boyfriend, Raphael, arrived from Jamaica. They got married in 1978 and he moved into the apartment. We were living near College Street in the west end of Toronto at the time. It was a nice apartment, quite spacious, with two bedrooms and a separate dining room. Olive had furnished it with all the modern conveniences and modern furniture. But she and Raphael just could not get along. They argued constantly. Their kind of arguing – hurtful, personal – preys on the mind of a teenager. It's the time of life when you need things to be solid, and when they're not, you can't walk away from the people supporting you. Your anger builds, seethes, and explodes at all the wrong times.

Olive and I have tried over the years to improve our relationship. She once came to live with Tony and me when we bought the house near High Park, but it didn't work out so she moved away. Now she lives with one of her cousins and his girlfriend. I take Sasha to see her nearly every Saturday. I like seeing Sasha with her grandmother, but Olive and I are better off apart.

During that first winter in Canada, I suffered a setback at school. We lived near some of my mother's cousins, a few of whom were my age. On a cold morning in January 1975, I tagged along to Western Technical with my second cousin, a boy named Clifton. I wanted to get into a technical school, as I still had a strong desire to become an engineer. I wanted to take drafting.

That first trip to school was an experience. I had never seen a subway train. Clifton and I were standing on the platform and the subway suddenly shot out of a hole at the end of the platform like a train hurtling out of a mountain tunnel, lights ablaze, metal wheels scraping metal tracks. As it passed, a rush of air from the train took my breath away. It crashed by, inches away, then screeched to a stop and all the doors wheezed open by themselves. It scared the wits out of me. Even now, I am nervous in the subway, especially when I'm with my daughters. I worry about Sasha falling through the space between the platform and the train.

That first morning, Clifton took me to the administration office to register for school. I was excited until I realized that they were going to put me back a year. In Jamaica, I had been preparing for my third form examinations. Now I was being put back to grade nine.

They do this to a lot of Jamaican kids. I'm convinced it's because we speak broken English, a Jamaican patois. We have our own expressions, like "in the island" instead of "on the island." I still catch myself using a plural subject with a singular verb or vice versa. And some of the sounds of the language here fool me. For years, I referred to the University of Toronto as "UFT," not "U. of T." I think they interpret this language difference as a form of stupidity. So, rather than offer special English classes, they put you back an entire academic year. I was devastated. I had always considered myself a bright student, an achiever. After a few minutes in the administration office, I felt like a dumb immigrant. I couldn't tell Olive how much this upset me.

I also found myself in what the sociologists love to call a visible minority group. All my life, I had been a black among blacks. I never gave it any thought. It's not like I get up in the morning and look in the mirror and say, "Hey, I've got black skin! How about that?" At Western Tech, I was black in a sea of white. But that was fifteen years ago and things have changed, especially in west-end Toronto; high school kids mix with each other more comfortably today. Back in 1975, though, the blacks clung to one another and the whites . . . well, the whites seemed to live in another world.

When I was on Team Canada and still in high school, the white kids would go out of their way to say hello or congratulate me. But I always knew that if I hadn't made the team, if I hadn't been exceptional, they would have walked right by. Stared through me as though I didn't exist, just as they always had.

I registered in shop classes at Western Tech, which made me a double minority, the only girl in a class of boys. There was another black in the class, however, and we got along well. His name was Miguel Nash; his brother Marvin was one of the best sprinters in the country. Marvin ran for Canada at the 1976 Olympic Games.

For the rest of the school year, and during the summer of 1975, I had nothing to do with track and field. It seems hard to believe, but I didn't know anything about the 1976 Olympics, which were to be held in Montreal. The papers were full of news about the mounting costs of the new Olympic stadium, the deficit, the cost overruns, and everyone was hopping mad because the roof wasn't ready on time. But I wasn't interested in any of it.

Not being involved in track and field, or in any serious hobby, I found all sorts of ways to waste time. That's what struck me about Canada those first months, all the things you can do, the choices: television, movies, record stores, malls, cars, restaurants, rock concerts, dances. Every day was an exhausting kaleidoscope of experiences, like a merry-go-round spinning faster and faster. There were so many choices that after a while I felt overwhelmed, they became a blur, and I ended up doing nothing. I doubt I could have concentrated on track and field even if I had tried.

By the fall of 1975, I settled down and got involved in after-school track and field activities. Most of the kids I knew played basketball, but I went with the sport I was familiar with from Jamaica. My dream of being an engineer began to crumble because I was having difficulty with drafting. In the summer of 1976, I went to summer school for another course in drafting, but it didn't help. I switched to academics at the start of the 1976 school year at Western Tech. That didn't seem to work out for me either, so after a few months I switched again, this time to Parkdale Collegiate. With all this fiddling around, I ended up losing another academic year. It didn't bother me as much this time because in my second time around in grade ten I met Mike Hawryluk.

Mike Hawryluk was my first coach in Canada. He was a phys ed teacher at Parkdale. A lot of athletes went through Parkdale: Carrie Smith, the sprinter Marvin Nash, and our best shot-putter, Bishop Dolegiewicz. Parkdale had a history of good track and field athletes. Mike Hawryluk didn't conduct year-round training for his track team, however; most years he was fortunate to get a month of training in before the outdoor season began.

I ran for Mr. Hawryluk and our team made it to the Ontario Federation of School Athletic Associations' province-wide high school track and field championships in 1977. The meet was held in another Kingston – Kingston, Ontario, a stately, treed, university city by the lake, halfway between Toronto and Montreal. Mr. Hawryluk drove me to the meet, just like my phys ed teacher had driven me to that big meet at the national stadium in Kingston, Jamaica.

In the car, I carried my stuff in a plastic shopping bag. When Mr. Hawryluk saw it, he asked, "Jeez, Ange, can't you get a gym bag?" All I had in the shopping bag was a hairbrush and my running shoes, what runners call flats. I didn't own a pair of spikes.

I learned something that day about competition, training, and track and field organization. Some kids think they can just show up and run and their natural ability will make them champions. It doesn't work that way. Running, or sprinting, may seem like the most natural athletic feat – what primitive man did when hunting or hunted – but it's not as natural, or as easy, as it looks. It is a rare runner who can make it to these meets on his own; it is rarer still to excel in competition.

You have to join a club and get proper coaching. At the meet in Kingston, it was obvious that some of the high school athletes had been training longer and harder than I had. They belonged to clubs, and they worked out under expert guidance five days a week, year round. Even so, I won the 100-metre final against the best high school sprinters in the province.

With help from Mr. Hawryluk, I made up my mind to join the track club at Michael Power High School for the summer of 1977. Michael Power is a Catholic school, now known as Michael Power–St. Joseph's High School, in Islington, a suburb west of Toronto. It was the high school that almost always came in as the overall winner in the Ontario high school championships. I trained with the club all that summer, while my friends worked at supermarkets, or played at summer camp, or hung around malls. There was one girl in the club, Diane somebody, who was very good. I could never beat her.

In the fall of 1977, I was back at Parkdale for grade eleven. In December, when the indoor running track opened at the Canadian National Exhibition grounds, I returned to the Michael Power club to resume training.

That was my introduction to Canadian track and field training, indoor-style; aspiring track stars had to wait for the Royal Winter Fair to finish before we could get inside a building called the Swine Pavilion. We called it the Pig Palace. The place reeked of horse shit, pig shit, and cow shit.

Before it was available, I trained in the gymnasium at Parkdale, which was used primarily for basketball. Up above the court, there was a circular gallery where you could stand and watch the game. I used that gallery as a track. I don't know if it was eighty metres around. It had no seats, which was a blessing, and there was a railing. For all I know the gallery might have been a track in the early years of the school.

My first time at the Pig Palace, I ran for Parkdale High. The meet was held on a blustery Friday evening. It's always brutally cold and windy in winter down by the lake in Toronto. We didn't have enough girls for the competition, so I ran in a relay team with three boys. And we did quite well. I can't remember if we came first or second, but we ran well and my split – the part of the relay that I ran – was right up there with the guys. I can't remember my precise time, but there was a man in the stands that night who thought it was damned good.

He came up to me after the relay and told me that he thought I'd run a fabulous race. He told me about a track club that met regularly at the Pig Palace, and he invited me to come out and train there. I was flattered, but I didn't take what he said seriously because I belonged to the Michael Power club. I went home that night and I didn't even tell Olive about the race, or what this man had said. Two days later, talking to Mr. Hawryluk, I mentioned that this guy had told me I'd run a great race and had invited me to train at the Pig Palace.

"What guy?" he asked.

"Some guy named Peter Cross."

Mr. Hawryluk looked impressed.

Peter Cross was the major coach with the Scarborough Optimist Track and Field Club. It was already one of the biggest and best-funded clubs in Canada, though it was only three years old. Cross had coached all the runners from the club who had made the 1976 Canadian Olympic team. When I heard this, I lost my nerve and didn't go to the first practice the following Monday night. But the next Monday, I did.

When I got there, I couldn't find Peter Cross. He was on a road trip with some of the club's senior runners. That night I heard he was phasing himself out of the Scarborough Optimist Club and bringing along another coach by the name of Charlie Francis. Cross went on to coach at Clemson University in South Carolina, and the last I heard he was working as a school principal in British Columbia. So, that first evening at the Pig Palace, with the Scarborough Optimist runners, my coach was Charlie Francis. I swallowed my disappointment.

Charlie Francis is a pleasant-looking guy in an ordinary sort of way. He has sandy brown hair and slightly squinted eyes in an intelligent face. You wouldn't notice him in a crowd. He had a beard then, and he certainly wasn't the fashionable dresser that he is today. Charlie was an athlete too — a sprinter. He represented Canada at the 1972 Olympics in Munich. His best time in the 100-metres was 10.21.

He had recently separated from his first wife and had returned home to live with his parents. He worked for an insurance company, and he came directly from work each evening to coach us. He always had a cup of coffee in his hand. He was a very hyper guy. He drove an Aston Martin, which he had bought from a friend who was an ace mechanic with a special interest in exotic cars. Charlie got work done on his car in return for helping out, unpaid, in the body shop. Charlie was smart this way, making deals, not afraid of hard work. But I always thought that flashy car was out of character for him. Later he had to sell it for cash flow, and he bought a little put-put to get around. That was when BJ was driving a new Trans-Am — a few years before he bought the $108,000 Porsche and the $257,000 Ferrari Testarossa.

Charlie never let us in on what he did in his spare time. Between his job and his commitment to track and field, I don't think he had much of a social life. We had worked together nearly a decade when he brought around Angie, who later became his second wife, and that's when he started dressing in Italian suits and expensive shoes. At the beginning, on trips to Europe, Charlie took only a little bag with underwear, T-shirts, and a couple of pairs of jeans.

Charlie always was curious, eager to hear all the gossip, and he was easy to talk to. He listened. Anyone at the club with a problem, whether it involved training or something personal, could go to Charlie and he would find a way to help out.

Athletes develop a peculiar bond with their coaches, especially if the coaches start bringing them success. It's a parent-friend-lover relationship, though athletes and coaches seldom get romantically or sexually involved. In all the years I was in track and field, I saw only a few athletes get seriously involved with their coaches, and that was mostly in Europe.

Your coach becomes the one person in the world who you want to impress the hell out of – on all kinds of levels. You spend a lot of time with your coach, more than you spend with your parents, or boyfriend, or even your husband. It's different in the United States, where there seems to be a kind of militaristic "Yes sir, no sir," relationship between athletes and coaches. Charlie became our friend. There were times when he was my best friend.

This might surprise some people who watched our workouts, or watched us before a race at an important meet. James Christie of *The Globe and Mail* once remarked how Charlie and I fought like cats and dogs. Charlie and I always had some ongoing battle, always over technique or training. If my starts weren't going well, I'd go into a terrible funk. I could be miserable. Near the end of my career, I became convinced that Charlie's workouts were too strenuous, that he was overworking me, and it was hurting my performance in competition. Charlie and I had loud, raging fights about this.

One evening, when I was preparing for a big meet, I just didn't feel like working out. The meet was going to be held the next day, and I was in pain and exhausted. Charlie lit into me with a stream of invective he usually reserved for Desai Williams or Tony Sharpe if they skipped a workout. "You lazy good for nothin'! You're gonna get your ass beat! You think you're so good you don't have to work, well I got news for you."

I blew my stack.

The swearing got pretty hot between us, but that was nothing unusual for Charlie, whose every second word was fuck this, fuck that. Believe me, I gave as good as I got. I stomped off the track that night, left the practice, and swore I was never going to work with Charlie Francis again.

The funny thing about Charlie is, you could have a screaming match like that, and the next thing you knew, he'd be at your side talking to you as though nothing had happened. The first time it happened, I couldn't believe it. One minute I'm telling him to fuck off and he's yelling at me to fuck off, and the next minute he says, "What are we going to do about your A-skips?" Charlie couldn't hold a grudge. I laugh about it now, but the effect was to keep me focused on my goal of perfecting my technique.

It used to drive us crazy the way Charlie illustrated every point with a story. He had a library of stories in his head, one for every occasion. It might be about training, using the blocks, hamstring pulls, or it might be about how to deal with a bank teller or your mother. Charlie began each story by saying, "I remember the time something similar happened. . ." We used to try to guess which story he'd use for a particular situation. After a few years, we knew them all. His wife, Angie, is already groaning about Charlie's damned stories.

Charlie was exceptionally good with me when I was injured. When we had a masseur, Charlie would be there with me, hovering, fussing, making sure the masseur got the tightness out of the damaged muscle. He designed special exercises to help the healing, or techniques to get around an injury in time for a meet. He'd watch me like a hawk at the workouts to make sure I followed his instructions.

There is an easygoing charm about Charlie, a sweet insouciance, but if you weren't doing your best, if you were slacking off, he could shoot you a withering look that chilled you to the bone. He also had a fierce loyalty to his athletes. It was what made the Scarborough Optimist Club excel. If a meet organizer got lazy, if he forgot some minor technical detail, Charlie would be all over him like a dirty shirt. If we were forced to run into the wind, or if the blocks weren't exactly right, Charlie raised living hell. He was the squeaky wheel that got the grease for us. He made a lot of enemies in track and field with that attitude. Some people hate him.

I started with the Scarborough Optimist Club in January 1978. I'd go down to the CNE after school. It was just a streetcar ride away from home. I don't remember Ben Johnson from those days, but I do remember seeing his older brother, Eddie. Eddie and I took the same streetcar. Desai Williams, Val Gross, and Tony Sharpe also trained at the Pig Palace. Mark McKoy came later. I was one of two girls at the club, the usual ratio.

The workouts were much harder than anything I had ever done. We used to do a long warm-up, and then detailed drills. After that, those of us who had them put on our spikes and did sprints. I wasn't used to the relentless organization. The drills included what we called A-skips and B-skips, and Running A-skips and Running B-skips. A-skips are when you run on the spot and bring your knees up at intervals; B-skips are when you run on the spot, constantly bringing your knees way up. With the running versions, you do the same skips but in a full run.

I had trouble with the running B-skips. I'm actually not that well coordinated. With B-skips, you flick your legs out, almost like a chorus-line dancer. Trying to do this when you're running is that much harder, and I could never get the hang of it. There were great floor-to-ceiling concrete pillars in the Pig Palace and when it came time to do the running B-skips, I'd slink away and hide behind them. I thought everyone would laugh at me if they saw me trying the skips. Later, I watched a bunch of kids who came to the club for a workshop and they looked hilariously spastic trying to do running B-skips. I started practicing the running B-skips at home and eventually I managed to do them without embarrassing myself. I didn't have to duck behind those pillars anymore.

I finally broke down and bought a pair of spikes, but I didn't bother buying a good pair of flats. I used to sit on the floor at the Pig Palace and remove the spikes so I'd have flats for the warm-ups, drills, and circuit training, then I'd screw them back in for my speed work. Charlie still jokes about this. I could afford only one pair of flats, and they weren't for running. I had succumbed again to my vanity and bought a pair of Roots shoes, which were popular with the kids at school. I have never yet bought a proper pair of flats. Later on, adidas always provided them. The first pair of adidas I got was a big deal. I went to the Metro high school finals in the summer of 1978 and did well, won the 100-metre final, and I got a gift certificate from adidas for a pair of Tartans. They were snazzy, red with three white stripes on the sides.

Training with the Scarborough Optimist Club became a very intense experience. This is where they separate the wheat from the chaff. Every day, Monday to Friday, I went directly from school to the Pig Palace, and didn't get home until about nine o'clock. On Saturdays, we worked out in the afternoon, so it became a six-day-a-week commitment. I formed strong friendships with people at the club. I didn't mind being out until nine every night, either. Olive and Raphael were slinging the mud pretty good by then.

I never got much homework at Parkdale. I don't know whether it was a policy at the school, or a concession to track and field students. Either way, it worked in my favor. I was not the kind of student to go home and review the day's lessons anyway, which is why I had so much trouble with math. When I was taught mathematical formulas in class, I'd remember them for about three days, then forget them for the exam. I did well in history, though, and social sciences. I never seemed to forget a date in history. But I didn't bother much with schoolwork anymore. When exams rolled around, I stayed up the night before and crammed, memorized entire textbooks. I maintained an average grade and graduated from grade thirteen.

Charlie used to beat into our little heads that we should keep a record of our workouts. He insisted that we build a kind of blueprint for future training programs, so we'd be able to look back and see what had worked well and what hadn't. He wanted it to be detailed, including the time we took for breaks between drills. I took to this easily. When Molly Killingbeck joined the club, she began a journal, too. The guys never did. Charlie himself never kept a journal; years later, he was always looking through mine to find out what we had done.

Over the years, these journals, or diaries, would become personalized. For a while in 1980, I had a crush on a guy named John Smith. He was the world record holder in the 440-yards. He's now a successful coach at UCLA and two of his athletes won the men's gold and men's bronze in the 400-metres at Seoul. We went out together for a while, and my 1980 diary has a few references to him. Things like, "John Smith: letter." There is a telephone number written on the inside front cover of my first diary that indicates where he would be "as of Sunday," whatever that meant.

That first diary of mine evolved into a work of art. I kept it from my first workout with Charlie in January 1978 and wrote in it every day until February 12, 1981, when I ran out of space. It is a legal-sized Blueline notebook with hard covers and lined pages. On the front cover, there are several stickers from my travels around the world: a bright yellow adidas sticker; another one that is orange with a stylized winged figure as a logo from Meeting International Athletisme Nice/Nikaia, August 17, 1980; a blue adidas sticker that partly covers another sticker from Familiade '80, Show and Sport Rheinstandion, Düsseldorf; and a sticker with a stylized orange running track on a white background for the Memorial IVO Van Damme on August 22, 1980. On the back cover are two more stickers: Lac Quelle Fürth, and Parkhotel "Val-Monte" Golden Tulip Hotel Nijmegen (Berg en Dal) Nederland.

There are some scribblings on the front cover, too. My name is there in big letters made with a red felt marker pen. And there are three words that are hard to make out by now, worn and faded as they are. They are: Swifter, Higher, Stronger. *Citius, altius, fortius.* The Olympic motto.

On the first inside page, I have again written my name but, as I did with all my subsequent diaries, I have also written a couple of inspirational expressions:

Winning is Not Everything. It is The Only Thing.

That's from Vince Lombardi, coach of the Green Bay Packers.

The other is a short passage I memorized in grade school in Jamaica, from Henry Wadsworth Longfellow:

The heights by great men
reached and kept
Were not attained by sudden flight.
But they, while their companions slept
Were toiling upward in the night.

A few rather unpoetic expressions also grace the inside front cover. I kept a list for a while of years beyond 1981, when I had already started new diaries. In pencil, I've made a note relating to 1983 that reads, "Fucking stupid programme, disastrous." And in 1984, also in pencil, I've written, "Still feeling the effects of '83 – error will never be forgiven."

On the second day of my testimony at the Dubin Inquiry, March 14, 1989, the Toronto *Sun* ran a big headline in red underlined letters that read "Drug Diary." My journals were much more than that. There is a lot of pain in the neat rows of figures that make up most of the diaries.

There are brief notes on the inside front cover, recording my best times and including times from 1977 that I must have thought worth noting. These are 25.5, meaning twenty-five and a half seconds for the 200-metres, and 12.2, meaning twelve and two-tenths seconds for the 100-metres. By 1982, the last year in this short list, the times are 22.25 and 11.00.

For ten years, from 1978 to 1988, a few seconds here and there were the story of my life.

5

Little Ben

Before the first diary had a single sticker on the cover, when all the pristine, blue-lined pages ahead had yet to be filled, I made some notes on the workouts I was doing after the high school championship meet in Kingston, Ontario, in 1978.

A lot of things had changed since the summer before when Mr. Hawryluk drove me with my plastic shopping bag to Kingston.

Tuesday, June 6th, 1978

Warm up
Drills
4 x 40 m
3 x 100 m walk between
Stretch
100 jog 100, 100 jog 100
Repeat 4 times
Hills
4 A skips, 4 B skips, 4 bounding
4 bounding in acceleration, 4 running As
into acceleration, 4 Bs in acceleration
4 accelerations
Jog down

That year, 1978, members of the Scarborough Optimist Club met at Northern Secondary School in North Toronto to board a chartered bus. The bus took us to dormitories on the campus of Queen's University in Kingston, for the Ontario high school finals, scheduled for June 2 and June 3. I was entered in the 100-metre and 200-metre sprints.

I came third in the 200-metres, at 25.3 seconds. But that isn't what still burns in my mind from the meet. What I cannot forget is my first meeting with Angela Bailey.

I had just run the 100-metres and I was babbling away to some other members of the club that I had run it in 12.3 seconds. Privately, I was disappointed because I had run much better times, as low as 11.8 seconds — high elevens, we called them — at various high school meets. I didn't like the track in Kingston — I was used to a harder surface by then — but as I was blathering, Angela Bailey sidled up to our group and said, "If I ran 12.3, I wouldn't tell anyone."

Bailey has an English accent that grates on my ears. At least, it started to grate on my ears when she opened her mouth that sunny June day in Kingston. I said nothing in return, though I was deeply offended. At the time, Bailey was the fifteen-year-old prima donna of the high school circuit. Who was I to talk back? It was the start of a series of misunderstandings and mutual insults that plagued both of us over the next decade.

Another memory from that day was the performance of the girl who came first in the 200-metres, Grace Verbeek. Verbeek beat me handily, but the next time I saw her, a year later, she was running the 800-metres. I was astounded: a fine sprinter forced to be a half-miler by some harebrained coaches. This is one of the things wrong with track and field in Canada. So few of the coaches are paid for their work that it's the luck of the draw as to what kind of coach you get. Verbeek had obviously been taken over by people who neglected her natural ability with speed and concentrated on her mediocre talent with distance. Verbeek never distinguished herself in track and field, which was a deplorable waste of someone who might have become world class.

I returned from Kingston filled with resolve to work harder than ever before, and on Tuesday the sixth, following the weekend, I was onto the heavy workout noted in my diary above. Let me explain.

"Warm up" consisted mainly of stretching exercises, to loosen up, get the blood flowing, maybe work up a mild sweat. For "drills," I'd run 40 metres four times, then 100 metres three times. I walked around the track between the sprints. After more stretching, I ran the 100-metres flat out, followed by a light 100-metre jog. I'd do this four times. As for "hills," I'd find a rise, a hill in the park if I was outside, and jog up it, like running up a flight of stairs. Then came the A-skips and B-skips, and "bounding", which was jumping as high as I could while doing the skips. "Accelerating" just means going faster and faster, in bursts around the track. After all this, I'd do a gentle jog to cool down.

In the summer of 1978, we also started using medicine balls in our workouts. A medicine ball is like a leather beachball filled with sand to give it weight. Some weigh six pounds, some weigh more than twelve. They're terrific for conditioning. You throw them around in a choreographed exercise – overhead, side to side, chest passes. Sometimes we held them and used them like weights during sit-ups. If the day comes when I decide to get rid of this belly I've developed after having babies, I'll start with my medicine ball.

I'm explaining this because people, even those weekend athletes who think they're serious joggers, often haven't a clue what these drills are all about. I realized this during my second day at the Dubin Inquiry, when Robert Armstrong, the commission counsel, tried to get on record exactly what these rituals were. Armstrong had picked a date at random out of my diaries. You'd think he was sifting through Egyptian hieroglyphics. Once, Mr. Justice Dubin looked down over his glasses at Armstrong and said to him, "Obviously, you haven't done much track and field."

Armstrong soldiered on.

"After you do the 100-metre sprints as part of your warm-up, what comes next in your diary there?" he asked me.

"Three times 50-metre strides in my spikes, then I take a little break, and then I get into all my power speed drills."

"What's involved in that?" Standing down there at the lectern in front of me, Armstrong looked perplexed. "You fill half a page almost with it. Could you just take us through that, please?"

I tried.

"Six times ten-metre A-skips, six-by-ten-metre running Bs, six-by-ten-metre running As, three-by-thirty-metre heel-and-toe, three-by-ten-metre heel raises, three-by-thirty-metre triplings, three-by-thirty-metre B-skips, three-by-thirty-metre running As with leg up. And then I take a break and we had an accelerator – ."

"Let me just stop you there," Armstrong interjected. He looked like *he* had been doing running B-skips. Mr. Justice Dubin looked on, a smile forming on his quizzical, owlish face.

"What are A-skips?" Armstrong asked.

I said to him, as gently as I could, "Do you want me to show you?"

Armstrong said, "Sure." I think he actually wanted me to step out of the witness box and do A-skips for the gallery. And to think I used to hide behind a pillar at the Pig Palace.

Mr. Justice Dubin cut in and said, "No, we're only kidding. Just describe them, if you can."

Armstrong ventured, "I have the picture, in a sense, of you using some kind of skipping rope."

"No, no, no, no, no," I said. "They're *knee* raises."

"I think it would be better if she explained it herself," Dubin said.

At this point, my lawyer, Dennis O'Connor, sitting in the front row of the gallery, suggested, "Maybe Mr. Armstrong could show us." That provoked howls of laughter.

After more "three-by-thirties" and "triplings" and "accelerations," Armstrong said perhaps it would be best if some day he visited the track to learn firsthand about these drills. Judging from the entry he had chosen from my diary, he assumed these were complicated and rigorous routines.

"Actually," I told him, "you've picked one of my easiest days."

Armstrong said he didn't want to tire Mr. Justice Dubin so early in the morning.

"Just listening to it makes me tired," the judge said.

Like all kids who join a track club, my biggest motivation by that summer of 1978 was to try for a spot on the national track and field team. By joining a club, I was automatically registered with the provincial track and field association, in my case the Ontario Track and Field Association (OTFA). This meant I was entitled to go to the national championships to try out for the national team. I filled out a form telling them the name of my club, the name of my coach, and, after I paid forty dollars, they registered me with the national body, the Canadian Track and Field Association (CTFA) (now known as Athletics Canada).

At that point, the CTFA put me on their mailing list for publications from national sports organizations, such as the Sport Medicine Council of Canada and Sport Canada. That's when I began to wade into the complexities of amateur sport in this country. I was nineteen, and most of the names of the organizations meant nothing to me; it was years before I understood who the important officials were in Canadian amateur sport.

At various times over the years, most of these organizations issued pamphlets or brochures on the subject of the use of banned substances in amateur sport. The pamphlets were supposed to be Canada's Maginot Line in the battle against these practices.

By September 1989, for example, the CTFA was distributing a pamphlet commissioned by Canada's Ministry of Fitness and Amateur Sport, that listed banned drugs, including forty-one types of stimulants, nineteen narcotic analgesics, seventeen anabolic steroids, ten beta-blockers, and sixteen diuretics, and the prohibited practice of blood doping (loading up on your own blood with red-cell transfusions, which marathoners often resort to for endurance). Alcohol and marijuana were listed as specifically not prohibited, but it was noted that a concentration of caffeine over twelve micrograms per millilitre would result in a positive doping test. The brochure warned that most cough medicines contain banned drugs.

This pamphlet arrived in a big brochure known as the CTFA Anti-Doping Information Package. In it, the CTFA outlined its doping control policy, first approved at the annual general meeting in June 1982. The association's general position is that it is unequivocally opposed on ethical, medical, and legal grounds to the practice of doping in sport. It also says that the encouragement or counseling of an athlete to use doping by any member of the association is unacceptable and will not be tolerated.

I put aside much of this information, as did most of my teammates. A glossy brochure printed in 1984 by the Ministry of State, Fitness and Amateur Sport, and the Sport Medicine Council, outlined the ethical reasons for prohibiting doping:

> The use of doping substances in an attempt to gain an advantage is a clear violation of the rules of amateur sport. Such conduct is cheating and contrary to the most fundamental principles of sportsmanship and fair play. The integrity of both athletes and the sporting community is jeopardized by such practices.

> Athletes should also recognize the significance of their status as role models for younger members of our society. Theirs is a trust which should not be betrayed.

High-minded sentiments indeed, but in 1978, my interest in organized amateur sport had nothing to do with role models and fair play. What had won me a place with the Scarborough Optimist Club was hard work, and the track club gave me an opportunity to improve my skills and enter tougher competitions. While other kids stayed at home and did their homework or watched TV, or went out on dates, I was at the track. I began to realize that I had natural talent, but I knew I wouldn't get anywhere unless I outworked everybody else. At nineteen, I did not consider myself a role model to anyone.

I began to feel part of the gang at the Scarborough Optimist Club. Every teenager wants to feel accepted, and for me the club was an ideal combination of a group of friends and the solo sport of running. There are few things more solitary than running. Sprinting – technically, the 100-, 200-, and 400-metre dashes, and same-distance relays – is the purest form of running. You exert the maximum human effort, you don't hold anything back. It takes at least seven years to properly develop a sprinter. In that sense, it's a creative sport. Artists and writers must also spend huge amounts of time alone, with nothing but their will to keep them going.

If that first glossy brochure had been available to me in 1978, I would have been most interested in the section on the legal implications of doping. But even by 1984, the date of publication, the language was finger-wagging, tut-tutting bureaucratese:

> International Sport Federations and the International Olympic Committee have unequivocally prohibited the use of doping substances. Sport Canada and the Canadian Olympic Association have taken a strong stand on the question in order to eradicate the use of banned substances by Canadian athletes. As well, most national sport bodies in Canada have adopted antidoping policies, in line with their respective international federations. Many of these substances are drugs whose use and transmissions are controlled by civil and criminal statutes in Canada and other nations. Obvious social, sporting and legal costs may

> be incurred as a consequence of the use of banned doping substances.

I don't know who those guys up in Ottawa thought they were composing this stuff for, but I'll bet nineteen-year-olds today file it the same place I did when I got it – in the garbage.

Earlier in 1978, during the March school break, several of us had piled into one of Ross Earl's vans for a trip to a winter training camp in Tennessee. Ross Earl is the founder of the Scarborough Optimist Track and Field Club. He is a secondary school teacher in Scarborough, a suburb of Toronto, and he owns an antique business on the side. Ross has got himself and the club in a heap of trouble within the past couple of years with the way the club handled some of the funds raised. In those days, as now, he was just a friendly, hardworking man without whom we could never have achieved what we did. Ross ran bingo nights to raise money for the club. At one point he was running five bingos a week, netting $3,000 each week for us. This money went toward entrance fees to meets, uniforms, vans, and, most importantly, winter training camps.

I can't exaggerate the importance of winter training camps to a developing track and field athlete in this country. Perhaps some of you will understand if you think about the difference between golf lessons in a gymnasium and out on an open fairway, with real grass, real bunkers, and real trees. Canada has long, cold winters, as do East Germany and Russia. Athletes from those countries don't hang around waiting for spring thaw before they start to prepare for the next season. They go south, often to Mexico, to a country with a warm climate, so that they can train outside.

The most important part of a winter training camp is the track conditions. In Canada, the indoor tracks are 200 metres, they are banked, and, if you're lucky, they are made of synthetic resinous materials such as Chevron or Tartan. All these expensive details are terrific for competition but nearly disastrous for training. Chevron and Tartan, which look like plastic-coated, grainy concrete, are far too hard for the daily pounding a runner's knees and shins take in training. And the banked corners can cause serious ligament injuries as your body strains to make the curve eight, ten, twelve, twenty times a day. The fact that the indoor tracks are only 200 metres adds to the problem, for endurance training – keeping up your speed the entire length of a race – requires a distance of at least 400 metres.

Every autumn of my running life, I suffered terrible shin splints for the first few weeks of the season as I adjusted to the indoor track at York University's high performance center, in a suburb north of Toronto. Of course, that wasn't as bad as the times when the university closed down the center for public holidays. Can you imagine having a major presentation to make to a client on Tuesday morning, but the boss decides to lock the office for a three-day weekend? We would tear our hair out when York closed and find a way to get to either the Fitness Institute, or, if it was open, the University of Toronto. The University of Toronto has the hardest synthetic track surface of all – Mondo. Superb and fast for competition, but a nightmare for training. We considered ourselves lucky that the owner of the Fitness Institute was generous enough to allow top athletes occasional access to his facilities, but it's tough to train when you have to elbow your way past all these flaccid old guys out for a jog before a cocktail and dinner.

The average guy on the street probably scoffs at our need to go to a warm country in order to train during the winter. Perhaps it's the reason that other athletes – hockey players, skaters, and skiers – get such respect in this country, as though they've beaten the ice and snow with honor. I don't know what we would have done if Ross Earl hadn't raised that money from his bingo games to send the top Scarborough Optimists south every winter. There are many talented track and field athletes out there who will never reach their potential because no one can find the money to send them south.

As it was, I believe the money Ross raised was a two-edged sword: it helped to produce some of the most talented runners in the world, but it planted the seeds of jealousy in the rest of the Canadian track and field community. An arrogance began to develop in our tight little group. With Ross's money, we rose above most of the petty squabbles of amateur track and field. We chased excellence; we ran solo.

I was proud to be invited on the trip to Tennessee. By 1978, the Scarborough Optimist Club had more than four hundred athletes and at least a dozen volunteer coaches. It was a select group that set off in that van. The details of that trip will stay with me forever, long after the memories of more glamorous trips to Europe have faded. The van was white with a purple stripe down the side — the colors of the club. We wore uniforms according to our ranking in the club. I had on the purple shirt reserved for junior members. Younger athletes, the tykes, wore white. The intermediates wore yellow. The seniors wore an orange uniform with the crest of the club in the middle and two yellow stripes down the sides.

Uniforms were always important to me. No small part of my drive to make the national team was that it meant I could wear the red-and-white Team Canada uniform. I wanted a singlet and a tracksuit with "Canada" written on them. When I got them, I was so proud I wore them to school. When Ben Johnson got his, he wore it to Yorkdale Shopping Mall. What ruined it for us was when one of the department stores bought the rights to sell the uniform to the public. It was slightly different, lacking the official Team Canada logo, but it still took the thrill away. Another thing that eroded our pride in our uniforms was the fact that our Team Canada uniforms were made of cheap nylon. (We were embarrassed to show up in them in Rome because the Italian athletes had designer outfits. The West German uniforms looked like they were made of suede.)

Charlie Francis and one of the senior athletes took alternate shifts driving the van on the two-day trip to Tennessee. We stayed overnight at one of those Day's Inns on the way down. I noticed that Charlie kept popping Vibrants, powerful caffeine pills, to stay awake when he was at the wheel.

I was looking forward to the training camp. It made me feel grown up. I'd never even been allowed to sleep over at a girlfriend's house. I had never wanted anything so much in my life as to be in that van, on my way to what we eventually dubbed the roach motel, because of the cockroaches.

It was on this trip that I got my first impression of Ben Johnson. The training camp was set up so that we worked out twice a day, drills first thing in the morning, before breakfast, then a harder workout in the afternoon. Each day, we'd go to one of those American family-style restaurants for a late "breakfast special" — all across the United States there were "breakfast specials" — and for dinner we'd go to some joint like the Ponderosa for that other American culinary tradition, "the dinner special." We'd kibitz at mealtime, goof around a little, but BJ hardly ever said more than three words. His older brother Eddie, who was a talented runner in high school and has since gone on to weightlifting in Texas, did everything for Ben. He spoke for him, even ordered his food for him. I thought it was odd.

We came to the conclusion at the time that Ben was afraid to speak, partly because he had a bad stutter, partly because he had a thick Jamaican accent. He was easily embarrassed. Since then, I've concluded that Ben is also astoundingly lazy, that if he can get someone to do something for him, he will. He used to call me at all hours of the day and night to look up things for him in the Yellow Pages.

But maybe there's more to it. People who are functionally illiterate often exhibit manipulative behavior; they resort to complicated, subtle subterfuge to mask their illiteracy. Maybe BJ couldn't read very well.

One day, during that winter training camp, Ben somehow ended up in the restaurant without Eddie, and the waitress asked him what he wanted.

"Heggs!" Ben shouted. "Lots!"

We were shocked. It was one of the few things I had ever heard him say. Then all hell broke loose and we laughed ourselves stupid. "Heggs" is the Jamaican accented version of eggs, and hearing it so loudly, and so forcefully, in that American restaurant sounded hilarious.

Poor BJ. After that incident, a couple of the guys in the club, especially Desai Williams and Tony Sharpe, ragged Ben mercilessly. I had already formed my opinion of people who run in packs, so I stayed out of a lot of the razzing, though some of their jokes *were* funny.

They were always playing tricks on BJ. On our first trip to Europe, in 1979, they got Ben's watch and set it ahead so that he jumped up, got dressed, and stood waiting outside Charlie's door with a packed suitcase at four-thirty in the morning. The guys still howl about that one.

I hung around more with the guys on the team than with the girls. With the guys, I could share a laugh, relax a little. Unfortunately, I came to lose respect for West Indian men as a result. After a while, they considered me "one of the guys," so they didn't hold back much when they were having a good time. I came to loathe some of their crude behavior. They thought farting in public was the funniest thing invented. We were traveling on a plane once and one of the guys went to use the washroom, and the smell was so bad they had to spray it down. The captain came out of the cockpit, mad as hell. They still howl about that one, too.

Early on, I dated Desai Williams for about six weeks, after which I vowed I would never go out with another black man. If I was on a desert island and the only men available were black, I'd become a nun. The things they said about women, how they treated women, what they thought about the women they lured into their beds, were revolting. They didn't spare me any details. Sleep with a West Indian man, and you can be sure the minute-by-minute replay will be all over town the next day.

BJ was as bad as the rest of them. Once he told me that he preferred white women and that he'd probably marry only a white woman because West Indian women were "miserable." But the way he carried on, it seemed that anything in a skirt was fair game. One time, in Spain, he'd bagged some Spanish girl and had her in his room. Desai bounded down the hall, woke me up, and told me to follow him and get my ear to BJ's hotel room door, which we both did. We could hear this Spanish girl carrying on, "You black. . .! Oooh, you black. . . ." The rest was in Spanish. Something must have gone wrong, or Ben was the fastest man in the world even then, because the next thing we heard she was putting on her clothes, getting ready to leave. I wish someone had timed our splits running down that hallway to get back to our rooms before BJ's door opened.

There is a theory, explored by Heather Robertson in her book *Grass Roots*, about what she calls the Village Idiot. As she explains it, in a small town, personal relationships become so constant and well defined, so stratified, that people lose their individuality and become archetypes – the Banker, the Postmaster, the Village Idiot. Robertson explains: "Once thrust into a role, the person adopts it; he becomes exaggerated, like a character in a play, and ceases to perceive any difference between himself and the community's perception of him. As long as he remembers his lines and behaves in a predictable way, his acceptance is assured. The community gives him an identity and relieves him of the responsibility of working one out for himself."

Ben became our Village Idiot. He acted the part and we reinforced it, even when there was evidence to the contrary. BJ might have had trouble reading, but he was a long way from being stupid. On that trip to Tennessee, a few of the guys were lounging around in one of the hotel rooms when an attractive woman came to pay a visit to Val Gross, another athlete who later went on to become a coach. Ben said that if Val wasn't interested in this girl, he'd like to take a run at her.

"Jeez, Ben, and what's the first thing you'd do?" Gross asked.

Ben answered, "K-k-k-kick y-y-y-your ass out of the room."

And Ben never seemed to have any money for breakfast; someone else always paid the bill. We were still paying for his breakfast before the Seoul Olympics in 1988, when he owned a million-dollar home and drove a Porsche.

The thing is, Ben did get his chance to shake off the label of Village Idiot. All the guys on the team had a field day with him for years: practical jokes, mean jokes, imitations that would set them to rolling on the floor. But when Ben started winning, they began to leave him alone. Just before Seoul, it was fair to say that some of them were almost kissing Ben's ass. Of course, they turned on him like a pack of dogs when the steroid scandal hit, when Ben was disgraced. I guess it's up to Ben whether he'll get a second chance to show the village they've got the wrong idiot.

We came back from Tennessee revitalized and ready for the spring training period leading up to the 1978 championships in Kingston, and then the crucial national championships later that summer in Montreal. The National Championship Games represented the gateway to international competition, with the possibility of winning a place on the Canadian Commonwealth Games Team. After that, maybe the Pan-American Games, then — the Olympics!

The way it works is that track and field athletics are governed at an international level by the International Amateur Athletic Federation (IAAF). The IAAF compiles rules and regulations for amateur athletes and cooperates with the various organizing committees of the Olympic Games, such as the Canadian Olympic Association. The IAAF also ratifies world and Olympic records. An application for record acceptance is submitted on an official form to the IAAF by the national association of the country in which the performance took place. The record must have already been approved by the national association, it must have been achieved with official timekeepers or field judges present, and it must have taken place in bona fide scratch competition – meaning no allowance, penalty, or handicap for any competitor.

If I won a place on the Canadian Commonwealth Team, I would be competing against such nations as Australia, New Zealand, Jamaica, the United Kingdom, a number of African states, and other countries linked by historical ties as part of the former British Empire. Originally called the British Empire Games, they were first held in Hamilton, Ontario, in 1930. If I won a place on the Pan-American Games team, I would compete against athletes from North, Central, and South America and the Caribbean. These Games began in Buenos Aires in 1951.

As a nineteen-year-old girl, track and field represented a link with concepts that only statesmen and privileged citizens of the world embrace, concepts of history and nationality and a profound understanding of your fellow man and the way the world works. I knew, when I began to set my sights on international competition, that the Olympics were a star in the sky, that they might just as well have been the shrouded pathway to the ancient gods to a black girl from a tin-roofed house near a bauxite pit in Jamaica.

But I believed in fairy tales.There was dew on the grass the morning in July 1978 when we set off in one of Ross Earl's vans for the national championships at the Claude Robillard Centre in Montreal. I was entered in the 100- and 200-metres. My main competition would be the girls who had beat me the month before in Kingston: Grace Verbeek, Jeanette Wood, and, Angela Bailey.

I managed a personal best time of 12.07 seconds in the 100-metre heats, but I missed the finals by three one-hundredths of a second. Charlie told me that I had a bad start, that I was slow off the mark, a problem that would plague my entire career. I came to be known for my weak start and strong finish. Angela Bailey was second in the 100-metres final with a fabulous time, for a fifteen-year-old, of 11.52 seconds.

I made the finals in the 200-metres with the first important placement of my career – 23.87 seconds. I came second. I beat Grace Verbeek and Jeanette Wood; they would never be able to beat me again. Patty Loverock, the reigning Canadian champion, won the 200-metres with a time of 23.21 seconds.

It was there, at the National Games, that I first tasted raw ambition. I was just a high school kid who had only begun formal training in January. By July, I was second in the 200-metres – *in the nation.* I had not expected to do so well. Some people are frightened by success, but I am not one of them. Success makes me want more success. It's an aphrodisiac.

Charlie stayed behind in Montreal after we left: with CTFA technical director Lynn Davies, national track and field coach Gerard Mach, and several other coaches, he was choosing athletes for the national team to compete at the Commonwealth Games in Edmonton. This hierarchy of coaches was created by the Canadian Olympic Association and Sport Canada after Canada did so poorly at the 1968 Olympics in Mexico City. We didn't win any medals in track and field that year. The idea had been to put in place a "game plan," which meant federal and provincial funding, so that Canada would do well at the 1976 Olympics in Montreal. Gerard Mach, a coach from Poland, had been hired in 1973 to conduct sprint clinics. Derek Boosey was hired for jumps and multiple events, Jean-Paul Baert for throws, and Paul Poce for distance running.

But we still didn't do very well at the 1976 Olympics. Greg Joy won the only medal in track and field, a silver in the high jump. In overall team standings, Canada, the host nation, placed eleventh. Our biggest test of the official game plan would be the Commonwealth Games in 1978 in Edmonton, at the new Commonwealth Stadium. My standing in the 200-metres in Montreal that July weekend got me on the national team. As a newcomer, this meant I had won the right to try out for the Canadian Commonwealth Team.

Charlie called me with the news as soon as he got back from Montreal. Desai Williams from the Scarborough Optimist Club had made the national team, too. And, of course, Angela Bailey. Several throwers were selected, among them Bishop Dolegiewicz, who went on to become Canada's top shot-putter and later a coach.

I was thrilled. I knew that it had been "iffy" whether I would win the right to try out for the Commonwealth Team. But because the Games would be in Edmonton, I got a break. As host, Canada was assembling a huge team. It was a matter of national pride and, as always in this country, of economics. If the Games had been scheduled abroad that year, I probably wouldn't have made it. It would have cost too much. Other countries often send young, promising athletes to international competitions so they can build experience, get used to the rarified air at the world-class level. In Canada, we agonize over seat prices on international flights.

Lucky me, I got a seat on the flight to Edmonton.

Sunday, July 9th, 1978
200 m semi-finals, 24.37
Finals, 24.12, third place
Had lane 8, hated being on outside
Made Commonwealth Team

It is no excuse for my performance that day, but the note in my diary about having the outside lane in the Commonwealth Team tryout is an interesting technical point. Most runners hate the inside lane, lane one, and the outside lane, either lane six or eight. Lane one has tight corners, which destroy speed. The outside lane is more of a psychological burden – you can't see the other runners because the starting blocks are staggered to make each lane the same distance.

I wish I could say these things became less important as I became more experienced, but the opposite is true. When I was becoming a name in track, Charlie Francis fought to get me my preferred lane – lane three. Most meet organizers recognized the importance of giving the top sprinters the best lane so they could improve their times, perhaps set a world record. But sometimes we had to draw lots for lane selection. It is one of the tough breaks junior athletes must endure. What's the point in giving the better lane to someone with no hope of raising Canada's standing in the IAAF world records?

I did badly at the Commonwealth Games. In the first round of preliminary races, on Monday, July 24, I was entered in the 200-metres and ran 23.81, which wasn't good enough to qualify for the semifinals.

I was out of the competition in Edmonton, but I was acutely aware of my rise from high school to international competition in only seven months. I became part of a select group in 1978, and Canada's game plan was beginning to pay off. Our athletes placed first overall in Edmonton. In track and field, we won six gold, eight silver, and nine bronze medals.

A few years later, the movie *Personal Best* starring Mariel Hemingway, was released. It was a "coming of age" film in which Hemingway joins a group of runners training under a talented coach. Ernest's lithe, blonde granddaughter gave the movie a high profile. And there were some steamy lesbian scenes.

I identified with some of the things her character experienced, though I've never encountered any flagrant lesbianism at Olympic-level competition.

In one scene, the women are warned against having men in their rooms. Perhaps this is meant to explain their lesbian behavior. Let me tell you, athletes at the Olympic Games go to bed early, and alone. When you have a chance to win an Olympic gold medal, even a bronze – hell, just to *be* there – you don't need to party to feel high. There may be some wild times when the Games are over, but it's all business during the Games. The only people I ever saw being frivolous at any competition were two Canadian female athletes who went to the beach every day to get a tan, but they knew they didn't have a hope of winning anything.

The least accurate part of the movie showed the athletes drinking beer and smoking marijuana. Athletes don't do social drugs, not when they're competing at serious meets. Alcohol stays in your system too long; so does grass. Both make you feel slow and spongy for days. *Personal Best* showed a lot of hanky-panky – athletes fighting, getting drunk, smoking up, screwing around. That may be what normal people do, but athletes aren't normal. They live different lives, lives of deprivation, pain, and effort.

There was a lot of crying in *Personal Best*, which I was contemptuous of when I saw the movie. They cried in disappointment, cried in pain. Later, I came to appreciate that this part of the movie was *cinéma vérité*. There can be nothing more frustrating in the world than working six hours a day, seven days a week, year-round, only to be injured the day before an important race. The disappointment is crushing, and I cried with the best of them. I learned to work through excruciating pain. There were times when I worked through such bad muscle and ligament damage that I couldn't lie still on a bed. The pain would propel me up from my mattress as though I'd lain on a bed of nails. Bruce Kidd, a Canadian runner, once said, "Everyone knows it's often unhealthy to be an Olympic athlete."

I cried from 1979 until 1985. I stopped in 1986, when I began to take my infant daughter, Sasha, to the track. It didn't seem right for the two of us to be crying. And I began to get some perspective on things. By 1986, I was running for money.

6

Coming Clean

Like many other athletes, I became obsessed by the concept of control. I wanted to control my training, my diet, my body, my equipment, the track conditions. I did not want to leave anything to chance. I know now that this is a formula for obsessive behavior and inevitable disappointment.

In the fall of 1978, I wanted to devote myself to track and field, because I was ambitious, and because I knew I had started late. I had a lot of ground to make up. Most track and field athletes build steadily on training from the age of sixteen or fifteen, like my husband, Tony, did. I hadn't started serious training until I joined the Scarborough Optimist Club, when I was nineteen. .

By January 1979, I was working out hard every day except Sundays. I remember only one Friday when I didn't work out because I was nursing a twisted ankle. I competed in a couple of all-comers meets, where anyone who shows up gets to compete, and a Toronto Secondary School Athletic Association indoor meet at Etobicoke Centennial Stadium.

At the meet in Etobicoke, my old friend and former Parkdale coach, Mike Hawryluk, told *The Toronto Star*: "Taylor is a superb athlete and is a definite medal winner for us in Moscow next year. She has a unique training style and has cut three seconds off her times in the past two years, which is a hell of a performance for a woman athlete."

I was beginning to see solid results from all my work.

There were three more meets in February, including the Ontario Seniors' Meet for athletes eighteen and older, at the CNE. That's when I set my first record, the first of fifty Canadian and six world records of my career. I ran the 200-metres in 24 seconds flat, but it was hand-timed and didn't count with the international federation. Charlie and I didn't make that mistake again. By February 24, at the Canadian Indoor Nationals in Edmonton, I officially established a Canadian record of 24.47 seconds in the 200-metres, and another Canadian record of 6.46 seconds in the 50-metre sprint. In the next ten years, I never lost a 100- or 200-metre race at the Nationals.

In my diary, I made a note about my two new Canadian records and a lengthier note about the plane trip back from Edmonton. We saw an eclipse of the sun on that trip, total darkness for about two minutes. We were all straining to look out the windows. My diary says, "Great experience!" The world seemed full of promise, and I was full of wonder. I had regained the confidence I lost when I left Jamaica — I felt my life was falling into order.

In March, I ran in a dual meet with the Soviet Union in Montreal. I was on a relay team with Angela Bailey, one of the few times in our careers that we worked together well. We were often put together on the women's four-by-100-metre relays, though later in the year she didn't show up for the Pan-American Games and we couldn't assemble a relay team. I don't know why she didn't show. I heard it might have been mononucleosis, or because she had to go to summer school. No matter, she failed to appear and it cost us the competition. At the U.S.S.R. meet in March 1979, she and I ran the relay with Anne-Marie Mackie and Debbie Campbell. We came a respectable third.

The press has made a big thing about the antagonism between Angela Bailey and me, and it's time I set the record straight. I did not then and do not now dislike Angela Bailey. I respect her as an athlete. She gave me the only serious competition I ever really enjoyed in Canada. The problem with Bailey is that she could not accept that I was better than her. At the Commonwealth Games in Edmonton in 1978, she predicted, "I'm going be the best 100-metre runner in the country, and you, Angella Taylor, will be the best 200-metre runner." But after 1979, few could beat me between 50 yards and 600 metres. This really aggravated Angela.

Angela devoted most of her career to trying to get me. She became obsessed with beating me. Once I told her to forget about me and go after the rest of the world, because I wasn't number one. I can't understand why, if she wanted so badly to be number one herself, she was so obsessed with beating me. It was pathetic. I never trained to *get* Angela Bailey; I trained to get the world.

At the end of March 1979, several of the Scarborough Optimist group went to a winter training camp at Clemson University in South Carolina, where Peter Cross had recently taken up his new position as an assistant track coach. For a long while, Charlie and I thought I might try to get a scholarship at Clemson as the next, natural move in my training.

I often joked around with Cross about my performance against men. The first time Cross had seen me, at the Pig Palace, I was running a relay with men, and he had heard about a more recent incident at York University. I had run in an all-comers meet in a 400-metre race against male runners, and my time of 52.3 would have been another national record. The Canadian Track and Field Association didn't allow the time to stand, however, because when a woman runs against men, the race doesn't count. This was always a problem for me, and I believe I might have become an even faster sprinter if I had had better Canadian competition. If I had been able to compete regularly against men in Canada, my times might have been spectacular.

I never was offered a scholarship at Clemson, though I was offered a scholarship later in 1979 from a university in Arizona. I had decided against attending Clemson anyway, for a variety of reasons. I enjoyed working with Charlie Francis, and I didn't want to leave him. I also didn't like the asphalt track at Clemson, which was hard on my shins. And I didn't like the town of Clemson itself.

In 1979, Clemson was a red-neck Southern U.S. town. The good ol' boys used to get liquored up and go out to the fields and push over sleeping cows. That's how it was in Clemson. There was a shit-kicking bar across the street from the university. Dave McKnight had a bad experience when he showed up as the only black in the place. That's when he first heard the word *nigger* aimed at him. And so many things were off-limits to blacks, though segregation was never official. Tony Sharpe complained that he wasn't even allowed to talk to white girls. We all got dreadfully bored, having nothing to do after our workouts, with no safe place to go at night.

Sharpe, Desai Williams, and Mark McKoy went to Clemson on scholarships but eventually left in disgust and returned to Canada.

I could never live in the United States. I don't think I could survive there as a black. I don't like the unwritten system of segregation. Marita Payne went on a scholarship to the U.S. and it was sad to see the change in her when she got back. She picked up a Southern drawl and got caught up in this black stuff – you know, stick together, don't let outsiders in, huddle around your inferiority complex. The athletes are out there on the field training together, and they think they are getting along wonderfully, but at the end of the day they trot off in different directions to separate dorms.

In a perverse way, however, I sometimes almost admire the Americans for their up-front prejudice. Say what you will, but there's nothing hypocritical about being called *nigger*. We do things differently in Canada. Discrimination is much subtler, coated in niceties. In 1987, presumably to capitalize on the excitement building toward the Olympics in Seoul in 1988, a major Canadian insurance company aired a television commercial showing a male relay runner passing the baton. It was a feel-good commercial, conveying strength, courage, and commitment, all those things the insurance industry likes to identify with. The runner in the commercial was white. At the time, the top four runners in Canada were black. They had managed to dig up some little white runner at the University of Toronto field house.

Charlie was furious about it. Some time later, he got a call from a representative of the company. Apparently, they had bought a table at a Conn Smythe dinner and wondered if some of his athletes would like to sit at it? I guess they weren't expecting much television coverage that night; a good time to extend the olive branch. Let's face it, what is the image of Canadian Olympic runners? A bunch of black West Indians? Because that's what they are. Wake up, Canada.

In April 1979, I decided to see a doctor. I had a pain at the back of my knee and a lump near my groin, which I suspected was a small hernia, probably from muscle strain. I also had swollen glands in my neck, which might have been due to a virus. I never had a regular family doctor when I lived with Olive, so I asked Charlie to recommend one. Charlie took me to see his doctor, Dr. G. Helge

Koch. His office was down the street from Varsity Stadium in Toronto, in a lovely old 1929 brick edifice with Medical Arts Building etched in stone above the entryway. Charlie went to see Dr. Koch when he needed a medical examination to get a licence to drive Ross Earl's vans to the winter training camps.

Dr. Koch seemed a little more flamboyant than most doctors. He drove to work on a motorcycle and kept his helmet in the waiting room. Years later, when I saw Dr. Koch at the Dubin Inquiry, I barely recognized him. He'd put on a lot of weight.

That first time I went to see Dr. Koch, on April 3, 1979, he made a note that I had swollen glands in my neck and ordered blood tests. It was all very straightforward. Afterward, I walked under the tiny spring buds of the trees along St. George Street and hopped on the subway to go to my daily workout. When we got the results showing a low hemoglobin count, that is, a lower than normal number of oxygen-bearing red blood cells, Dr. Koch recommended that I start taking megadoses of vitamin B-12. He gave me an injection right away, in my thigh. It was the first injection I'd ever had.

For much of the month of April, all my joints were hurting — wrists, knees, ankles, even my toes. It may have been the same viral infection that caused my neck glands to swell, but it was a new experience to work through pain like that. We never stopped. On the same day I felt so sick that I first went to see Dr. Koch, I recorded the following workout:

Tuesday, April 3rd, 1979

Blood test taken
8 laps
4 x 20 m As, Bs, running As
2 x 600 m, 2 x 300 m, 6 x 100 m
Calisthenics
15 sit-ups, 10 push-ups
arm circles, hip rotations, 15 sit-ups
10 push-ups, running on the spot 30 seconds
bicycling 30 seconds
hops, 2 foot — 10 m, 1 foot — 10 m
alternating feet — 10 m
hops with heel touching ass
front with knee raises
6 x medicine ball
6 x 200 m

By the end of May, I had set two more records: 23.5 seconds in the 200-metres for a Canadian high school record, 23.8 seconds in the 200-metres for a Metro Regionals record. Mike Hawryluk told Al Sokol of *The Toronto Star*: "Taylor has the potential to become the first Canadian woman to win an Olympic track medal in fifty years."

But it was the first Monday in June that weighed heavily on my mind. On June 4, we were to fly overseas to Florence to begin a two-week trip covering three major competitions – a meet with Poland and Italy, a dual meet with East Germany, and another dual meet with Belgium. I had never been to Europe. I was nervous about competing against the Europeans on their own turf because we had been hearing rumors that they were all on steroids. The rumors had abounded at the Montreal Olympics in 1976, two and a half years earlier. There was a story in the *New York Times* back then on the success of the East German women swimmers. When asked why so many of their women had deep voices, an East German coach replied, "We have come here to swim, not sing."

Whenever we saw an athlete do exceptionally well, we suspected steroids. Runners had begun to clock very fast times, and every time another record fell, rumors flew about anabolic steroids. Charlie believed that international competition was rife with steroid-users. I didn't believe all the rumors – I was still young and idealistic – but it was one more thing to worry about.

In fact, my biggest worry turned out to be lack of sleep. Charlie had told us that the best way to prepare for the difference in time on the other side of the Atlantic was to sleep on the flight over, then stay up the entire next day in order to go to bed more or less in sync with nightfall. Otherwise, you'd get yourself into a mess by being sleepy all day and awake all night. I discovered I couldn't sleep on an airplane.

It was a problem that plagued me throughout my career because, often, within a day of landing, we would be in a competition. It was agony for me. I loathe feeling exhausted, sleepy, dragged-out; it makes me feel hollow to the core. It's why I'm not attracted to drugs like alcohol and marijuana. I have never been attracted to that drowsy, laid-back feeling. Charlie gave me some sleeping pills, but they didn't help much.

By Wednesday, June 6, we were at the first meet, and I came

fourth against Poland and Italy, running the 100-metres in 11.64 seconds. I was short of the Pan-Am qualifying time by five one-hundredths of a second. I was heartbroken. Charlie had brought us to Europe so we could get some tough competition as a way to prepare for the Pan-American Games in Puerto Rico the following month. It began to look as though I wouldn't be going.

It was at this meet that I encountered the great Irena Szewinska, the Olympic medalist from Poland. I am never able to say her name without adding the drumroll, "the great." I suppose that's what it feels like for little hockey-playing kids when they finally get to meet Wayne Gretzky. We learned to revere Szewinska at the knee of Gerard Mach, who had been head coach of the Polish sprint team before Canada persuaded him to become our national track and field coach. At the team meetings, which were always called before we headed off to an international competition, Mach rhapsodized about the good old days in Poland in the 1960s and about "the great Irena Szewinska." Mach is a dear man, a little odd-looking with Dickensian mutton-chop whiskers, but his musings got to be so long-winded that the coaches had to tell him to scale them down to fifteen minutes.

Mach admired Szewinska's incredible range – she seems to have won medals in almost every track and field event – and resiliency; she came back to win the 400-metres after having two children. Mach had worked with her in Poland. I think he admired Irena Szewinska most of all because she represented the pinnacle of his success as a coach.

When at last I saw her, the great Irena Szewinska was doing the most ordinary thing – tying her shoelace at the edge of the track. I stood off to the side, unobtrusively watching her. I felt I was gawking at a forbidden goddess, like the hunter Actaeon coming upon the naked goddess Artemis. In the unremitting heat of the Italian afternoon, I watched, and I committed every detail to memory. Szewinska was exceptionally tall, and she had a body that could have been sculpted from iron. It wasn't a masculine power she conveyed; it was a lithe, feline power, which I found bewitching. In the Greek myth, Artemis changes the spying hunter into a stag for his misdemeanor, and his own hounds pursue him and tear him to pieces. Only hindsight could have given me the wisdom to draw a comparison between the hunter's fate and my own then-and-there decision to emulate the great Szewinska — no matter what it might take.

Happily, that day, I rallied after the disappointing 100-metres to come third in the 200-metres with a time of 23.64 seconds. I had achieved the Pan-Am standard, but my hamstrings were sore.

Hamstrings are a group of muscles located on the back of the thigh. The muscles start from the buttock, or, specifically, that bony prominence you feel when you are sitting, called the ischial tuberosity, and extend to just below the knee. From behind, the lower thigh resembles a large ham, so the tendons and muscles that form this configuration are called hamstrings. However you describe them, the pain in these muscles was excruciating, like a comb with teeth of glass shards shredding my backside. We flew to East Germany on June 7, and by June 10, the day of the meet, I still was unable to run the 200-metres because of the pain.

I did not distinguish myself by running the 100-metres in 11.69 either, heroic though it was in my condition. I was up against Marlies Göhr, who held the world record of 10.88, and Marita Koch, who had just broken the world record in the 200-metres with a time of 21.71 seconds. They both beat me with ease. In that dual meet alone, three world records were broken in a single day. I wasn't the only one humiliated: the senior Canadian four-by-100-metre relay team was defeated by the junior East German relay team. We were completely outclassed.

We left East Germany for the final meet in Brussels — it always reminds me of Toronto, somehow, before Toronto's downtown became an ordinary crop of glass towers — and I had until June 16 to recover before running the 100-metres. I did reasonably well, finishing third in 11.68 seconds. The next day, though I did not place, I managed a personal best time of 23.59 seconds in the 200-metres.

We boarded a plane for home on June 18, and the following day I went directly to Dr. Koch's office. Charlie had to escort me because I was so exhausted. That day, Dr. Koch gave me an injection of 200 milligrams of Depo-Testosterone, half in each of my deltoid muscles, which are the triangular muscles covering the shoulder joints. Dr. Koch's record of the event reads: "Recently back from trip to Europe to compete and had lots of problems — wear and tear and fatigue."

Depo-Testosterone is an anabolic steroid, which is a synthetic derivative of the most powerful male sex hormone, the androgen known as testosterone. "Anabolic" means a substance used for growth or repair. "Androgen" means a substance that produces male characteristics. Both sexes produce testosterone, and it is generally acknowledged that testosterone produces the sex drive in both men and women. However, a woman's body produces only a small amount of testosterone naturally, in balance with the more dominant estrogens that create female characteristics and govern the reproductive cycle.

Dr. Koch thought the testosterone might increase my still-low hemoglobin level, and he also hoped it would combat some of the stress I had suffered on the European tour. We were looking for the anabolic repair qualities to give me a quick lift and work miracles on my still-sore hamstrings. The trials for the all-important Pan-American Games were scheduled for June 23, only five days away. I would have to work through the pain. I cannot say whether the Depo-Testosterone actually helped me physically, but it gave me a psychological boost. I felt I had a friend in my corner.

I made the team and ran for Canada at the Pan-Am Games in San Juan, Puerto Rico, in 1979. Evelyn Ashford of the United States was the big competition. She was already an established American track star. In a funny way, I was more intrigued by the contest with my old rival, Jacqueline Pusey, from that day long ago in Kingston, Jamaica. I ran the 100-metres in 11.36 seconds to win the silver medal. Ashford won the gold. In the 200-metres, I ran 22.80 in the semifinals, which set a Canadian record, then broke that record the next day with a time of 22.74 seconds. It was good enough for third place and the bronze medal. Jacqueline Pusey came fourth.

I was rewarded with some of the first press coverage of my career and two letters, which I have still. One was signed by Steve E. Paproski, the minister of state for fitness and amateur sport. "Dear Angela," he wrote – it took a long while before anyone could remember my name had two "l"s –

> I would like to take this opportunity to congratulate you on your medal-winning performance at this summer's VIII Pan American Games in San Juan, Puerto Rico. How gratifying

> it must be to have your hard work and self-sacrifices rewarded in this fashion . . . . Both the individual successes and the overall performance of the Canadian team as a whole are a solid indication of Canada's amateur sport development. There is no doubt in my mind that our athletes have established themselves as consistent contenders at the international level and will continue to be serious threats, even under the pressure of prestigious events such as world championships or the 1980 Olympic Games in Moscow.

The other letter was from Reuben C. Baetz, Ontario's minister of culture and recreation. He wrote:

> As I congratulate you, let me also thank you for setting an example that will inspire thousands of others to either reach the same levels of competitive excellence or to simply keep fit. 'A healthy mind in a healthy body.' That ideal remains as valid as ever and your accomplishments will keep us all aware of it.

My head was spinning with my success, but my body was hurting, again. Looking back through the pages of my diary, I realize I was nearly always in pain. Sometimes I think track and field, and the sprints, are mostly about pain, seldom about joy. There is so much hard work, and the work begins when your eyes open in the morning, and the morning after that, and all the mornings you see stretched ahead of you. There are not many surprises. You work too hard to be surprised. If conditions are right, you know pretty well how you will do in a competition. There are no "lucky bounces" in track and field. Even breaking a record rarely comes as a surprise.

If there are surprises, they usually are disappointments — a fall, an injury, a virus, a poor lane, a strong headwind. When you're working hard, reaching a peak of performance, when your training times indicate a predictable level of accomplishment, maybe a significant breakthrough, something can, and often does, go badly wrong.

In a book titled *Sport: A Philosophic Inquiry*, published in 1969, author Paul Weiss tries to capture this truism. In a chapter on the attraction of athletics, he writes:

> Athletes usually submit themselves, often with enthusiasm, rarely with reluctance, to long periods of training. They do not seem to mind having to engage repeatedly in dull exercises and tedious practice sessions. Nor do they seem to take amiss the need to control their appetites, even those that are imperious and insistent. Willingly, athletes sacrifice opportunities to be lax, give up occasions to be irresponsible, and put aside a desire simply to enjoy themselves.
>
> At times they risk injury, and in some cases death. Fatigue is a familiar. Sooner or later every one of them comes to know that he is preparing himself for defeat, and perhaps humiliation. His days are numbered, his successes rarely momentous, and his glories short-lived; he works hard and long to prepare himself for what may end in dismal failure.

By the end of July 1979, I had competed in three more meets – the Ontario Relay Championships, the Jim Buchanan Memorial Meet, and the National Championships in Sherbrooke, Quebec. (Jim Buchanan was an athlete from Ottawa who became a national champion in the long jump. He died in a car accident in the 1970s.) It was at the National Championships that I suffered a nauseating and terrifying experience peculiar only to women athletes: I got my period.

It was the first time my period had coincided with a major competition. The National Championships were the stepping stones to the crucial World Cup competitions to be held at the Olympic Stadium in Montreal in August. The World Cup was a new global meet for track and field and it would be the closest thing to a rehearsal for the 1980 Olympics in Moscow. My competition would be Evelyn Ashford; her competition would be Marlies Göhr and Marita Koch of East Germany. If I did poorly at the Nationals, I would not be entered in the World Cup.

A period usually causes no more trouble than a slightly tired feeling and maybe a mild headache the day before it starts. Sometimes, however, and more often in a time of stress, a period rears up like a dragon in your guts. When it does this, it feels like food poisoning, diarrhea, and a kick in the intestines all at once. It makes you light-headed, even dizzy, and the flow of blood might be a lot heavier than usual. This time, I felt *sick*. And I was terrified that the blood might seep through my shorts, in front of thousands of spectators, maybe live on television. Out on the track, at the starting blocks, I wouldn't be able to slip into a convenient washroom and find a fresh sanitary napkin in my handbag.

I got through the Nationals, cramps and all, though my times were not sensational: 11.49 in the 100-metres; 23.43 in the 200-metres. I'd put the handicap of a bad menstrual period at about half a second.

When we got back from Quebec, I went to see Dr. Koch again. I cried on his shoulder that day. I was in the middle of the first season of my life as an athlete and I was in a constant state of desperate exhaustion and nerves. Every muscle in my body ached. I told him about the World Cup coming up in Montreal and how important it was to me, and he was quiet for a moment, thinking, before he told me what he planned to do. Dr. Koch gave me another injection of 100 milligrams of vitamin B-12. He was convinced that my continuing low hemoglobin level was sapping my strength.

I didn't think of it as significant at the time, and perhaps he didn't either, but this would be the first time that I had received an injection *before* a competition, as an aid. Until then, any injections of B-12 or even the Depo-Testosterone had been made to correct an existing health problem and there had been no direct link to a specific competition. Dr. Koch wrote in his notes that he had given me vitamin B-12 in June and that it had given me a two-day lift. "Therefore, try again for this meet in Quebec," he wrote.

We decided to enlist the help of another drug that day. The World Cup was scheduled for August 24 and 25, almost a month to the day from the start of my last, disastrous menstrual period. Dr. Koch gave me two samples of tiny lilac-colored pills in a round dispenser of grey plastic: Ortho Novum 180, the birth control pill.

They've made some changes to the pill in the decade since I got my first samples that day, but essentially, they are made of a combination of estrogen and progesterone, the female hormones that control the reproductive cycle. They work by signaling the pituitary gland, the body's "master gland," to stop the ovaries from releasing eggs. The pill also produces mucus at the opening of the uterus, which helps to prevent sperm from entering. At the time, I didn't have much need of the sperm-blocking benefits, but I was most grateful for the ability to stop ovulation.

It meant I would be able to stop one package of pills and immediately start another in order to hold back my period until after a competition had ended. The pill also tends to make each period shorter and the flow of blood much lighter. It was my first real weapon in the fight to control the circumstances of my body. Dr. Koch may have told me about the possible side effects of the pill – the increased risk of heart attack, stroke, or thrombosis, which is the formation of blood clots in the circulatory system. If he did tell me, I wasn't listening.

The Canadian trials for the World Cup were held in Quebec City on August 11, and I managed to set a Canadian record in the 100-metres at 11.20. I had to beat Jackie Pusey and Merlene Ottey to win my position on Team Americas. We returned to Ontario, then headed out to a training camp in Quebec for a week before arriving in Montreal for the World Cup. I managed to come fifth in both the 100-metres, with a time of 11.50 seconds, and the 200-metres, at 22.83 seconds. It was a major achievement, against the best in the world.

When I got home, I picked up a copy of the Toronto *Sun*, and I couldn't believe my eyes. George Gross had written a story that made me out to be a big disappointment for placing fifth. In 1978, I had run the 100-metres in 12.07 seconds and didn't even make the final in Canada. Only a year later, I was running with the best in the world. I ran against Marita Koch, the world record holder, and Evelyn Ashford of the United States. In the 100-metres at the World Cup, Ashford came first, Koch second, the West German Olympic champion Annegret Richter, came third, and the Soviet Champion, Lyudmila Kondratyeva, came fourth. I came fifth. It was the same in the 200-metres – fifth against the best in the world!

And then this stupid newspaper story when I arrived back home. I was hurt, then I was enraged.

I left home that fall. Olive and Raphael were not getting along very well by then and I couldn't stand the tension in the house. I came and went, keeping to myself most of the time. Olive left me alone. I spent most of my time at the track. One day, Ross Earl came around with a van, and we moved my bed and clothes to a room in the bungalow he owned next door to his own house in Thornhill, north of Toronto.

The only other things I took were two posters Charlie had given me. One was a dramatic shot of the men's 100-metres finish at the 1972 Olympics in Munich, with the Russian, Valery Borzov, in the lead; the other showed the men's 100-metres finish at the 1976 Olympics in Montreal, with Hasely Crawford of Trinidad breaking the tape. The posters were thumbtacked to the wall in my bedroom, the way other kids put up posters of their favorite rock stars.

Charlie was a generous soul. In 1979, because he was pleased with my work, he gave me a beautiful gold bracelet to honor my tremendous progress. It was like a length of textured rope with a delicate white-gold chain intertwined. I lost it at the World Cup meet in Montreal. It must have just slipped off my wrist. I was heartbroken, because I loved that bracelet. It took me a year to replace it, and when I did it cost me nearly $600. This time Charlie fastened a safety chain to the clasp so I wouldn't lose it again. He was always doing things like that. He bought Desai Williams a handsome ring once, in Switzerland, because he had run well. Another time, he bought me a pair of diamond stud earrings because my hamstrings were hurting after a race in Zurich. Charlie also drove me to the pound one day, to help me pick out my beloved orange tabby, Kaya.

The day I left home, I told my mother that I was going, picked up Kaya, and walked out the door. We never did have much to talk about. If things had been better at home, I would have preferred to stay and save money, but in September 1979, I had been approved for a C-card and decided to strike out on my own. Ross Earl charged me $200 a month for the bungalow, which was a bargain in 1979. It was all I could afford.

My C-card, my passport to freedom, was part of a system devised by Sport Canada in the early 1970s to provide direct funding to athletes, part of the old game plan to improve Canada's chances of winning medals in international competition. It is based on a system set up by West Germany. It is a good system for recognizing that amateur athletes need money for food and a roof over their heads; what's not so good is that the standards are brutally high.

These days, each card category includes a tuition-paid university education, though many athletes are unable to juggle the academic and athletic loads. Most athletes know that it would take them ten or twelve years to get through a Bachelor of Arts program, taking a couple of courses a semester, maybe another during the summer. That's about as long as most of their athletic careers.

In 1979, Sport Canada paid $50 a month to working athletes, plus "lost time" payments to full-time athletes without jobs. For a full-time athlete still at home with parents, this would be an additional payment of $75 per month for a total of $125. For an athlete living on her own, the monthly "living support" payment was $215, for a total of $265. I didn't think of it then, but there was a sort of built-in incentive to leave home. By 1981, the living and training payments were combined to be $350 a month. I don't recall there being any difference in payments to A, B or C-carded athletes.

To get an A-card by 1988, my last year of competition, I had to equal the performances of the top eight athletes in my event in the world. This was worth $650 a month, or $7,800 a year in income, plus a travel allowance from the Canadian Track and Field Association for winter training camps. The *top eight* in the world, so I could earn what a high school kid makes flipping burgers at McDonald's.

To get a B-card, an athlete had to be as good as the top sixteen athletes in the world, to be entitled to $6,600 a year. A C-card, worth $5,400 a year, meant the athlete was one of the best in Canada, equal to the top fifty in the world, with the potential to beat out international competitors.

In the March 1990 issue of *Saturday Night* magazine, writer Varda Burstyn cited statistics that show fewer than a thousand athletes in Canada are carded and that as of 1989, 66 per cent of them relied on their card money as their sole source of income. As Burstyn points out, "Though Sport Canada's budget grew from $8.9-million in 1972 to $58.5-million in 1988, athletes as a group have not been getting rich."

As it was, the money owed to me in 1979 on my C-card took so long to come through that I fell badly behind in the rent I paid to Ross Earl.

In September 1979, I got my own faradic muscle stimulator. Charlie had done some research into these machines because he had read in the papers that the Russians were using them. They are popular with women who want a svelte, firm body without working up a sweat. A faradic stimulator generates a discontinuous, alternating current which activates the nerve to contract the muscle. Nerves function by an electrical current system, and by stimulating the nerves by machine, it is possible to attain a stronger contraction than would otherwise be possible with training aids like weights. Call it a short-cut to developing muscle. We were worried about the cost of such a machine, about $1,000, until Charlie came up with a brilliant ploy.

At the World Cup, I had stepped up to the podium at the end of the meet wearing a T-shirt with a huge adidas logo on it. You are not supposed to do this. The IAAF expressed their disapproval. Apparently, I should have turned my T-shirt inside out to hide the logo. adidas was happy, of course: millions of people had seen the logo at the stadium, on television, and in newspaper and magazine photographs. Charlie went to adidas and told them I'd managed to get myself in hot water over all this, so how about coughing up the money for a muscle stimulator to show some appreciation? adidas paid. My education on how to survive as an amateur athlete was beginning.

I had taken two weeks off at the end of August, after the World Cup and before leaving home. It was the last holiday of my running career. I had some hard thinking to do, considering my rapid progress from a high school kid to fifth at the World Cup, despite what the Toronto *Sun* thought. The next season I would be training for the 1980 Olympics in Moscow. I would be training harder than I'd ever trained in my life.

By attending the European meets and the World Cup, I had rubbed shoulders with the best sprinters in the world. It gradually dawned on me that I had also seen a lot of people at these meets who had been struggling for years and couldn't crack the top ten in the world. I did it in one season.

If I could go from absolute zero, from the joke of not being able to make the final in the 100-metres in Canada, to fifth at the World Cup, then I must be able to do well at the Olympics. I must be able to win a medal! But I had seen the Europeans. I felt sure that the best of them were on steroids, and I would never be able to beat them without playing their game. It was not humanly possible to train harder than I already did.

Unless . . .

On September 24, 1979, on a golden, early autumn afternoon, Charlie and I visited Dr. Koch and told him that we wanted to start a program of anabolic steroids. He was the logical choice; he had given me the Depo-Testosterone in the summer. We needed a prescription. Charlie went downstairs to the pharmacy to have the prescription filled and returned to the office with 100 little pink pills in a bottle. The pills were manufactured by Ciba-Geigy and the label said each pill contained five milligrams of methandienone, the generic name for the brand Dianabol.

That afternoon, in Dr. Koch's office, I was nervous but very determined. I kept thinking how I wanted to become the fastest woman on the planet. Dr. Koch briefly discussed the side effects of Dianabol, but I wasn't really listening, and he didn't seem all that concerned. He recommended five milligrams a day for a six-week period. He gave me a big blue hardcover book called *Compendium of Pharmaceuticals and Specialties*, which is published each year and contains information on drugs available in Canada. It would become an invaluable guide.

Everything I did that day was aboveboard and legal. I wasn't in a clandestine meeting with some pusher in a back alley. This was in my doctor's office, across from the verdant lawns and shaded walkways of the University of Toronto's St. George campus.

One of the few times I got angry during the three days of my testimony at the inquiry was when Dr. Koch's lawyer, Linda Rothstein, had me on the stand. It was her manner that irritated me; there was something schoolmarmish about her.

There were lawyers at the inquiry on behalf of the Sport Medicine Council of Canada, the College of Physicians and Surgeons of Ontario, the Canadian Track and Field Association, and the Canadian Olympic Association, and they all had serious ass-covering to do. The Sport Medicine fellow wanted it on the record that the council sent out a brochure telling us all about drugs. The College of Physicians and Surgeons wanted it on the record that most of the prescribing and supplying of substances banned by the IAAF had been done by Dr. Astaphan, who is from St. Kitts, which is a long way from Ontario. But this Rothstein woman kept hammering away that Dr. Koch prescribed Dianabol only for my anemia. Dianabol, an anabolic steroid, is one of the banned substances.

She began by mentioning my first visit to Dr. Koch, in April 1979. "Do you remember, Ms Issajenko, that when you first went to see Dr. Koch one of the things you were complaining about was fatigue?"

"Exactly."

"Chronic fatigue?"

"Chronic fatigue."

"And I believe you have told us already that Dr. Koch sent you to get your blood work done?"

"That's correct."

"And indeed one of the things he was concerned about was that perhaps you had some mononucleosis. Do you remember that?"

"We thought that was the problem, but obviously it wasn't."

"Right. It was subsequently determined that it wasn't mononucleosis."

"It was fatigue, because I was running around all over Europe. . ."

I was getting testy. I felt she was being patronizing, spoonfeeding me her questions, trying to manipulate me.

She described Dr. Koch discussing nutrition, changes to my diet, as if really that was all that was bothering me. Then she asked, "Do you remember that he suggested that you take vitamin supplements, and that, in particular, he cautioned you that when you take vitamins you have got to take them with meals or they don't have any effect? Do you remember that?"

I wondered if she was going to tell me I should chew my food sixteen times before swallowing.

"I was already a world-class athlete," I told her. "I knew that I needed vitamins."

"Well, I suppose doctors are always giving us advice we don't always need, but it's certainly possible he said something like that."

"It's possible, yes, it's possible."

She worked up to my meeting with Dr. Koch in June 1979, when he gave me 200 milligrams of Depo-Testosterone. "And that. . .was to combat the low hemoglobin problem?" she asked.

"And the stress, yes," I replied.

"And the fatigue?"

"Yes."

On and on it went, until Mr. Justice Dubin himself got lost, confusing low hemoglobin level with low blood pressure. "Is Dianabol a remedy for low blood pressure?" he asked. Maybe he thought he was back in kindergarten. That's how I felt.

By this time Rothstein was up to September 1979, when I went to Dr. Koch to ask about taking Dianabol. She mentioned again that my hemoglobin level still was below normal. Exasperated, I asked if she was suggesting that Dr. Koch was giving me Dianabol only to raise my hemoglobin level. That got her all stiff-necked, but she cleared her throat and started again, this time appealing directly to Mr. Justice Dubin.

"Dr. Koch's evidence will be that he believed it would assist in treating her anemia," she said.

I couldn't let that one go. "I went there with the intention to use it as a performance-enhancing drug – not to cure anemia."

We fenced some more, and then Rothstein said, "Well, let me suggest to you then, and I realize it's a long time ago, that what Dr. Koch said was he thought the Dianabol would be of some use in treating your low hemoglobin, in treating your anemia. Do you remember that?"

"Let me give you a scenario," I said. "What if I kept taking the Dianabol, I show up at the Olympics . . . and I test positive. Would Dr. Koch come to the IOC and say, 'Well, Angella Taylor, I only gave her this because she had anemia.'?"

"I can't answer that question," Rothstein responded.

When I saw Dr. Koch back in 1979, there were no random doping controls, so the message from the governing sports bodies was clear: do what you will to train, but don't show up at meets with banned substances in your veins. Don't show up "dirty." They could see as well as I could that the Europeans had extraordinary muscle development, that the women had hair on their chins and some of them had voices like Henry Kissinger's, and they were smashing records that had stood for decades.

So I went to my family doctor and he gave me a prescription for Dianabol. It was as easy as getting a prescription for an antibiotic. Four days later, on September 28th, I turned twenty-one. I worked out, as usual, and made a note that I weighed 129 pounds. By Christmas Day, I weighed 138.

That fall, the magazine *Track & Field News* came out, as it does every year, with the world rankings for amateur athletes. I was seventh in the world in the 100-metres. That was for the 1979 season, when I was "clean."

7
Wall of Fame

On December 24, 1979, I wrote in my diary: "Indoor track closed until Tuesday. I am a serious athlete. What the fuck do they expect me to do? Take four days off? Well, they can kiss my dead granny's ass."

People often ask, do anabolic steroids make you aggressive? They wonder if steroids have changed my personality. I used to tell them that any aggression from the steroids affected only my desire to train, so I could win races. I used to tell them that steroids did not make me want to punch out someone's lights.

This was not entirely true.

When I started to take Dianabol for the six-week cycle in the fall of 1979, I had just turned twenty-one. I was still the Cayenne Pepper of my youth. I had a bad temper and a short fuse. I took offense at the slightest provocation. As I've said, Charlie was the ideal coach for me because he never held a grudge. This helped to defuse my violent and sometimes childish outbursts.

The entry on Christmas Eve was the first time I used foul language in my diary. The reference to my great-grandmother is obscene. But those few lines are only a mild indication of the rage that was inside me. I didn't realize it then, but the steroids were exacerbating my temper. Years later, I did, in fact, go around looking for someone to punch and most often I'd land a few on Tony. It shames me to say it today, but, like most spouses, he happened to be a convenient target for my uncontrollable anger.

I grew to fear my rages, especially when I became a mother. It wasn't until I had a baby that I began to make the connection between Dianabol and my mood swings. Besides an ugly temper, it could also cause an extreme depression. Dianabol, or any other artificial hormone, suppresses your own body's natural production of hormones, so that when you finish a cycle, it takes a little while for your body to get the message to start producing again. In that period, a couple of days, a couple of weeks, you have no mood-balancing hormones. You're flat. We called it crashing.

When I had my daughter Sasha, I became much more attuned to the cause and effect between steroids and my moods. Like any loving parent, I was afraid that one day I might lose control, I might lash out at my helpless child. I became cautious in my use of steroids and I worked to control my moods. I no longer excused myself for merely having a bad temper. I am happy to say that today, Tony and my children have reason to respect my temper, but no reason to fear it. Since I stopped using steroids, I have discovered that my normal adult mood is remarkably calm and even. It's a nice thing to learn about yourself when you turn thirty.

But on Christmas Eve 1979, I had a long way to go before I hit bottom.

I had begun serious training for the 1980 Moscow Olympics in the fall, and Charlie had introduced a once-a-week "special endurance" training session every Wednesday. For sprinters like me, special endurance means adding long-distance runs to a normal workout. On a routine day, we might run alternating distances of 100 and 200 metres, interspersed with shorter spurts of 60 or even 10 metres to practice acceleration. Longer runs of 500 or more metres are hard on a sprinter; they're meant to build up strength and endurance for the times you need power near the end of a race.

There were plenty of times during the endurance runs when I "hit riggi." I don't know where this expression comes from; it is like the expression "hit the wall" that a lot of joggers use to describe the moment when your legs seize up and go dead. We heard it often around the track. When your muscles quit, when you just cannot go on, when your body collapses, you've "hit riggi." What happens is you exert so much energy that you literally starve your muscles of oxygen. As a result, lactic acid begins to build up in your muscles and they feel like they are burning.

I hit riggi one day in January 1980, when we had an all-comers meet at the newly opened Metropolitan Toronto Track and Field

Centre at York University. I ran 37 flat in the 300-metre race, a Canadian record. At the time, 37.4 was the world indoor best.

The Track and Field Centre had made us all very excited. We felt suddenly elevated into a kind of professional realm. For years, we had been pounding around outdoor parks in all kinds of weather, waiting for the Pig Palace to open in November, and now, suddenly, we had this magnificent new facility up at York. York, I must admit, seemed to be in the middle of nowhere, and the campus, especially in winter, was vast, desolate and windswept, but no matter, the conditions inside were superb.

Later, after the Scarborough Optimist team members did so well at the 1984 Los Angeles Olympics, the center was designated a "high-performance center," with special privileges for carded athletes like me. It was never exactly clear, however, what those special privileges were. From 10 A.M. to 3 P.M, it was open for use by York University students. From 3 P.M. to 10 P.M., carded athletes could use it, along with the general public. At the Alan Eagleson Sports Injuries Clinic, just inside the front door, if we pulled a hamstring we had to make an appointment just like any Joe off the street. At first, we were all excited by the concept of an on-site clinic, but it didn't work and we ended up going elsewhere for physiotherapy. Maybe the clinic was too profit-oriented; it treated a lot of people from the outside.

I loved the place. For ten years it was my home away from home. All the cares of the outside world fell away when I swung through those doors. I was in my element, like a fish in water, like a bird on the wing. I knew everyone and everyone knew me. And it was quiet as a church. The only sounds were the faint whir of ventilating fans and the plap-plap of runners' soles. The walls were painted golden shades of beige, darker at the bottom and, layer by layer, lighter up to the high ceiling of painted girders and conical hanging lights. It was pleasing to the eye, restful. The lights made long shadows on the walls, so you never really knew what time of day it was. We measured only seconds anyway.

The track was four lanes, like all indoor tracks, with a banked fifth lane on the outside for casual joggers. It was 200 metres long and made of rust-colored Chevron synthetic rubber surface. The center of the track was marked out with the distinctive rounded-end triangle of the shot put section. To the left was the pole vault pit, and the long/triple jump pit was to the right. The high jump area was in the middle. There was a weightlifting room at the far end. We did our warm-up exercises on blue mats at the side of the track.

After 1984, someone at the center put up big blue plastic letters on a wall just to the left of the entrance to the indoor track that spelled out WALL OF FAME. Underneath was a row of mounted photographs of Ben Johnson, Angela Bailey, Molly Killingbeck, Tony Sharpe, and Jillian Richardson. They never did get around to putting up photos of Desai Williams, Charmaine Crooks, or me. Under each of our names, there were plaques commemorating some of our outstanding performances. There was one plaque under each athlete, except for me and Ben. Ben had nine plaques; I had three:

Silver Medalist
4 x 100 relay 42.77 sec
1984 Olympic Games
August 11, 1984
Los Angeles, USA

Indoor World Record
50 m 6.06 sec.
Winternational Indoor Games
January 31, 1987
Ottawa, Canada

Silver Medalist
60 m 7.08 sec
1987 World Indoor Championships
March 8, 1987
Indianapolis, USA

In February 1990, long after the Dubin Inquiry ended, a friend told me that the Wall of Fame still existed and that students still stopped to look at the pictures and study the plaques.

That made me sad. I wonder if I will ever set foot in the place again.

On January 20, 1980, when I hit riggi with 37 flat, I identified the problem as a poor start. If I could get a better start, if I could explode out of the blocks like Ben, I would not have had to burn myself out trying to make up time at the end of the race. The extra push I needed for the finish line always risked injury. I was beginning to see a pattern.

Unlike Ben, and even Angela Bailey, I suffered with the problem of poor starts for most of my running career. BJ was blessed with an innate instantaneous reaction to the sound of the starter pistol. The rest of us used to say that Ben and Angela Bailey had different-looking muscles, not like the rest of us, and maybe this was why they could power out of the blocks. Our muscles – Desai Williams', Mark McKoy's, mine – even at their most developed, were more supple. Ben and Angela had this iron-like musculature. A few of the U.S. athletes used to call Ben RoboCop after some movie with a half-human, half-robot character.

Ben was so quick that sometimes his starts were ruled technically illegal because he could break from the blocks within a tenth of a second of the starter's pistol. An old rule classified this as anticipating the gun, not reacting to it. But Ben wasn't cheating, he was just that quick. In the mid-1980s, mainly because of Ben's lightning instincts, there were recommendations that the rule be updated to conform with modern athletic capabilities.

It might have been physical makeup, it might have been some psychological response to the pistol, or it might have been a combination, but whatever it was, I didn't come by it naturally. Charlie worked with me, sometimes for hours at a time, trying to find a solution. Once, we included hand claps as part of my training routine. At the sound of Charlie's sharp hand clap, no matter what the circumstances, I was to instantly start running. It helped, a little. Charlie thought it was possible that I was concentrating on the wrong thing in the starting blocks, that perhaps I was preoccupied just waiting for the sound of the gun. The idea, he said again and again, was to focus on what I wanted to do *once the pistol cracked.* And what I wanted to do was fly out of there.

Another training aid we used to try to improve my starts, or what we called explosive power, was the weighted vest. I'd strap on this vest – it was like a flak jacket – with rows of pockets into which one-pound lead weights could be fitted. I used that for hill work, running up hills, to help build up explosiveness. I'd keep adding a couple of lead weights every two weeks, until all the little pockets were filled. The vest had twenty-six pockets.

I have had to ask myself some tough questions about the whole direction of my career, in light of my trouble with starts. It is possible that I should have been steered toward longer-distance running. I really did possess the gift of the fabulous finish. But I was a sprinter, though it took me nearly seven years to get it right — my starts did not significantly improve until about 1986.

The one thing I did have in common with BJ was that we were both what you might call highly coachable. I can't speak directly for Ben, but in my case, it meant that I had offered up my life to track and field. There was nothing in my world that didn't relate directly to running, whether it was the clothes I bought or the friends I made. I developed an insatiable appetite for winning. I did not merely want to "go out there and do my best," in the words of Abigail Hoffman, the director general of Sport Canada. (As a former athlete, and a winner, she knows better than that, but maybe we all become platitudinous in a bureaucracy.)

What made me coachable was that I believed that Charlie Francis could help me win. Most athletes share the desire to win, but it's exaggerated, intensified, in an individual sport such as running. When you have a bad day, there is no team behind you to take up the slack. You can blame it on the wind, or the track, or a hamstring, but, in the end, either you're on the winner's podium or you're not.

Earlier that January, I got a morale booster in the form of an invitation to the plush downtown offices of a wealthy patron of sports. This scion of business once ran the 400-metres and he was entitled to distribute funds to athletes through the Canadian Track and Field Association from a trust account specified by his father's will. I believe the family was connected to a big firm in the transit industry. I was singled out as the recipient of $2,000 from the foundation, to be paid half in January and half in February.

I was ecstatic. The money meant that I would be able to attend two training camps for Scarborough Optimist athletes destined for the Olympics. We were to leave for a week in Florida on March 14, and there was another, two-week camp in California scheduled for May. I don't remember whether the money was paid directly to me or if it came through the CTFA.

In February 1980, I established seven Canadian records, usually breaking my own to establish the next. At the Maple Leaf Indoor Games, held at Maple Leaf Gardens, I clocked 5.95 seconds in the 50-yard dash. In the 50-metre race, I set a record with 6.33 at the Ottawa Citizen meet, broke that a week later with 6.28 at the Ontario Seniors' meet, broke it again the next week with 6.22 at the Edmonton Journal Games, then broke it again at the end of February with 6.21 at the National Senior Indoor Championships. In the 200-metre race, I established a Canadian record with 23.42 seconds at the Ontario Seniors' meet, then broke it with 23.15 at the National Senior Indoor Championships for the new world's indoor best.

I paid for my successes in February with pain in March. I strained my right hamstring badly at the Indoor Championships and stupidly went on to compete in a dual meet with Belgium in Montreal. I broke my previous record in the 50-yard dash with 5.87, another Canadian record – seven one-hundredths of a second short of the world record.

As a result, I wasted time and money going to the Florida training camp. We worked out at the University of Florida campus, where I suffered through the week with both hamstrings cramping and the start of trouble with my feet and shins. By the end of the week, I was unable even to run slowly for warm-up.

On March 10, I had started another six-week cycle of Dianabol, five milligrams and ten milligrams on alternating days. Dr. Koch had prescribed only five milligrams, but I was convinced that my astounding progress in February was directly attributable to my first cycle the previous fall, and that a tiny increase in dosage might produce even bigger miracles. I thought of it as "my little secret."

As I did throughout my career, I combined the drug cycle with regular sessions on the faradic stimulator. I'd attach my legs to the pads, which are in turn connected to the machine with electrodes, and turn up the dial to the highest level of intensity I could tolerate. The level at which I used it was painful. After the first session each season, I was usually very sore and stiff. I used to count the muscle contractions by placing a set of plastic shower rings on top of the machine and knocking them off one by one after each contraction.

Much later, in 1986, I managed to get a promotional contract with Bio-Med Systems Corporation in Toronto for using their much improved updated stimulator. Theirs was a computerized machine, so I could set the program for the correct number of contractions and even the rest periods in between. No more shower rings. (They were to sponsor me with $500 a month, through a couple of years including the six months after Seoul, in return for recommending their machine and appearing at press conferences as a representative. We know what happened in Seoul. I never did get paid after they pulled the plug on Ben.)

By the time we left in April for a meet in Knoxville, a pretty little city on the Tennessee River, I had a catalogue of physical problems. My hamstrings were still tender, my back was sore, my shins were in such bad shape that I had strained the ligaments in my right ankle and had to tape them, and my pelvic girdle had begun to throb in a mysterious, recurring ache that would haunt me for much of the following year. I ran 53.87 seconds in the 400-metres, nothing special. I blamed it on the weather.

I paid no attention to my growing physical problems. The Olympics were coming and I was going to be there and I was determined to excel. On an unseasonably cold day back in Canada, in April, before the Tennessee meet, I recorded the following workout in my diary:

Tuesday, April 15th, 1980

135 lbs.
Morning:
worked out at U of T
4 laps, 6 x 20 m , A & B skips
1 x 600 m, 1 x 300 m, 3 x 100 m
Medicine Ball
10 + 50 m running As, 40 m accelerations, jog back

Afternoon:
8 laps, 6 x 20 m, As, Bs, running As
1 x 600 m, 1 x 300 m, 3 x 100 m
10 + 50 m tempo into 20 m running As, jog back
Short Break
6 x Medicine Ball I + II
100 + 200 + 100 m
200 + 200 + 100 + 100

100 + 200 + 200 + 200
100 + 200 + 200 + 200
100 + 200 + 100
Short Break
50 m into 20 m running As, jog back
50 m into 20 push ups
50 m into 20 sit ups
50 m into hip circles
50 m into 20 m running As
50 m into 20 push ups
50 m into 20 sit ups
50 m into 10 m running As
50 m into 10 push ups
50 m into 10 sit ups
Warm down

Earlier in February, *Maclean's* magazine had a story by reporter Hal Quinn on the growing reaction to the recent Soviet invasion of Afghanistan. Quinn wrote, "Three weeks ago, the U.S. ambassador to Moscow was recalled to Washington to confer with President Jimmy Carter. He was asked what would have the most punitive effect on the Soviets – withdrawal from the Olympics or trade sanctions? The ambassador replied, 'There's no question. The Olympics would.' "

It was the first and last time that I ever exercised my citizen's right to vote, but that freezing February I had rushed to the polling booth at the end of my street to put an x beside the name of the Liberal candidate in the federal election. The occasion was a strange blip in Canadian politics when Prime Minister Joe Clark was forced to call an election after his Conservatives had won a minority government eight months earlier. Trudeau, whom I had long admired – something about his cerebral statesmanship made me proud of Canada – was against boycotting the Olympics in Moscow. I believed he would stand up to the Americans, should they go ahead with the boycott, and send Canadian athletes to Moscow.

Most other athletes kept to the sidelines on the issue, but I spoke out. I remember telling one reporter, "If Brezhnev has his eye on the oil fields, boycotting the Olympics won't stop him. The West should just get together and tell the Russians that if they take one more step they'll knock the crap out of them." It wasn't as if I majored in political science. I was only an Olympic athlete, but my opinion on Russia and Afghanistan seemed to matter, and what I had to say was dutifully reported. I told another reporter, "People are trying to use the Olympics to teach the Russians a lesson. But it's not going to work. If the boycott goes through, so what? The Russians would lose face, but they're used to losing face. And if the boycott goes through, the Communist bloc countries certainly aren't going to be here in 1984."

That's exactly what happened; maybe I should have been a pundit.

Trudeau won the election, but perhaps his heart was not in politics anymore — he resigned before the end of his term — because on April 22, three days before a scheduled meet in Martinique, we received word that the Canadian government had announced its decision to boycott the Olympic Games. Our only hope, that the Canadian Olympic Association would independently decide against the ruling, was dashed four days later. The COA backed the government.

I was deeply disappointed by the decision. Even today, I am convinced that the boycott had no effect at all on the Soviets. What made them eventually pull out of Afghanistan was the stubborn spirit of the Afghanis themselves and the new mood in the Soviet Union under Mikhail Gorbachev.

I comforted myself at the time with the knowledge that I was one of the younger athletes and that the boycott was much more damaging to the older athletes who might have competed for the last time in 1980. It turned out that 1980 might well have been my brilliant lost opportunity. At the 1984 Olympics in Los Angeles, I was so badly injured that I experienced one of the worst years of my career, though I managed to win a silver medal as part of the four-by-100-metre relay team. Then came the debacle of Seoul in 1988. I will probably be watching Barcelona on television in 1992, sitting on my couch. Funny how time slips away.

Plans had already been made, and deposits paid, for our pre-Olympic training camp in California, so we left on May 9. I was happy to go. My living arrangements with Ross Earl had not worked out and I had had to return home to Olive. The money from my C-card allowance was so late coming through that I owed about $400 in back rent. To make matters worse, a couple of resident Siamese cats had ganged up on my poor declawed Kaya. They nearly killed him. Ross was good about it, and I arrived on Olive's doorstep with my bed, my clothes, my posters, and a maimed cat under my arm. Olive didn't say much. I was seething.

May is a wonderful month to be in California. The pink and white adobe houses and Spanish-style curlicued public buildings are exotic to the eye and bright as candies in the sweet spring air. The smog comes later, in the heat of summer. Every morning was spiked with a heady excitement because we were working out at the UCLA campus where Evelyn Ashford and the other big American track stars trained. On a perfect May day, during a scheduled meet with Nigerian athletes, I clocked another Canadian record, breaking my own again – 22.68 in the 200-metres. I was twenty-one. I felt wonderful. I'm trying to explain why romance was in the air.

The night before we left for home was a Saturday. The injuries, the aches and pains, seemed to be in blissful abeyance. I had had an excellent workout that afternoon. Everyone had made plans to go downtown to one of the clubs, and one or two Canadians even skipped the Saturday workout to go and see the beach at Malibu. As for me, I had my eye on a tall, handsome runner with the unbelievably ordinary name of John Smith. Whenever I wrote his name in my diary, I couldn't resist putting quotation marks around it. I suppose it could have been worse – his name might have been John Doe. When he asked me for a date that Saturday night, I felt tongue-tied, but I said yes.

We went out for dinner and then came back and sat in the hallway of the student dormitory. We talked for hours. He was charming and inquisitive and I didn't really believe him when he said he would write to me in Toronto.

John had recently separated from his wife, a pretty Mexican actress. I saw her in a movie some years later, and I can see they must have made a striking couple. John is black, so I was going against my instincts to find him attractive, but what can I say? These things happen. He had been to Australia, looking for work as a model, and he did have those magazine-cover good looks. I saw him recently in a bit part on an American sit-com television show, so I guess he is still pursuing some kind of second career to capitalize on his looks.

Two days after I got home from California, on May 28, I paid $35 for 100 five-milligram Dianabol tablets from Charlie. I wanted to begin a third six-week cycle immediately. I was unconcerned about the National Championships, which were scheduled for the weekend of June 13 because, at the time, there were no doping controls in place there.

Four days before the National Championships, I visited Dr. Koch, and he gave me an injection of 30 milligrams of testosterone. He injected me again on July 7, with 150 milligrams, and again on July 30, with 75 milligrams. I didn't mention the Dianabol I'd gotten from Charlie, but in some kind of deference to his earlier advice, I limited myself to five milligrams a day.

I was convinced that steroids had something to do with my astonishing progress. Looking back, if there is a flaw in the argument, it would be that I had raw talent and speed to begin with and that a year of coaching would have produced some results anyway. But at the time, I began to perceive the steroids as an integral part of my training – another aid, like the muscle stimulator, the vitamin B-12 injections, the multi-vitamin pills (which I was gulping by the handful), the massages, whirlpools, the birth control pills, a proper diet, and the social life of a cloistered nun.

Perhaps more importantly, I had begun to fear my workouts and the steroids became a kind of shield against my fear. I was afraid of what I had to endure; I was terrified of injuries. And the myopic focus on my daily workouts was beginning to flatten my personality. In California, John Smith's overtures genuinely surprised me. What did I have to offer except my ramblings on track and starts and building endurance? I didn't read books anymore, didn't go to movies. I was bored, but obsessed by the very thing that bored me: the unrelenting daily workouts. It took a tremendous amount of mental energy to turn this into the will to win, day after day, meet after meet. The steroids helped, like a magic elixir, even if it was all in my mind.

On top of this, I had spent nearly two years in track, and the message about European athletes was strong and clear. They *all* used steroids. There were other, grisly stories, too. We heard that the Russians had discovered that when a woman is pregnant, she produces high levels of progesterone and estrogen, but also testosterone, the male hormone, which builds muscle. The testosterone level can double in a pregnant woman. After the 1964

Olympics, the Russians had admitted that ten of their twenty-six medal-winners were pregnant when they competed. The rumor we heard was that the pregnancies were planned so that the athletes would be six to ten weeks pregnant during the Olympics. I wondered, how were they inseminated? Did they get state-funded abortions when the Olympics were over? Questions, questions.

When I had been back from California a week, I got home late one afternoon to find a special-delivery letter from John Smith. We began to correspond.

On June 6, 1980, I received a strange letter from Cecil Smith, the executive director of the Ontario Track and Field Association:

> Dear Angella, Congratulations on your fine running recently. I am sure your European Tour will be extremely beneficial to both yourself and your coach, Charlie. Just remember, your *[sic]* as good as any European, the difference is only opportunity.
>
> Keep in touch.

Smith was referring to the European meets set up by Canadian and American track officials for the summer of 1980, though I did wonder exactly what he meant by my apparently inferior "opportunity." Some people called them the Alternate Olympics, and they took on the overtones of the Cold War with the free world going its own way and setting its own records, independent of the Olympics in Moscow. We were scheduled to leave for Europe on June 30, and before we left, we had a special endurance timetable set up with an all-comers meet in Ontario, then the National Championships in Sherbrooke, Quebec, and finally the Colgate Games at Centennial Stadium in Etobicoke.

At the National Championships I ran a Canadian record with 11.03 in the 100-metres, but the wind stole it from me. The IAAF stipulates that for a record to be registered, the wind factor must not exceed two metres per second. That means that if there is a wind from behind, propelling you along the track, the wind must not affect your time by more than two metres per second. They use an anemometer to measure the speed of the wind. At Sherbrooke, the wind measured +3.1, so my time was disallowed.

The wind can sometimes blow against you, and that affects your time, too. The way they keep a record is to note the time in which you ran the race with the wind factor beside in parenthesis (minus or plus). I never paid much attention to wind readings before Sherbrooke, but after that episode, I recorded all of them faithfully.

In track, you learn by doing. Early in my career, I was continually frustrated trying to beat the times of runners like Evelyn Ashford. I'd carefully note their times, even to the third decimal point. I stopped bothering when I realized that wind conditions were so variable that even Evelyn Ashford couldn't possibly beat some of her own times. The wind is a capricious friend. You might run the best time of your life one day in no wind, only to beat it the next day with a wind-assisted mediocre run. On blustery days at an outdoor meet, the runners sniff the breeze like nervous foxes.

Despite the fact that my time was not registered as a Canadian record, I came home from the National Championships in Sherbrooke with the gold medal in the 100-metres and the 200-metres, at 22.98 (-2.1). In the 200-metres, the wind was against me and again, at more than two metres per second, the time was not registered. BJ, who spent the first few years of his career trying to keep up with Desai Williams and Tony Sharpe, came away second to Desai in the men's 100-metres. He ran 10.38 that day, an interesting benchmark against his 9.79-second 100-metre race in Seoul eight years later.

Unfortunately, I had done some damage at the Sherbrooke meet. By June 16, I was forced to visit Dr. Koch, and he diagnosed the pain as strained tendons in my knees. Add to this my still-tender hamstrings, and I could hardly walk properly. Dr. Koch recommended alternate applications of ice and heat, and an anti-inflammatory drug called Indocid. As is the case with many anti-inflammatories, the Indocid was very hard on my stomach – it felt like the lining was bathed in acid – so he switched me to another anti-inflammatory called Naprosyn. (Both Indocid and Naprosyn are permitted by the IAAF as nonsteroidal anti-inflammatories.)

By the time of the Colgate Games on June 22, my injuries had improved, but I was horrified to feel a twinge in my tendon with the first warm-up stride. When a runner gets a warning signal like this, with no choice but to go ahead, it's like submitting to having a tooth pulled knowing the anesthetic isn't working. To make matters worse, the meet organizers were overwhelmed by the number of entrants that day, and the start of my race, the women's 400-metres, was delayed by seventy-five minutes. I was in pain, and I had lost my warm-up by the time the race started. I was furious.

Charlie was in a temper that day, too. He had put a tape mark in my lane at the 40-metre mark as a guide to where I should stop accelerating and start to hold the pace to avoid hurting my knee. The race officials made him remove it for no particular reason other than they'd never seen it done before. There was nothing illegal about it. I suppose we could have used a blade of grass to mark the spot, but it would have been hard to see. What's worse, the Canadian Olympic Association had decided that the Colgate Games would be the last race for women athletes to register times before the European tour, and the qualifying times they decided upon were higher than those set by the International Amateur Athletic Federation. The Colgate Games were designed to bring novices up against top Canadian and American women, so concessions were made for the 1,400 inexperienced runners – like the seventy-five-minute delay – and our guests, the Americans. It was the wrong place for the Canadian Olympic Association to impose such standards.

I managed to set the 400-metre record for the Colgate Games with 52.50, but it wasn't high enough for the Canadian Olympic Association. As a result, the European tour did not have a qualifying four-by-400-metre Canadian women's relay team.

The whole thing blew up in the newspapers, with Charlie fuming that none of his top athletes would ever compete in the Colgate Games again. He told Al Sokol of *The Toronto Star*, "Everywhere else the organizers try to give the advantage to the top athletes, but here we penalize them." My old friend Cecil Smith, from the Ontario Track and Field Association, said that national-caliber athletes would never again be invited to the competition. It was the beginning of a series of run-ins between Charlie and track officials in Canada that only got worse in the years ahead.

It must be rooted somewhere deep in the psychology of Canadians that we must show the world we can withstand incredible odds in order to come second, even if we have to manufacture odds to do it. In any other country in the world, track meet officials would say to themselves, you've invited a talented citizen, a world record holder, to your meet. Both you and the athlete are looking for top performance. It would be beneficial to all concerned – the athlete, the meet officials, the country itself — to guarantee excellent conditions to encourage top performance. In this fashion, world records are registered with the International Amateur Athletic Federation. A country's athletes have an incentive to strive for excellence, especially on their home turf.

In Canada, we do it backward. When we invite top athletes from another country to compete against our top athletes, we defer to them, giving them the most advantageous lanes. They go away happy, with excellent conditions contributing to another top performance. Someone like me, for a curious reason based either on ignorance or deference, often gets lane one, the inside lane. Lane one won't bother a slowpoke, but because of my speed, lane one throws me out on the curves. I lose time. Often I lose the race. The meet officials are happy: another second-place finish for another great Canadian!

By the time we left for the European tour, I had received word that my ranking had been upgraded to an A-card and that I had been accepted as a first-year student at York University for the 1980–81 academic year. Of course, these benefits applied only as long as I maintained my level of achievement, which would be reviewed every year. I wrote in my diary, "I hope I am better by The Hague meet. I need to run so that I can get a good world ranking in the fall — will depend on how I work out at York next year."

But it wouldn't all depend on my income as an A-carded athlete. For the first time in my life, I was to receive "appearance money" at the European meets. I have no idea how long the practice had been established, but it was understood that organizers would pay to have top athletes appear at their meets. I suppose it makes sense. Surely I couldn't be expected to pay for winter training camps, national competitions, and a two-week tour of Europe, plus keep up my rent and feed myself on what Sport Canada gave me.

It was not until the next year, 1981, that the International Amateur Athletic Federation finally acknowledged that appearance money was being paid. They introduced a ruling that permitted amateur athletes to earn more than $250 U.S. per meet, providing the money went directly to a national sport governing body trust fund.

Ross Earl set up an independent trust fund for the Scarborough Optimist Track and Field Club in 1980. The idea was that we could go to Ross for any money we needed and he would keep a running tally of what we deposited versus what we withdrew. Ross was a benevolent banker. At one time or another each of us would have lost an apartment or a car, or gone hungry, because of late payments from the Canadian Track and Field Association carding system. When we were desperate, Ross advanced us money. We trusted him.

Athletes of my caliber in 1980 could make as much as $600 U.S. per meet, but we found it hard to get endorsements. Charlie bumped into Alan Eagleson one evening and tried to arrange a meeting, but nothing came of it. Later, when Ben began to pull in big money, he called Eagleson but by then, Eagleson was wary of Ben's already complicated agenting arrangements. It was too late. Other people had shouldered in.

8

The Nice Life

We arrived in The Hague, a city in the west Netherlands by the North Sea, on June 30, 1980. Since the inquiry in 1989, I have often thought back to Mr. Justice Dubin's remark to the weightlifter Denis Garon about his "nice" life and the perks of being an athlete. You get to travel to other countries, Dubin said. To an athlete, travel is a grind, an interruption of training, a marathon of stress, as you try to adapt to strange competition conditions. All you get in return are glimpses of airports, suburbs, and stadiums. But occasionally, as happened in The Hague, we did enjoy the benefit of a closer look at life abroad.

The Hague is an important city, site of the South Holland government, the royal residence, and the International Court of Justice, established in 1899. The Hague Peace Conference of 1907 defined prisoner-of-war treatment, maritime warfare and war-time neutrality for the wars to follow. One of the city's most famous residents was Vincent Van Gogh, who lived there in 1883. Vincent had fallen in love with a prostitute named Sien. Five years later, in Arles, he cut off an ear and gave it to another prostitute. Reading Vincent's letters from The Hague to his brother, Theo, I found a line that I thought applied as much to athletic as to artistic aspirations: "What I want and aim at is confoundedly difficult, and yet I do not think I aim too high."

The connection to Vincent Van Gogh is easy to make as you wander the streets of The Hague. The depth of color he described to his brother is there, and so are the prostitutes.

It was like nothing I had ever seen. There were magazines showing women with men, women with dogs, women with pigs. (I remembered the pigs in Jamaica, how I used to throw the feed at them because I didn't want to get too close.) Our North American society uses women as symbols of sex so that people will buy cars and hydraulic lifts and beer, but in The Hague, the mannequins in the windows are flesh-and-blood human beings and the product is sex itself. As a woman, I felt ill seeing women so openly, blatantly, for sale. I can't speak for my male colleagues. I never asked where they went at night.

I won the meet at The Hague on July 4 with 11.42 in the 100-metres, but the competition wasn't tough and I was still favoring my injured tendons. In fact, I jogged in from the 60-metre mark and still didn't see anyone until the finish line. The next day, we left for the *Sturm und Drang* of the official/unofficial Alternate Olympics in Stuttgart, West Germany.

The West Germans had also boycotted the Olympics in Moscow, and they wanted to show the world what it was missing. The timing of the track and field events, to be held at the 71,000-seat Neckar Stadium, was designed to upstage the Russian show by three weeks. I worried about my tendons and Charlie repeated again and again that I should accelerate only for the first 40 metres, then hold the pace, to avoid further injury. Gerard Mach, the national coach, who was accompanying us, stroked his whiskers and said philosophically, "You know, Angella, every sprinter gets hurt."

I won the 200-metres with 22.92, to beat my own personal best time of 23.18 seconds. I "dusted" Australia's Denise Boyd, who came second with 23.21. Translation: she was so far behind, she had to eat the dust I kicked up. I didn't dare run the 100-metres, fearing my tendons could not react that quickly to the shorter, more powerful burst of speed. I decided I wouldn't run the 100-metres in Philadelphia, either.

The plan for the Alternate Olympics teams was to break up after Stuttgart and attend a number of simultaneous meets scheduled between July 14 and July 17 in all parts of the world, including London, Warsaw, Oslo, Paris, and Philadelphia.

On July 14, my teammates and I arrived in Philadelphia, City of Brotherly Love, home of the Liberty Bell and site of the signing of the Declaration of Independence in 1776. In a city famous for its architecture and its sculpture, I was amused to find that there was a statue of Sylvester Stallone's character Rocky in front of the Spectrum arena. This is where Rocky boxes his way to victory in one of the countless sequels.

I won the 200-metres with 22.77, bettering my personal best again. I felt dizzy coming around the final curve, but it had nothing to do with the race, or my tendons or hamstrings or glutes. Maybe *dizzy* isn't the right word; *fluttery* might be better. I knew John Smith would be arriving in Toronto the following night for a short weekend visit. I was smitten, so much so that I took a day off that Saturday to spend some time with John. I made a note in my diary that I was not disappointed by my times during a special endurance workout on Sunday. I simply wrote, "Went to bed late." I was on cloud nine all the next week. John and I ran up some hefty long distance charges.

It helped me get over the nagging feeling of being left out when the Olympics, the real Olympics in Moscow, were held. I made careful note of all the winning times, however. Lyudmila Kondratyeva of the Soviet Union won the 100-metres with 11.06. Marita Koch of East Germany won the 400-metres with 48.88.

There were a lot of international shenanigans that year of the boycott. Italy was bursting with pride over the performance of its athletes in Moscow, and a meet called the Golden Gala was scheduled for the first week in August to show off their talents. The Italians had to find a way to soothe the bruised egos of the countries that had honored the boycott, so they billed the Gala as a "revenge meet." Nineteen countries would take part, including newly-minted Moscow champions and revenging boycotters from the United States, West Germany, Japan, Canada, and Kenya.

I arrived in Rome on August 1, carrying my faradic stimulator. Mentally, I was confident, thoroughly prepared for the contests ahead. In my diary, after I had noted the Olympic times, I printed in large square letters: "MY DAY WILL COME." Physically, I kept my fingers crossed that my tendons would hold up. They were the only thing between me and victory.

On August 5, John Smith's thirtieth birthday, I won the 100-metres with 11.27 against Natayla Botchina of the Soviet Union, who was second with 11.29, and Alice Brown of the United States, third with 11.36. The Olympic champion, Lyudmila Kondratyeva, had pulled a leg muscle and didn't run. If the Afghanis could have used the energy and passion of the crowd of over 100,000 people in the Rome Olympic stadium at the "revenge meet," their country might have been freed in a day.

I could do no wrong on the rest of the European tour in that glorious August of 1980. I was flying. In West Berlin, I won the 100-metres with 11.25 to beat West Germany's Annegret Richter, the former world record holder. The same day, I won the 200-metres with 23.02, beating France's Chantal Rega, who ran 23.09. In Cologne, I won the 100-metres with 11.38 over Jeanette Bolden of the United States, who ran 11.51, and Annegret Richter, who ran 11.52.

My toughest test was in Switzerland. Nine Olympic champions were entered in the Zurich meet and so was my nemesis, Merlene Ottey of Jamaica. I had been unable to beat Ottey in the 200-metres so far, though we shared none of the rancor that existed between me and Angela Bailey. I rather liked Ottey. She could goof around before a race, chit-chat, but when we crouched in the starting blocks, she was nobody's friend. I admired her concentration. Charlie was riding me hard about Ottey. Before the race, perhaps sensing I was psyched-out by Ottey, Charlie called me a chickenshit. It was his own psych job; he thought I'd do better against her angry than cowed. He had a bag of tricks, that Charlie.

In Zurich, I placed second in the 100-metres with 11.25, behind Marlies Göhr of East Germany, who ran it in 11.18. In the 200-metres, I came third, with a time of 22.61, which set a Canadian record. Marita Koch won with 22.34, and Merlene Ottey came second with 22.43. The only note in my diary is, "Ottey beat me by .18." I was furious at Charlie. He never tried that "chickenshit" stuff on me again.

Switzerland was important for another reason. In track and field circles, the Zurich meet is regarded as second only to the Olympics in world importance. Zurich attracts the top athletes because meet organizers pay top dollar for them to appear. In years to come, BJ would pull in as much as $25,000 U.S. per race in Zurich.

My brush with the way the payout system worked came at the end of the meet, when the organizers hosted a dinner for the athletes and their entourage of coaches, trainers, assorted sports officials, and agents. Around midnight, a line of people began to form in the hallway outside the dining room. Some of them sat on the floor, a few stood holding their drinks from the party. It was a congenial queue, like kids waiting for tickets to a Rolling Stones concert. Some athletes stayed inside the dining room, sipping a last drink, anticipating a day off for travel. Most athletes, like myself, decided not to hang around and wisely went home to bed.

Charlie told me later that he saw Adriaan Paulen, the head of the International Amateur Athletic Federation, walking along the hall where the line of people waited to collect their appearance money. The line led to a door and inside, at a long table, sat the president of one of the biggest insurance companies in the world. On the table in front of him were stacks of paper money in bundles secured by elastic bands. It looked like there could have been a million dollars on that table.

When Charlie reached the table, he read out the names of the athletes he had brought to the meet. The insurance man consulted his list and then counted out the appearance money due in snappy $100 American bills. I never knew exactly how much Charlie collected in total.

The International Amateur Athletic Federation's definition of an amateur is "one who competes for the love of sport and as a means of recreation, without any motive of securing any material gain from such competition." It is a definition formulated when rich men took sabbaticals from their positions to run a foot race or ride a horse or throw a stick.

Paulen obviously knew what was going on. That's the sham of it. The appearance payouts were made openly, and they were made *over* the table in places like that small room. Only in Czechoslovakia and Hungary was no cash given — they didn't have any to give. Instead, the athletes were paid in crystal vases.

It was the second clear instance of hypocrisy I had encountered in track and field. The first was that it was perfectly acceptable to take an anabolic steroid prescribed by your doctor so long as it had cleared your system by the time of competition. The second was that even though you were not supposed to make money as an amateur, there was money to be made, and the head of the IAAF knew it and did nothing to stop it. I began to wonder if everyone in track and field knew about these things, or if just some knew. I began to wonder who I could trust.

In the beginning, I carried the cash around with me in my wallet. So did BJ and the others. They used those fancy leather over-the-shoulder bags that European men favor. Once, we jumped off a shuttle bus that had taken us to the airport and we had hurried up the ramp before Ben realized that he'd left his bag in the bus. It was another great moment in sport when he broke the sound barrier getting back to the bus to retrieve his bag. Ben must have had $50,000 in $100 U.S. bills in that bag.

Customs officials were often amused to see us toting the large, unwieldy trophies that we also won. A successful tour would mean a lot of excess baggage. There was so much hardware that some of it had to be left behind, but I have an impressive collection in my laundry room.

One time, we were going through Canadian customs, returning from a meet in Japan, when a customs officer came upon cash in my wallet. A thick wad of new $100 U.S. bills. Uh oh. (Often, going through customs, the officers recognized us. Sometimes, they'd mention that they had read about our races in the newspapers or watched us on television. Usually they smiled and waved us through.) This time I thought, "This is it, I'm sunk." I worried perhaps this would jeopardize my amateur status, have me kicked off the team – what did I know? The officer finally leaned forward, over the counter, and said in a quiet voice full of concern, "You know, ma'am, you really ought to get traveler's cheques."

"Yes, yes, of course," I said. "Silly me."

There still were another four meets scheduled for the European tour, starting with the fifth annual Nikaia track and field meet in the beautiful city of Nice. I came second in the 100-metres with 11.36, behind Natayla Botchina, and third in the 200-metres with 22.61 behind Botchina in first and Merlene Ottey in second. In Nijmegen, back in the Netherlands, I won the 200-metres with 22.88 against some mediocre competition. But I was driving myself hard. I was not pleased with my times; I thought I should be running 22 flat.

By August 22, we were in Brussels, and I won the 100-metres with 11.24 and the 200-metres with 22.80. Suddenly, I wanted to go home. The constant traveling and unrelieved pressure was getting to me. But I rallied for the last meet, in Düsseldorf, to win the 100-metres with 11.23 and come second in the 200-metres with 22.93.

My performance in Europe showed up in the 1980 fall rankings by *Track & Field News*. I was rated fifth in the world in the 100-

metres and seventh in the world for the 200-metres. The Sports Federation of Canada named me female athlete of the year for 1980, and I had my picture taken with a young blond hockey player named Wayne Gretzky, who had been chosen in the Canadian Press poll as male athlete of the year.

My immediate concern, the minute I stepped off the plane from Europe, had been to find an apartment of my own. Classes at York were to start in two weeks, and I was determined to rent a place near the campus. I have never learned how to drive, so commuting from Olive's apartment would have added an hour each way to my day. I went out one morning and did a quick tour of some buildings up in Downsview, on Niska Drive, within sight of the university. I wanted a one-bedroom apartment, but there was only a two-bedroom available in the building I eventually settled on. I was in such a hurry, I said I'd take it.

My apartment was on the thirteenth floor. There aren't many occasions in modern North American life when you get to see a display of good, old-fashioned superstition, but most builders do what they can to ward off bad luck by renaming the thirteenth floor. This time, the thirteenth floor had been renamed "PH," which did wonders for my social status. Everyone thought I lived in a penthouse.

There was a little Jewish woman, Mrs. Kaplan, sitting in the rental office. I described in detail my being an athlete and the way the rent would be paid. Mrs. Kaplan wasn't having any of this, so I had to send for Ross Earl to come and sign a guarantee. The funny thing is, we all took a liking to this area, and later, Molly Killingbeck and Desai Williams moved into an apartment there, then Eric Spence, another athlete, moved in, then Jillian Richardson. Charlie moved into the twin building next door, and Tony Sharpe took a place in a building down the block. Every time someone moved into Niska Drive, Mrs. Kaplan had the same question: "How are you going to pay the rent?" Every time she had to hear the story about the carding system. And every time she insisted that Ross Earl sign a guarantee.

Mrs. Kaplan turned out to be an important part of my life for the five years I lived in the apartment. She got to know us all quite well, and there is nothing like an interested property manager to provide top security. Nobody got in or out of that building without a thorough grilling from Mrs. Kaplan.

The day I was to leave Olive's, Ross Earl came by with one of his trusty vans again. I packed my clothes, swept Kaya into my arms, and left. Olive didn't mention that she had seen any news reports of the European tour. It was the usual leave-taking.

This time I didn't take my bed with me. I felt flush, what with the windfall from Europe, the money from my A-card status, and another $500 a month from adidas. Charlie had negotiated a promotional contract with the sporting goods company that included bonuses tied to performance. My first-place finishes were each worth $200.

I wanted to buy all my own things. I spent about $1,200 to have neutral beige broadloom installed. Naturally, I expected everything to be perfect, so I slept on the floor for three weeks because I couldn't find a bed I liked. I took Ross Earl's advice and began to scan the newspapers for auction notices. His house was full of intricately carved antique furniture, and I took a real liking to it, so I was on the prowl for antiques I could afford. Ross always said antiques maintain their value, perhaps even appreciate over time. I bought a television set to keep me company.

Eventually, I broke down and bought an ordinary couch and two lamps for the living room. They made the place look lived in. Later, I did very well at an auction, buying a five-piece Duncan Phyfe dining-room set with six matching chairs for $1,900. When I saw the graceful curves and rich finish in my own apartment, I was immensely proud of myself. Going to weekend auctions became a hobby, and I would always pick up one small thing or another.

On my twenty-second birthday, in September 1980, Charlie and I drove to an auction house in Mississauga. Ross had said this particular auction might have some worthwhile bedroom furniture. As soon as I walked in the door, I saw the bedroom suite I wanted. It was carved from gleaming mahogany, and it included two oval mirrors, two chairs, a desk, a makeup table, a man's chest of drawers, a headboard, and a footboard. I had to have it. The auctioneer started at $900, and I was dismayed to hear another woman bidding against me. I had arranged with Ross to have his wife meet us at the auction with a cheque, and we had set a ceiling of $2,700. The bidding heated up: $1,000... $1,500... $2,000...

then in increments of $100. I was sweating, but I finally got it – for $2,600.

At the same time as I was pulling my apartment together, I had started to attend classes at York. With workouts at the track and field center every day, I couldn't handle any more than three first-year courses. I decided on a social sciences course, in which I did very well, and a pure science course on the biology of sex. I did reasonably well until we hit genetics, which baffled me. My third course was classical studies. I wanted to pick up on my love of literature and ancient history, and it seemed a good combination of the two. It was daunting, though. I had already been out of school for two years and I never did learn how to type. I used to write out essays one night, then spend the next two nights rewriting them legibly. It was probably a good process for editing – my essays emerged quite polished – but it was very time-consuming.

One of the things I loved most about those years at York was going to classes in the mornings. Most days, I was able to trot out the front door of my apartment building – "Morning, Mrs. Kaplan!" – tramp down a little hill, tiptoe my way over stones to get across a creek, then jog up another little hill to cross the campus, round the man-made pond where all the Canada geese floated, then slip inside the building for my first lecture. Occasionally, the creek would be too swollen with spring rain to cross, and I learned to avoid this route after a heavy snowfall. The creek bed would fill up with snow and there I would be, floundering around up to my armpits. One luscious spring day, when the sun was sparkling on the water and the leaves were beginning to bud, I tripped lightly across the stones on the creek, lost my footing, and scattered all the notes I needed for a nine-o'clock exam. I left a muddy trail of water all the way to my desk that day.

It was my luck to attend university at a time when track wear was fashionable. I managed to get the very latest outfits from adidas – sweatsuits and running shoes – so I never had to spend much money on a wardrobe. I met a young woman at York who designed and made gold jewelry, and I had her make up a long, dangly earring with three gold strands. I wore this in my right ear, with matching studs in the left ear. It became my trademark. Some reporters considered me a fashion plate.

It became a pleasant routine. Every morning, I'd cook up a nice breakfast of bacon and eggs. I've always rationalized my love of bacon, and bacon fat, as my need for protein. I even treated myself to steak and eggs every once in a while, though I have since eliminated red meat from my diet. The fact is, I was kind of lazy about cooking and I often skipped lunch. I sometimes wonder if I didn't cause myself problems with hypoglycemia due to poor eating habits. At night, after a day of classes and a grueling workout, some of us, too bushed to cook, headed down to one of the local fast-food restaurants. Most often, I had chicken at Swiss Chalet.

I love coffee, but I rarely allowed myself to have it in the mornings or any other time during the training season. I had weak tea instead. Rightly or wrongly, I had this idea that the stimulation of caffeine should be reserved for competition. I'd drink lots of coffee on race days.

As the fall progressed, I found that the dual load of training and school got very heavy. There were weekends when I went home Friday night and didn't emerge from the apartment until Monday morning. All I could do was sleep. Around Thanksgiving, I was plagued by an incredibly painful arch in my left foot. I went to have it X-rayed and began seeing a chiropractor three times a week. I started taking anti-inflammatories again. For some reason, exhaustion probably, I felt like crying all the time. I went off the birth control pill for a while, thinking maybe it was the culprit. In a nice piece of irony, around this time I was invited onto a CBC children's show called "Yes You Can". The idea was to show kids that with determination and hard work, anyone can reach a dream. I limped home after the show to cry myself to sleep.

In early December, I started another six-week cycle of Dianabol in preparation for the indoor competitions. It was December 8, 1980, a date I won't easily forget. That was the night John Lennon was murdered in New York City.

My spirits improved the day I handed in my final first-term essay, and I started to get excited about Christmas. I had decided to spend two weeks at a winter training camp in California. John and his brother had asked me to stay with them. On December 21, John's sister was getting married, and I had been invited to the wedding.

I worked hard those two weeks at UCLA. I was rewarded for my efforts on December 30, back in Canada, when I won the 300-metres with 36.91 at the Saskatoon Indoor Games, setting a world record. And I finally beat Merlene Ottey of Jamaica. She came second with 37.23. I pasted the newspaper photograph of the two of us crossing the finish line in my scrapbook and spent one of the most pleasant New Year's Eves of my life staring at it until I fell asleep.

By the second week in January 1981, I was back into the swing of things at York, and I managed to set a Canadian record for the 400-metres at an all-comers meet, with a time of 51.99 seconds. At the Toronto Star Maple Leaf Indoor Games the next month, I set another Canadian record, for the 50-yard dash, with 5.85 seconds. I was invited to be the mystery guest on CBC-TV's "Front Page Challenge" with Betty Kennedy, Gordon Sinclair, and Pierre Berton, but they failed to guess who I was. They asked me what it takes to be a world champion runner, and I gave them an answer that seemed to make them happy. Even Sinclair, the curmudgeon of the panel, didn't dig too deeply. Not much truth gets told on television. That morning, I had started a new anti-inflammatory called Tandearil.

By the end of February, I had set two Canadian records at the Edmonton Journal National Games, with 6.19 in the 50-metres, and a team record of 3.41.37 in the women's four-by-400-metres relay. I had also started a new cycle of Dianabol. By March 24, I had begun to use a cream we called DMSO, short for dimethyl sulfoxide, to relieve the pain that was beginning to build in my tendons.

I managed to get a prescription for DMSO, though I knew it really wasn't meant to be used as a pain reliever. Most of the time, it's prescribed for people with herpes sores; it's actually a cleansing agent. DMSO is dangerous to work with, though it was approved for use in hospitals in Florida. It went through my system in seconds. The minute I put it on my skin, I could taste it in my mouth. In one of his famous stories, Charlie used to tell us about the rumor that some spy had been murdered when someone sneaked into his car and smeared his steering wheel with DMSO with some sort of poison in it. I don't know if I believed him, but I used DMSO sparingly.

The biggest story in my life that winter was neither new track records nor exotic new pain killers, but the saga of John Smith. John and I were still going strong when he came up to Canada to stay with me in my new apartment for a while. He had decided to make a comeback and went to the trouble of having his Achilles tendon scraped. The Achilles can calcify, and it takes surgery to have it repaired. After he arrived, he began to train with Charlie at York.

John told me that there had been the possibility of a coaching job at UCLA but that it hadn't panned out. He and I were thinking of making a go of it. To my surprise, and chagrin, he got word that the coaching job had come through, and in two days he was gone. Something screwed up in California, though, and he landed back on my doorstep about the end of February. I got tired of the situation. A lot of my disaffection had to do with the cavalier way he'd taken off, but there were other problems. It's hard to put your finger on exactly what goes wrong in a relationship, but I'm not the sort of person who can fake feelings. When it's over, it's over.

My resolve to end the relationship with John was bolstered by a little outside help, a cute little blond guy at the track at York. Cute, little, blond, and very young. His name was Tony Issajenko, and he had started working out with Charlie a year earlier, when he was fourteen, a skinny kid. He used to show up at our workouts at Lawrence Park the odd time. I never paid much attention then – I mean, *fourteen years old!* – but one afternoon I noticed him at York and he had obviously been doing a lot of work with weights. He looked bigger, stronger. And twice as cute. He'd gone to a salon in Yorkville and had his hair styled. Molly Killingbeck and I teased him; I ran my fingers through his hair, messing it. Besides, Tony Issajenko was an older man now; in another six months he'd be sixteen.

Tony's nickname was Antosha, or Tosha, for short. One day, I lent him a pair of spikes and realized I had an excuse to call him and ask him how things were going. I looked up his number in the telephone book. The fact is, I was flirting.

On another level, I respected this kid for his talent. I had seen him run earlier at one of the high school meets, and he'd won the 100-metres. He ran a fabulous race, and he had very quick reactions. Charlie told Al Sokol of *The Toronto Star* that he thought Tony could become a nationally classed sprinter. By then, Tony had run the 100-metres in 10.8 seconds, tying Ben Johnson's record in the fifteen-year-old age category. This was remarkable for a white kid. "Tony is a big talent, but I sometimes wonder if he's aware of it," Charlie said.

To this day, I have regrets about Tony's running career. My theory is that he was too good too young. When you are so fast so young, you tend to think that you'll just keep improving at the same rate, year after year. To a degree, I had problems with this attitude, too. After a certain point, the only thing that will lead to improvement is constant training, and this takes patience and commitment that I don't think Tony had. But that winter, it wasn't his running that was on my mind.

It started out as a fling. I don't think either of us really thought anything would come of it. Some of the people at the track thought we were nuts. I heard rumors that Tony would leave me because he was just in it for material gain. I've had the last laugh at the rumors, I guess; Tony and I are still together, with two beautiful daughters.

What cemented our relationship was the fact that Tony's parents got a divorce when he turned sixteen. I had given him the keys to my apartment when I was on tour in Europe the summer of 1981 and he was supposed to look in and water the plants and keep an eye on Kaya. He never left. I think the fact that his parents were divorcing made it difficult for him to stay at home. He had had epileptic seizures before, when they separated. Tony took the divorce very hard.

Tony is a true Slav in many ways. He has a difficult time talking about his feelings, and although he has a good sense of humor, he doesn't often smile. I recall hearing the actress Jacqueline Bisset talking about her relationship with Alexander Godunov, and she mentioned this Russian aloofness. I find it attractive in the way that it calms me down. I can be a very emotional person and I will let the pots and pans fly, but usually Tony is calm and even-tempered. I went through a stage when I wished he was different and I was sad to realize that after years together, I never really could tell if he was upset or happy about something. But it's the way he is. At this point, I don't think I'd know what to do with a man who gushed all over me. Tony's aloofness appeals to my sense of independence.

We have developed an unusual relationship, one that I believe will last. I've always respected the difference in our ages, and I give him what others would consider a lot of freedom because he's so young. If he wants to go out to clubs until five or six in the morning, it's not a big deal to me. I got over the jealousy thing a long time ago when I realized women would never really leave him alone. They're always passing him notes and making eyes at him. What am I going to do – send him out the door with a bag over his head? I've never had a brother or a sister, but I suppose you could say Tony and I have a very close relationship that must be something like siblings. A happy, supportive, incestuous sort of relationship. We've done a lot of growing up together.

I hope we'll be together forever.

In the spring of 1981, rumors began to fly around the track that a number of track and field athletes were using cocaine to improve their performance. I was curious.

Someone told me I could get cocaine through a man who worked for a major corporate sponsor of track and field. I was surprised, but it turned out to be a good tip. One night, a friend of a friend appeared at my apartment door, and he sold me a small vial of cocaine for $150. I put it to the test in a meet in Guadeloupe on May 30.

We felt a few drops of rain at the beginning of the 200-metres, and by the end of the race it was a torrential downpour. The water streamed down our bodies, and we had to squint to see as we ran. It was a close race; I was running against Chandra Cheeseborough of the United States, and she was breathing down my back in all that rain. Ordinarily, under these circumstances, I would have tightened up. I'm not saying I would have lost the race, but I might have injured myself by putting on the burn at the finish line with tense muscles. With the cocaine, I had a marvelous sense of well-being, a feeling of strength and lightness. I was relaxed, though the rain was almost suffocating and I could sense Cheeseborough with my skin, she was so close. I won, with a time of 22.55, setting another Canadian record.

My experiment with cocaine was a success. I tossed it in my bag and headed overseas for the first swing through Europe that year. Cocaine was the glamor drug back then, the social drug of choice in Hollywood and among talk-show guests. Those were the days before crack. Still, I was uneasy using it. It was the first illegal drug I had tried.

In the next few meets, I began to see that cocaine wasn't working for me. It made me unconcerned with the competition, but I was so much better than anyone else in the races I entered that I didn't need to worry anyway. I detected a certain mellowness coming over me, and I decided it must be the cocaine. As I've mentioned, I dislike most social drugs like marijuana and alcohol for the way they induce a laid-back sense of well-being. I ultimately decided to give the cocaine away to one of the other athletes on the tour. If anything, I wanted a drug that would make me feisty. I found it in Fürth, in Germany.

My graduation to higher dosages and stronger drugs came about for the innocuous reason that I'd run out of Dianabol. It was an oversight on my part. I suppose I had thought I could get by with the Dianabol I still had and that I would continue to use the cocaine throughout the European tour. There were no doping controls in Europe then. When I realized I didn't have enough Dianabol to properly complete my cycle, I asked Charlie for help, and he scouted around the circle of throwers to see if he could find anything.

(At the Dubin Inquiry, Robert Armstrong, the commission counsel, asked why we would go to a thrower for steroids. I told him, "One assumes that the thrower is always on steroids.")

The thrower was a top American shot-putter Charlie had known for years. He gave us a steroid called Anavar, and I simply substituted it for Dianabol, so that I took five milligrams of each every other day. But he also gave me something he called black beauties. I had told him about my experience with cocaine, and he said that if I really wanted something to give me a kick at the start of a race, I should try these black beauties. They were little capsules filled with tiny granules of speed – amphetamines. Guaranteed to produce a hyperactive response.

On June 5, we arrived in the small city of Bratislava in Czechoslovakia, on the Danube River. The running shoes I took with me were bothering me, sliding up and down on my heel, so I took them off and curled my toes into the grass field before my workout. It was a lovely summer day with puffy, drifting clouds in a blue sky. It was silly, but I decided to do my workout in bare feet, just like the old days. I started a long warm-up session. By the end of the workout, I was hobbling. I had reinjured my tendons. I was furious with myself. We had only a day to go before the Bratislava meet, and I was expecting good competition from, among others, Merlene Ottey.

The thrower came to the rescue. He mixed up a concoction of 150-milligrams of Deca-Durabolin, spiked with Primobolan, another anabolic steroid. It was based in a heavy oil, and the idea was that the regenerative effects would slowly seep through the body over three or four weeks, speeding up my healing process. As well, the testosterone would give me some extra aggression, something I worried chronically that I lacked, especially in comparison with European athletes. The thrower injected this concoction into my thigh. Charlie couldn't do it; he said needles made him squeamish.

For the meet itself, I decided to rely on the kick start of a black beauty to overcome my dread of pain from the injured tendons. I followed instructions on the Saturday morning before the race and faked a slight cold with sniffles. One good snort into a hanky before the pre-race warm-up and I was hyper as could be from the speed. In fact, I was so hyper – *wired* might be a better description – that I failed to warm up properly. I just jumped around, then went straight into the race. I broke the Canadian record in the 100-metres, but I didn't win the race. Worse, I strained my left hamstring.

The next day, I couldn't walk properly. I was terrified. There were still another three meets in the European tour. I had to get through the next two weeks somehow. I applied some DMSO to the hamstring, and we took off for East Berlin.

By the time we arrived, I was in such pain that Charlie took me to see a local doctor. The doctor gave me an anti-inflammatory cream I had never heard of called Hepathromb, to be applied once every hour. If this didn't stop the pain, I was to take some pills called Gelonida. I didn't know what was in them, either. I had a restless night and spent the next day attached to the faradic stimulator. I put the pads on my glutes, my feet, my biceps, my triceps, and my stomach. The bombardment of ointments and pills and muscle stimulation began to take effect, and by the afternoon I was able to complete a short workout.

I was still in too much pain to be able to compete in East Berlin, and it was unlikely that I would be able to run in the scheduled Potsdam meet, either. We were supposed to fly out of East Germany for Paris on June 12, but even that didn't work out. The Canadian Track and Field Association was supposed to have had our tickets waiting for us at the airport, but someone had messed up and poor Charlie realized he was going to have to put us up in hotels on the other side of the wall, in West Berlin, for another two days. He did what he could afford to do and sent us out in taxis to some places he found listed in the newspaper.

Charmaine Crooks and I arrived at a fleabag hotel by nightfall. There was no point in complaining; we knew Charlie was out on a limb for money, and no one seemed to know if we'd end up paying our airfare to Paris and home ourselves. There was what looked like a strip joint beside the hotel. The word *seedy* doesn't do justice to the sheer filth and degradation in that part of West Berlin. But Charmaine and I were curious, and we had time to kill. What would we see behind those crumbling walls next door?

We put our bags in the hotel room and walked over to the strip joint. It turned out to be a peep show where they had little booths with slot machines you dropped coins in to watch pornographic movies. I hadn't seen anything so awful since the magazines in The Hague. I wondered what would make these wretched human beings do those things. In the dark, I whispered to Charmaine, "Jeez, a pig can bite your hand off!"

And all the time, a wizened old man pushing a mop and pail patrolled the grimy room, washing semen from the sticky tiled floors.

Newly arrived in Canada.

After a successful season that included establishing seven new Canadian records and wins at national and international track meets, I was named Female Athlete of the Year for 1980. Wayne Gretzky won Male Athlete of the Year.

The Toronto Star/F. Lennon

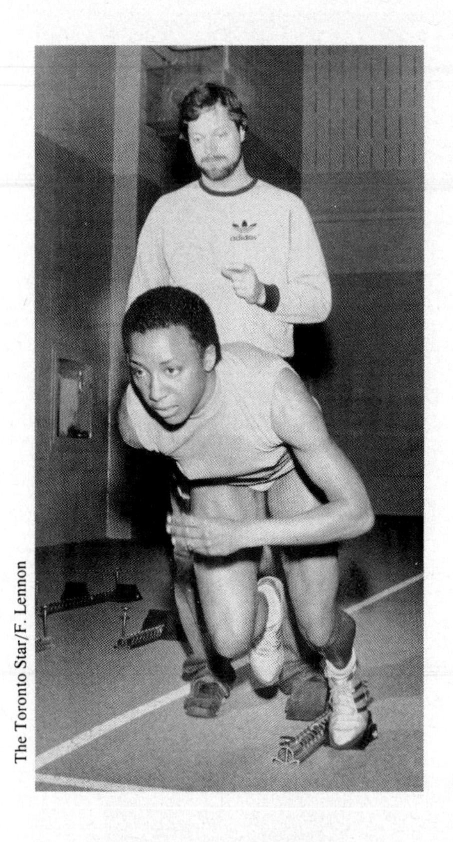

The Toronto Star/F. Lennon

Coach Charlie Francis and I constantly worked to improve my weak starts – a problem that plagued me throughout my career.

Hostility erupted into a confrontation with Angela Bailey in 1983, after she told me I was "washed up" at the age of 24. Charlie Francis (right) and coach John Mumford intervene.

The Globe and Mail/J. McNeill

CanadaWide Features/G. Hershorn

"Sprint Empress Angie." The Australian press gave me the title at the Commonwealth Games in 1984 in Brisbane. I won four medals: the gold in the 100-metres, a bronze in the 200-metres, a silver in the 4-by-100-metre relay and a gold in the 4-by-400-metre relay. The 4-by-400 finish was one of the most exhilarating of my career.

Allsport/Claus Andersen

The relay team of Angela Bailey, France Gareau, Marita Payne and myself won a silver medal at the 1984 Los Angeles Olympics. We were honoured in front of a Toronto crowd at the Toronto *Star* Indoor Games in 1985.

The Toronto Star/T. Bock

Alexandra (Sasha) was born on September 1st, 1985. Tony and I showed her off to the world a few days later. After a few months off, I resumed training and Sasha became a regular at workouts and international track meets.

On the comeback trail. By August of 1986 I had regained some of my winning form, defeating Kathy Cook in the 200-metres final in Scotland.

Allsport/Claus Andersen

In the World Championships in Rome in 1987, I competed against one of my great rivals – Merlene Ottey (left), and Heike Dreschler.

Allsport/Claus Andersen

CanadaWide Features/C. Robertson

The team was in high spirits when we left for Seoul in 1988. Mark McKoy, Desai Williams and Ben Johnson posed with me before we got on the plane.

CanadaWide Features/Goldstein

Our agent Larry Heidebrecht was under seige – just like the rest of us – after Seoul.

The Toronto Star/J. Hryniuk

Jamie Astaphan came back to Toronto to testify at the Dubin Inquiry.

CanadaWide Features/C. Robertson

Waldemar Matuszewski, the team's masseur and physiotherapist also appeared before the Inquiry.

Reuters/G. Hershorn

Robert Armstrong and I sort out details of the various drugs at the Dubin Inquiry.

Tony and I face the world after the inquiry.

Reuters/G. Hershorn

9

Hotshotting and Crashing

By the third and final day of my testimony at the Dubin Inquiry, feathers had begun to fly south of the border. A story in the Toronto *Sun* quoted Pat Connolly, a high-profile, well-respected American coach and former athlete, as saying, "I think Dubin has gone beyond justice in allowing this thing to go on. He's not getting the truth. He's getting a lot of garbage."

Pat Connolly was angry because I had testified that John Smith told me he had supplied Connolly with Dianabol. Connolly had coached Evelyn Ashford around the time of the 1984 Los Angeles Olympics.

I was emotionally exhausted by the inquiry. I knew by then that I would lose many of my longtime friends. The hostility from the Canadian West Indian community was frightening, not to mention the roasting I was taking from the likes of Pat Connolly. But I was convinced that truth-telling would win the day in the end. I did not know that I would be one of the few to take the oath to tell "the whole truth" to heart. I did not know that with every word I said, I drove another wooden spike into my future as a runner.

I let the lawyer representing the Sport Medicine Council of Canada have it. Of all people in the room that day, I wanted Thomas Barber to get a grip on the reality of drug use in international amateur competition. It's been my contention from the beginning that it was completely predictable that Ben, of all people, would be caught for steroids at Seoul. It was inevitable that if a Canadian athlete became number one in the world, the Canadian would be caught. It's because amateur athletes in Canada must figure out for themselves what drugs to use and how to use them undetected. In most other countries, certainly in Eastern-bloc countries, athletes are assisted by teams of qualified doctors, therapists, and officials. Drug use is not the guessing game it is in Canada.

Barber had been grilling me on drug dosages when I told him that the trouble with my use of performance-enhancing drugs was that it was trial and error. In other countries, there are federations and medical committees in league with the athletes, advising them on anabolic use. "They get their programs down pat," I said. "They know what to do. But in Canada, nobody is here to help."

Barber responded, "Well, here it's prohibited, of course."

"It's prohibited everywhere, they say," I answered.

Barber cleared his throat and shot Dubin a nervous glance before going on. He asked me next if I had read the Sports Medicine brochure regarding the use of steroids. I told him that I had not, in fact, gone over the brochure. Why would I? The council was squarely opposed to anabolic steroids and I was looking for advice on how to use them properly. The brochure was about as useful as watching the movie *Reefer Madness*, officialdom's view of the evils of marijuana.

I told Barber, "The way to stop athletes from taking steroids is not to send out brochures trying to frighten them about side effects, because they don't believe in side effects. They don't see athletes dropping dead from anabolic use. They don't believe it."

"The only way to stop athletes from using steroids," I continued, "is to implement random doping controls. At competitions, at training camps, at campuses — all over the world, in every country, and all at once."

"Thank you," Barber said. End of cross-examination.

I wondered if he had really heard what I said.

There were no doping controls that could not easily be circumvented in the dog days of August 1981. I had come away triumphant from the National Championships in Regina on August 1, with first place in both the 100- and 200-metres. On August 6, I went to Dr. Koch for another injection of 200 milligrams of Depo-Testosterone in preparation for the all-important World Cup trials in Cumana, Venezuela. To qualify for the Americas Team in the World Cup competition, scheduled for September in Rome, I had to win either the 100- or 200-metres race in Cumana.

Before we traveled to Venezuela, everyone had to get a yellow fever shot and take a series of antimalaria pills. I had an allergic reaction to the malaria pills, so I had to start taking an antibiotic. I was worried. The allergy was bothering my eyes and I got dizzy during workouts. We left on schedule, however, and on the first night, a few of us gathered in Mark McKoy's room. I went into the bathroom and noticed that Mark had already unpacked his shaving kit. There were everyday toiletries spread out on the counter: toothpaste, shaving cream, a razor — and a bottle of Propionate.

I was surprised to see it. Propionate is testosterone based in a much lighter oil than the Primobolan I'd had in Bratislava earlier. Rather than the slow, regenerative effect of Primobolan, Propionate moves quickly through the system. Mark was casual about my finding it and I suggested that he sell it to one of our throwers. Earlier in the afternoon, I had asked for an injection of testosterone and was told there wasn't enough to spare. I don't know if Mark did sell his supply, but I do know I managed to get an injection of 350 milligrams of Propionate later that evening.

Two days later, I noticed a marked increase in my aggressiveness. My nerves felt jangly. The next day, I won the 100-metres with 11.17, and the day after that, I won the 200-metres with 22.71. I made the World Cup for both races. Unfortunately, from a technical standpoint, I ran both races badly. I had a slow start in the 100-metres and had to strain to the finish. My hamstring began to twinge. In the 200-metres, I favored my leg on the curve and made up for it with an all-out effort on the straightaway. By Monday morning, when we were due to leave Venezuela, my hamstring was hurting badly and I was forced to apply some of the cleansing agent, DMSO.

All during the brutally long flight to Europe — eight hours to Lisbon, two and a half hours to Frankfurt, one hour to Berlin — I used the muscle stimulator on my hamstrings and quads. I passed on the meet in Zurich and managed to get a couple of workouts in before the meet in Cologne, where I came second to Evelyn Ashford's 11.02 with 11.17. I entered another meet in Koblenz, but it was too much for me. My whole body — hamstrings, quads, back, pelvic girdle — throbbed. The World Cup was coming up fast. I was getting desperate.

At the Athletes' Village in Rome, I asked the thrower for help, and he gave me another injection of Propionate. I also managed to get an injection of vitamin B complex with vitamins B-12, B-6, and B-1. None of it helped. My hamstring was not mending. The World Cup was three days away.

For the first time, I decided to try a technique called hot-shotting. To an extent, it was the same thing I had tried to achieve with the cocaine and the black beauties – the kick start just before a race. Cocaine and amphetamines were minor versions, however, of the true hot-shot, an injection of aqueous-testosterone. This is testosterone based in water, so the effect on your body is instant. I wanted to come out of the blocks like a missile with a rocket engine boost.

It turned out that Evelyn Ashford was the big winner at the World Cup. She won both the 100- and the 200-metres. I came fourth in both races, and my relay team came fourth in the women's four-by-100. As far as I was concerned, my experiment with hot-shotting had failed. Every time I tried it, I injured my hamstring.

I was sick to death of trying to sort out a program of drug use based on rumors from strangers and the availability of drugs from friends. I decided to take things into my own hands. The first step in my self-styled program was to clear out my system. I decided to take no drugs at all after the end of the 1981 outdoor season and no drugs in preparation for the indoor season to follow. I began to read everything I could get my hands on about steroids, stimulants, ointments, and treatments. I took books on anatomy out of the library. And I began to compile a list of experts. If the experts couldn't come to me, perhaps I could go to the experts.

That fall, the annual *Track & Field* magazine rankings put me at fifth in the world for 1981 in both the 100- and 200-metres.

In the fall of 1981, I enrolled at York for the second leg of my first-year courses. I began to entertain the dream of eventually teaching history. Nothing too ambitious, not a professor or anything. I realized that to be a professor I'd need a doctorate, and it would take me forever to get it if I continued with track. I thought it would be nice to teach high school history, and so I enrolled in British history and political science courses.

I really liked my history professor, a balding, square-built fellow by the name of Willard Piepenburg. He was tremendously energetic, and he'd leap around the classroom and bellow out the lessons in a way that took me back to the preachers at the Church of God. I still have all of my notes from Professor Piepenburg's class. He has since retired and become a professor emeritus with the history department. I loved his classes, and I never missed a single one until the day I quit in February of 1982.

I had been working out over the winter, harder than ever before, up to six hours a day, when I injured my left calf muscle. I couldn't walk, much less hike over the campus to classes at York. I can't blame it entirely on the injury; I just never went back to class. Even though any athlete in track and field will tell you that ten or twelve years is all you can expect from that career, for some reason it seems like forever when you are young and starting out. I chose athletics thinking I could always return to school and get my degree. Quitting university is a decision I regret to this day.

It was during the winter of 1982 that Tony and I began to sort out our unusual living arrangement. He enrolled in grade eleven at C.W. Jefferys Secondary School, and I bought him a car so he wouldn't have to take the bus all the time. It was a 1972 Mustang, a neat little buzz-bomb. I bought it from Mark McKoy for $1,200 and we fixed it up. It still is a legend among all the track team members who lived around Niska Drive — you could hear it a mile away when Tony started it up to go to school in the morning. It had a hole in the muffler that made it sound like the start of the Indy 500. Tony parked it close to Charlie's window, and every morning Charlie would holler, "Jesus Christ, can't you do something about that muffler?"

I had high hopes for Tony that year, with regard to his track career. There was a good possibility that he might make the junior national team. We often trained together at the track. Tony had turned seventeen the previous November — he still had plenty of play in him.

We used to have some raging fights. I threw him out on his ear at least once that winter. A little bird told me that some girl at his school had a crush on him, and I took it badly, but I recovered. I can laugh now. I had one good fight on the telephone with Tony's grandmother, whom I've come to know and love. I call her Babushka Helen. One afternoon she called me up and told me Tony was just a baby. She demanded to know how I expected to support him.

I told her, "Don't worry!"

"Good for you, I won't," she said, then she hung up. It was the only fight we've ever had.

Tony's mother, Nadia, arrived at York University one day and gave Tony a good smack over the situation, but we got past that, too. After a while, Tony and I were regular Sunday afternoon visitors at the house Babushka Helen shared with her husband, Misha.

By March of 1982, I had formulated a program of drug use for myself that I felt confident about. For lack of a better word, I called the program pyramiding. It involved increasing and decreasing dosages starting with five milligrams of Dianabol per day at the beginning, rising to twenty milligrams, then back down to five. At the inquiry, commission counsel Robert Armstrong asked me to explain it to Mr. Justice Dubin.

I told Dubin I had discovered that on straight dosages of anabolic steroids, there was a tail-off effect, or what I had referred to previously as crashing. This occurs when you stop taking the steroids. Your body has stopped producing naturally the hormones that the steroids provide, and it takes a while for the body to start producing again. The crash could be severe, with a terrible lack of energy and severe depression. The higher the dosage of steroids, the more severe the crash. I thought that if I went in a pyramid where I slowly went up and slowly came down and leveled off, I would not experience tailing off or crashing.

I also told Dubin that my research had revealed it was advisable either to increase the dosage or switch steroids every year because the body became used to the intake and the drugs became progressively less effective. I wanted to increase my dosage of Dianabol in 1982, but I didn't want to be on a six-week program that would lead to a bad crash.

The way it worked was on April 1, 1982 — April Fool's Day — I started taking five milligrams of Dianabol per day until April 8; then I increased the dosage to ten milligrams per day until April 22. Between April 23 and May 7, I took fifteen milligrams per day, then twenty milligrams a day until May 13. And here, my finely tuned plan fell apart. I had miscalculated, and I didn't have enough Dianabol to properly complete the second week of twenty milligrams per day. Charlie got me a substitute anabolic steroid from a different group known as stanozolol. The brand name was Winstrol.

At the peak of my pyramid, then, I took fifteen milligrams of Dianabol and two and a half milligrams of Winstrol. Then I continued down the other side of the pyramid with fifteen milligrams of Dianabol from May 21 to May 25 and further down with ten milligrams of Winstrol until June 2. For the last week, I took five milligrams of Winstrol per day until June 10. At the time, I thought Winstrol was a milder steroid than Dianabol, but I was wrong. Trial and error.

When we left for the first European tour of the 1982 outdoor season on June 30, I felt supremely confident. My workouts had gone well and my drug program appeared to be working. The one wrinkle was that the clearance time for oral anabolic steroids was understood to be twenty-eight days, and the first meet of the tour – a dual meet with Yugoslavia – was only twenty-four days away. You'll excuse my contempt for Canada's commitment to drug-free amateur athletics when I say, as I did at the Dubin Inquiry, that Charlie set my mind at ease by calling Don Fletcher, who was the director-general of the Canadian Track and Field Association. Fletcher told Charlie that there would be no doping controls at the meet with Yugoslavia.

Every detail of training, every meet we entered, every drug we took, in 1982, was aimed at the one important goal of winning at the Commonwealth Games scheduled for October in Brisbane. I did well on the first European tour and even better at a July meet in Colorado Springs, setting Canadian and Commonwealth records – 11.03 in the 100-metres and 22.25 in the 200-metres. My teammate Tony Sharpe did well for himself, too, by winning the men's 100- and 200-metres. His time of 10.19 in the 100-metres was just two one-hundredths of a second off the previous Canadian record, unbroken since 1960, set by Harry Jerome of Vancouver. Ben Johnson came third in the 100-metres, with a respectable 10.31.

It wouldn't be fair to take all the credit for the excellent times in Colorado. Colorado Springs is a lovely resort town in central Colorado near Pike's Peak, part of the Rocky Mountain range and about 14,000 feet above sea level. This makes Colorado Springs a sprinter's dream: a high-altitude town. Imagine trying to run under water, then breaking out into the atmosphere; that's what it feels like sprinting in thin air. It benefits only sprinters, however. Long-distance runners suffer from lack of oxygen by the end of 1,500- or 3,000-metre races. Like wind readings, it is another factor to consider when you aim at a world record.

In July, I won the Canadian championships in Ottawa with 11.07 in the 100-metres and 22.37 in the 200-metres. Shortly after, I went on another, abbreviated, pyramid cycle of Winstrol. Charlie and I had come to the conclusion that Winstrol presented fewer problems with water retention than Dianabol. We still believed it was a milder drug, meaning I could expect less stiffness and tightness in my muscles during training. I ignored the warning signals about Winstrol or, more likely, I misdiagnosed a growing soreness in my muscles. By August 9, I had to cancel a workout. I was too stiff. At the time, I figured it was because I had come straight from the championships into a heavy workout period in preparation for the second European tour of the summer.

It was about this time when the first reliable test for testosterone was introduced at meets. I had been reading about testosterone and had copied a few items about it in my diary. I noted that it was considered an "extremely dangerous" drug for women and that the side effects might be irreversible. These side effects might include facial hair, a deeper voice, clitoral enlargement, and cancer of the kidney, liver, or breast. Testosterone might also affect the absorption of calcium in the bones.

I had noticed no physical side effects other than a slightly hoarse voice for a couple of days after I began a cycle. I reasoned that I was a sensible user of anabolic steroids like testosterone. Outside of my limited experiments with hot-shotting, I did not rely on the drugs for competition. And, in comparison with what I had heard about European athletes, I used modest amounts. I did, however, begin to take megadoses of calcium, up to 3,000 milligrams at a time. And I stepped up my dosages of vitamins. As for cancer, well, so far so good. Cigarette smokers take bigger risks than I ever did.

I babied myself on the second European tour, dropping out of some meets and entering others more for special endurance workouts than anything else. Tensions in the Scarborough Optimist group were high; we were all on edge about the Commonwealth Games. One day, in Koblenz, a picturesque city at the junction of the Rhine and Moselle rivers, Ben came with Desai and me on a shopping excursion downtown. When we got back to our quarters, Charlie was livid. He didn't want us walking around like that, using our feet and legs to no good purpose. Some very bad words were exchanged that day, and in my diary I swore I wanted nothing more to do with Charlie.

This is one of the worst parts about being an athlete. I was constantly aware of "saving myself" for competition. In all the ten years that I kept diaries, I made a single reference to going out to dance one night. It makes for long, boring nights in strange hotel rooms. I could be in a place as exotic as Paris, and the world went on outside while I wrapped my legs in a massage ointment and plastic bags and propped myself up in front of the television set. Even when I had a day or two off at home, when I might get out to an art gallery or a movie, I tended to rest up or run long-overdue errands, like shopping for food. There didn't seem to be much point to sightseeing at home when I'd just returned from another month-long trip to Europe. The trouble was, I didn't get to see much in Europe, either. Time off became a problem for me. I had no hobbies. It has taken me a long time to adjust to a proper home life.

September was a grueling month. We returned from Europe only to fly out again on the fifteenth to the first-ever Harry Jerome meet in Vancouver, en route to a special Eight Nations meet in Japan. I have dismal memories of Vancouver; it rained from the moment we landed till the moment we left. Japan, however, was delightful. The team was invited to the Canadian ambassador's house, which was a fabulous place with a Japanese garden and goldfish ponds in a courtyard. Three days later, I came second in the 100-metres to Marlies Göhr and beat European gold medalist Barbara Wockol in the 200-metres.

My time in the 200-metres was not particularly fast at 22.73, but I did beat Wockol by about two metres. Gerard Mach was with us, and he told me later that he screamed so hard he lost his voice. Oddly, I felt a peculiar twinge in an area that I had never felt before. Just at the finish line of the 200-metres, I'd felt a jab where my hamstrings began, deep in the buttock, close to the groin. It was mysterious. I let it go.

We got to be known as Charlie's Angels at the Twelfth Commonwealth Games in Brisbane. Eight of the eleven-member Canadian sprint team were Scarborough Optimists. For the first time, some reporters began to take note of the fact that we were black and that most of us had been born in the Caribbean. Allen Abel wrote in *The Globe and Mail*, "A smart aleck might attribute the nation's sudden rise to sprinting prominence to a single factor – immigration." Mark McKoy won a gold medal in the men's 110-metre hurdles and Ben Johnson won a silver in the men's 100-metre sprint. He also took part in the men's four-by-100-metre relay team, with Tony Sharpe, Desai Williams, and Mark McKoy. The Canadian team came second at 39.30, for a silver medal, just fifteen one-hundredths behind Nigeria.

At a press conference, BJ said that a few years before, he had weighed ninety-three pounds and couldn't run twice around a track without expiring. He seemed a little cocky, I thought, referring to people like Hasely Crawford as has-beens. "Those guys, that's the past," Ben said. "I'm talking about now."

Someone asked him what he would have become if he had stayed in Jamaica.

"In Jamaica, I'd be a bum," said Ben.

Charlie, who was watching from the back of the room, just shrugged. Ben's growing confidence was contagious. I got a little cocky myself. I told Abel, "Next year I think I can beat everybody in the world. I *have* to. Canadian track and field people never really set the world on fire before. Now, people are seeing how good we are. They're seeing we're as good as the swimmers, as good as the skiers. This is a big meet for Canada. We did well in Tokyo in the eight-nation meet, but this is on television back home. Now I'll go home and people will say, 'Oh, that's Angella Taylor. She won the Commonwealth Games.' "

And I *did*. I won four medals in Australia, more than any other Canadian athlete at the Games. I ran my fastest time ever to win the gold medal in the 100-metres – 11 seconds flat. I won a silver in the four-by-100-metre relay, running with Angela Bailey, Marita Payne, and "little Molly Killingbeck" as the Australian press dubbed her. I came third in the 200-metres, with a time of 22.48, which meant the low point of the Games for me was a bronze medal. Merlene Ottey won the gold in that race.

The press called me "sprint empress Angie Taylor," mainly because of my performance in the four-by-400-metre relay. The newspapers were still writing about it when I returned to Australia five years later. It was a thrilling race, one of those memories you can relive for a lifetime. It was the final event of the meet. At the last minute, Charlie had substituted me for Marita Payne, and I was to run the last leg of the relay, taking the baton from Molly. It meant I would be running against Raelene Boyle, known as "Australia's golden girl." She was heavily favored to win. She had already won a gold medal in the 400-metres, a distance I had attempted only twice that year, and it would be the last race of Raelene Boyle's splendid career. The race was televised worldwide, which meant Tony and my friends back home would be watching. There were 62,000 spectators at Brisbane's Queen Elizabeth II Stadium, one of whom happened to be Queen Elizabeth II, regally ensconced in the royal box.

With me on the four-by-400-metre relay team were "little Molly," Jillian Richardson, and Charmaine Crooks. When Molly passed me the baton I had a few metres on Raelene Boyle, but she pressed me. I could *feel* her behind me, gaining. The crowd roared. At the finish line, I pushed through, and won by two one-hundredths – by a nipple. It was such an exciting finish that the Queen herself, I'm told, gasped.

Years later, I watched a television documentary made by Australian producer Jack Thompson, and he focused on my bronze medal race in Brisbane, the 200-metres. Thompson used this particular race to illustrate a point about how athletes don't always listen to their coaches. Obviously, he had heard the story about Charlie being angry at me for staying out late the night before the race, but that's not why I came third.

I had simply gone to a boxing match with a couple of boxer friends, John Calvin and Sean O'Sullivan. It was a match between a couple of African fighters, and John told me one of them had trouble making weight, so he'd been sitting in the sun all day trying to sweat a few pounds off. It was the first and last boxing match I will ever see. The violence appalled me, and it made me cringe when the boxers got tired and bloody and the crowd bellowed for more. They had to wheel the sunbather out of the ring at the end; he was a mess. When Charlie gave me his tongue-lashing the next morning, I reminded him I hadn't used my precious legs or feet at all – I'd just sat in a chair and watched two pathetic human beings bash each other in the face in the name of sport.

The reason I came third in the 200-metres is recorded in my diary: "Race was lost from the start. Wrong kind of nervousness, shouldn't have been nervous at all. But, one learns as one goes along and I will have to learn to bounce back after having done one terrific performance. Trouble."

The "terrific performance" meant the gold medal in the 100-metres earlier. "Trouble" referred to a disturbing recurrence of the stabbing pain I'd felt close to the groin in Japan. It seemed to come from somewhere deep inside.

No amount of pain could dull my happy outlook that golden autumn. I was on top of the world, Down Under. When the *Track & Field* magazine ratings came in, I was listed as fourth in the world in the 100-metres, behind Ashford, Göhr, and Wockol. A few months later, the Sports Federation of Canada named me the outstanding female amateur athlete of 1982. Steve Podborski, the skier from Don Mills, was named top male amateur athlete.

On December 6, 1982, I had started the third of my experiments with pyramiding drug use. Originally, I had thought that I wouldn't bother with steroids for the indoor season, but then Charlie changed the training program and I found the workouts harder than they had ever been. I was using heavier weights and running farther and killing myself with explosive work trying to perfect my starts. I got shin splints that wouldn't go away, my hamstring was hurting, and my ankles ached. I decided I needed the steroids to help me through. For seven and a half weeks, I started with five milligrams of Dianabol per day, all the way up to twenty milligrams and back down. I had pinpointed Winstrol as the cause of tight, stiff muscles in my previous pyramids, and I promised myself I would never take it again. It was too powerful.

By the middle of January 1983, my weight had shot up from a svelte 133 pounds in Brisbane to 140. The steroids were responsible, of course. Weight fluctuations were one of the things athletes watched for in each other. Stretch marks and a moon-face are good indications that an athlete is using steroids. (I have also heard the moon-face referred to as the Cushing's syndrome look, though Cushing's syndrome can be caused by either excessive long-term steroid use or an overactive adrenal gland.) In my case, the weight I gained during training put extra pressure on the muscles and ligaments in my lower back. It started to throb, so I went to a chiropractor for a satisfying spinal crack, or manipulation, before setting off for a meet in Sherbrooke, Quebec.

I won the 200-metres with an unimpressive 23.72, but the sluggish win was the least of my problems that month. Shortly after arriving home from Sherbrooke, I was at an all-comers meet at York when Angela Bailey came out with a stunning bit of thumb-sucking rubbish. I had just finished running the 60-metre dash and I came second to Molly Killingbeck. Bailey sidled up and informed me that, at twenty-four years of age, I was "washed up." She, being only twenty, was still on her way up. I was speechless. The only explanation I could imagine for her saying this was bitterness over all the attention I had been getting since Brisbane.

Bailey wasn't finished. Next she accused Molly Killingbeck of taking steroids. That's when I exploded. I actually tried to give her a good shove. The reporters loved it. We became known as the Battling Angel(l)as. What is amusing is that my diary for that afternoon, regarding my race performance, says, "no aggressiveness."

At the Toronto Star Maple Leaf Indoor Games two weeks later, Bailey pouted to the press, "I'd rather walk away than fight, but if I'm cornered, what can I do? I'm too short to fight." This prompted me to pull a mean, silly stunt. Soon after the games, I followed Bailey into a public washroom at York and stood there in front of the row of sinks for a very long time, waiting. There was absolute silence in the washroom. All I could see were Bailey's feet under the door of the cubicle. She must have been terrified, because all the time I was there, she never came out. I knew then that this feud had gone too far.

On the first day of February, I awoke with an annoying headache. I don't ordinarily suffer from headaches, and I recall thinking that it was an ominous sort of pain. By the end of the day, I was unable to complete my workout, despite taking Aspirins and 250 milligrams of Naprosyn, an anti-inflammatory. My left hamstring had begun to twinge, and I took the anti-inflammatory as a precaution. But the pain that stopped my training that day was a return of my old friend from Japan and Australia, that strange, enfeebling jab deep inside.

I wasn't listening to my body. I had lived through so much pain and injury; I thought, this, too, will pass. I was more committed than ever to my career as a runner. I could see a straight line of glory from my triumph in Brisbane to the 1984 Olympics in Los Angeles. Any businessperson would understand. I had a goal, an objective. I wanted to be the fastest woman in the world.

By February 26, we were back in Sherbrooke for the Canadian national indoor track championships, where I won the 200-metres handily, with 23.59. But I found the track difficult to run on for some reason, and I was beginning to come emotionally unraveled. I had decided that the mysterious pain must be a kind of nerve condition. Tony and I were having problems at home, with some serious screaming matches. I know the pain contributed to our problems. My diary entries for that time are bleak. I described my emotional situation as "a mess"; I described my spirit as "broken." Occasionally, I would rally and write, "Pain worse, but decided I would not let it conquer me."

On a cold, windy day in early March, when even the indoor track at York seemed frigid, I spent a couple of minutes talking to Molly and Mark McKoy before a workout. We were comparing muscle flexibility when I decided to do the splits. For no particular reason, I slid to the floor like a ballerina to show them how flexible *I* was. It was one of the biggest mistakes of my life. I heard a *pop* and a wicked pain raced from my groin down to the bottom of my left hamstring. Charlie ordered me off the track for a week.

I visited Dr. Koch, who referred me to a chiropractor in the Medical Arts Building. I got the impression, between the two of them, that they didn't really know what was wrong. There are always some "by guess and by golly" diagnoses, but this time I began to lose confidence in Dr. Koch. I decided on a second opinion and went to Dr. Charles Bull, an orthopedic surgeon and a sports medicine specialist with the Fitness Institute. Dr. Bull determined that the problem was a severe form of hamstring tendonitis. He prescribed rest whenever I felt pain and recommended that I see a Dr. David Wise for physiotherapy sessions on a super-stretching and stimulating machine. I increased my intake of anti-inflammatories.

When I did see Dr. Wise, he said that the "pop" I had heard when I did the splits might have been the breaking of scar tissue where I had damaged the top of my hamstrings. He did not consider it a major injury. I promised to see him again for regular visits when I returned from the winter training camp in Florida.

At the same time, Charlie scouted around and found a chiropractor at the Columbus Centre, a big, impressive complex in northwest Toronto built by the Italian community for the arts and fitness. The chiropractor's name was Dr. James Meschino, and he turned out to be an extraordinarily pleasant person. I made a mental note to see him, too, when I returned from Florida.

I didn't want to go to Florida. Tony and I had reached a crisis point in our relationship. I was in constant pain and my nerves were stretched past any appeals to reason. I went to an official banquet in Toronto and Tony was supposed to pick me up at the end of the evening. He never showed up, and I was infuriated by his explanation that he'd been at the library. I was finding the half-sister, half-wife role difficult. On the one hand, I resented carrying Tony financially; on the other, I honestly wanted him to do well and finish high school. I had a terrible feeling that the trip to Florida would push us over the edge and he'd be gone when I got back. It felt like we were ready to call it quits. Then Charlie called to say that the van would leave for Florida at four o'clock in the morning and we'd drive straight through.

When we arrived in Florida, it was cold and raining. My period had started and it was nasty, with cramps. My whole body ached, and I was miserable. We'd come a long way from the joyous trips south three years earlier. Now, the Scarborough Optimists were in the big time.

Again on April Fool's Day, 1983, I began a six-week drug pyramid. I was wary by now. My injuries were not healing, and they were beginning to affect my training. I started with five milligrams of Dianabol, rising to ten milligrams a day, then back down to five. My commitment was wavering, so I took less. But I was certain that my meteoric performance in 1982 was directly connected to rigorous training that I would not have been able to do without steroids. By April 11, I was home from Florida, crippled with pain.

From April through June of 1983, I went through a ceaseless round of physiotherapy with a faradic stimulator, ultrasound, and hydrocollator packs – fancy heat packs. I took huge doses of calcium and vitamins, rubbed DMSO on the sore spots, popped Naprosyn daily, and tried deep friction massage, which is painful in itself. At the Columbus Centre, Dr. Meschino started me on a machine called a Diapulse. It is supposed to deliver deep heat to sore spots, though I don't think it made any difference. I tried a laser treatment called neuroprobe system II, which is similar to acupuncture. I changed my running technique. I thought if I ran more on my toes, it wouldn't hurt as much.

In the middle of June, we were in Vancouver for the Harry Jerome meet. As usual, it was pouring rain and too cold for training, much less competition. I have always thought I am more sensitive than others to cold, and this was confirmed in Vancouver when a local doctor told me my body temperature was below normal. He suggested I might have something similar to Raynaud's disease, a circulatory disorder that results in a restricted flow of blood to the limbs. However, the blood flowed back into my limbs as soon as we arrived in sunny California, where the temperature was a respectable seventy-five degrees Fahrenheit.

We were in Los Angeles for a thirty-two nation meet organized by the Americans to test the 1984 Los Angeles Olympic Coliseum course. Personally, I found the track a little too soft underfoot, and I was surprised to feel a strong headwind coming around the corner of the 200-metres, though I managed to win with the unremarkable time of 23.03. I ran fourth in the 100-metres; I was afraid of pushing too hard into the pain. I made an appointment to see a visiting East German doctor in California, but he never showed up.

When I arrived home from Los Angeles, I could not work out at all because of the pain. Gerard Mach heard about my condition and called to suggest that maybe the deep massages I had been getting were doing more harm than good. I got out of bed one day and tried to do my usual morning stretches, but my hamstrings were so tight I couldn't touch my forehead to my knees. Crying time, again.

We left on July 3 for Universiade '83, the World University Games in Edmonton. Ben and I had pulled a fast one in order to qualify for competition. We both enrolled in university, with no particular intention of going, in order to be classed as students. I imagine a few others did the same thing.

Our relay team in the four-by-100 metres did well with 43.21 and a silver medal. The four of us — me, Tanya Brothers, Molly Killingbeck, and Marita Payne — had some exceptionally good passes. Molly and I had worked out a new word for passing the baton. Runners on most other relay teams shout "Hye!" as they pass the baton, like a football quarterback calling for the snap. We shouted "Stick!" In the excitement and roar of the crowd, it individualized our team. It worked.

The relay was the high point of the games for me. I came third in the 100-metres with 11.17. I just was not reacting to the starting gun. The prospect of pain made my body instinctively pull back. In the 200-metres race, I couldn't force myself to run the corners properly. My body was rebelling. At the end of the race, I broke down and wept, again.

By July 19, we were in Colorado for another meet, and the best I can say is that I came fourth in the 200-metres. My performances in the 100-metres and the four-by-100 relay are not worth mentioning. I was hurting so badly that I began to consider getting a bone scan. Worried that my hormones might be out of whack, I also thought I should see an endocrinologist. In a desperate moment, I even mapped out a strategy for pumping myself full of Propionate. In my diary, I mentioned, "one-half a cc every two days. . ." When it came up at the Dubin Inquiry, I had a hard time convincing them that I never did follow through. Instead, I switched to another anti-inflammatory: Feldene.

Charlie began to consider not registering me for the World Championships in Helsinki, to start August 7. It was a devastating blow. The World Championships were an inaugural event, hosted by the International Amateur Athletic Federation, and to miss the first such competition was unthinkable, especially after my performance in Brisbane. They would not be held again until 1987, in Rome. The World Championships were the single most important event in track and field for 1983. Performances in Helsinki would determine which athletes were selected for the 1984 Olympics in Los Angeles.

We got home and, perfunctorily, I began to prepare for the tour of Europe, which would lead to Helsinki. Charlie advised me not to run for six weeks, to go on a program of calisthenics only, but Gerard Mach suggested that I accompany the team and consult some European sports medicine doctors. At least I'd get to watch the meets in Finland. I changed my mind about going several times, more for the sake of my relationship with Tony than anything. Just before we left, I wrote in my diary: "There is no way anything will come from this relationship. This is the best time to gradually break it, because when I get back from Europe and get over hurting from track, I will also be over him. Boy, when it rains, it pours."

On July 22, we arrived in Europe, and I immediately regretted my decision to go. Stubbornly, I stopped taking anti-inflammatories and immediately went into even deeper pain. I wondered what the hell I was doing over there anyway. Considering I was going to have to forgo any break at the end of the season and work right through the year to try to save 1984, I might just as well have stayed home for the six weeks and wallpapered the apartment. On July 25, Gerard scheduled an appointment for me with a doctor in Munich. He didn't show up. I began to take a dim view of the legendary German efficiency.

On July 26, I went back to try to see the doctor again. His name was Professor Manfred Klimper. According to Gerard, he was reputed to be the best sports medicine doctor in the whole of Europe. His office was sparsely furnished with wood-paneled walls the color of buckwheat honey. It was cool and quiet and peaceful compared with the hubbub on the blistering sidewalks outside. Klimper welcomed me into his examining room with a slight sweep of his hand. He nodded, but didn't say much, and began to probe my legs and my back with surprisingly strong, blunt fingers. Finally, he spoke.

"Go and perform a full workout, a hard workout. Give it 100 per cent of your effort. Come back to me after."

I couldn't believe my ears. A hard workout? I wasn't even supposed to do a light jog for six weeks. I nodded, my mind reeling with doubt. Before I left, Klimper gave me a nerve injection of a narcotic analgesic.

The next morning, I got up at six-thirty to get in a full workout before I arrived at his office. He shrugged when I told him about the pain and set his fingers to work again. Then, he gave me a shot of Delphimix.

"Go and run a race," he said.

"But what about my hamstrings? My tendons?"

"There is nothing wrong with your muscles or your tendons. Do as I say."

I went back to Charlie and presented myself for a 100-metre race scheduled for that afternoon. "Doctor's orders," I told him. Then I ran the 100-metres heat and came second with 11.33. The message kept shooting to my brain: *Nothing wrong with your muscles, nothing wrong with your tendons.* I ran the final and won, with 11.22. The pain was gone.

Professor Klimper diagnosed my problem as a damaged sciatic nerve. The sciatic nerve is the biggest nerve in the body. It begins from branches of the spinal cord located in the low back to form a nerve the circumference of your thumb that runs through a bony notch in the pelvis to continue down the leg. The bony notch is close to the ischial tuberosity. The ischium is a bone at the bottom of the pelvis; tuberosity refers to the protuberance of the nerve from the ischium. The nerve can be compressed in this area by the lower back and hip muscles, which is what Dr. Klimper thought had happened. From what I have read since, it is possible that it was damaged by the pounding of the weighted vest or overwork. This is why I had felt the pain in my groin.

Klimper also said I needed minerals, enzymes, and more sleep. The list of elements I scribbled in my diary included pancreatin, papain, bromelain, dipeptidase, amylase, trypsin, chymotrypsin and rutin, all in small amounts from one to one hundred milligrams. He gave me a pill called Spandylonal to take three times a day and some injectable vitamin B-12. He also gave me enough Delphimix to inject myself once a week and a different anti-inflammatory made from human rather than synthetic sources. I was to take a pain killer called Osmogit only if I actually felt the pain.

Finally, Klimper told me that I had developed the muscles in my legs, back, and buttocks to such an extent that they were overpowering my stomach muscles. As a result, I was literally pulling back on my body all the time and it would be especially noticeable when I ran. It was true. Charlie and I had been discussing my technique only a few weeks before when he noticed that I seemed to be leaning backward at the finish line. It had cost me a race when the winner simply lurched forward to break the tape. My odd posture also contributed to the pressure on the sciatic nerve. Professor Klimper gave me a series of sit-up exercises that would strengthen my stomach muscles.

On the bright, clear Saturday morning of July 30, we left for Helsinki. I felt alive again, though I knew I might not set the world on fire after such a disastrous training season. I was free of pain, and the first-ever International Amateur Athletic Federation World Championship Meet was nine days away.

A lot can happen in nine days.

10

The Steroid Guru

On August 5, 1983, three days before the 100-metre final at the World Championships in Helsinki, Finland, I caught my finger in a door. The nail snapped at the base, and I would definitely lose it.

I had the finger X-rayed and it wasn't broken, but it hurt something fierce. It was an unfortunate bit of bad luck. You might not think a single finger is important to a sprinter, but you need all of them, and your thumbs, to position yourself at the starting blocks. If you can't lean your weight into your fingers, you'll wreck the start. And you know the trouble I had with starts.

I hurt my finger during a short sightseeing trip. Finland had seemed extraordinarily attractive to me from the airplane window; the south part of the country looks like clusters of jewel-green islands rather than mainland because there are so many lakes and rivers flowing into the Gulf of Finland and the Baltic Sea. Finland gained recognition from the Soviet Union as an independent republic in 1920, and it held on to its identity through the Second World War. The history of this feisty little country intrigued me. A few of us visited the local Evangelical Lutheran church. Charlie was disgusted, of course; we should have been resting.

Later that same day, we got some interesting news: a couple of top athletes from the United States would not be running the 200-metres at Helsinki, despite good performances at the American national championships. Then we heard that Diane Williams, a hurdler with the American team, wasn't going to run the 100-metres. I wrote "strange bunch" in my diary, though their actions were anything but strange. Rumor had it that they had used steroids to compete at the nationals and that they had crashed.

Ultimately, Diane Williams did decide to run in Helsinki, and she managed to win a bronze medal. Years later, she revealed publicly to a U.S. Congressional Committee that she had used steroids before the meet.

At last, the first day of heats for the 100-metres arrived, and, bandaged finger and all, I did well enough to advance to the semifinal on Monday, August 8. I came third with 11.22. I felt no pain at the ischial tuberosity, the hamstrings were holding up, all was going well, until I heard the starting pistol for the final. The way to describe my start might be, kindly, "delayed reaction." I had a terrible start, and then Evelyn Ashford's hamstring popped and she fell to the track in the lane beside me.

In the glossy official handbook for the Helsinki meet, one of the most popular photographs shows medics applying ice to a nearly comatose Ashford lying next to a stretcher. The adjacent photograph shows Ashford grabbing at her leg as she crumples to the track. I am in the picture, running in front of Ashford and only inches behind Marlies Göhr. We are both suspended in midair, knees up, showing good form. Only if you look closely can you see that Göhr's eyes are closed as she strains ahead. Mine are momentarily diverted by the camera, my face slightly turned. Göhr won the race, in 10.97 seconds. I came seventh, with 11.30. Even Bailey beat me that day, with 11.20.

I had pushed too hard too soon after my miraculous recovery at the hands of Professor Klimper. I was never really in the race; I had no accelerating power at all. I had a flash of pain at the top of my hamstrings, and by the next day I couldn't sit down. I went to see a Polish doctor traveling with his team, and he confirmed Klimper's diagnosis. It was the sciatic nerve. He could tell from my posture that it was under a lot of pressure. The solution was simple: strengthen the stomach muscles with sit-ups.

We left Helsinki on August 11. Charlie said he didn't want to see me at the track for two weeks. I returned home for the showdown with Tony only to find out he'd gone to stay with a friend. One evening at sunset, when the shadows were long, he came for coffee to talk things over, but we didn't get much talking done. The next morning, I tackled the laundry while Tony did the shopping. There were times when I thought I couldn't live with Tony, but other, piercing moments when I knew I couldn't live without him. Besides, he was eighteen years old now, and he was almost through high school. Things could only get better.

Near the end of summer, there was disturbing news that many athletes had tested positive for drugs at the Pam-American Games in Caracas, Venezuela. The rumor was that a new steroid detector had been invented that could find anabolic traces in an athlete's system up to a year after discontinuing use. We were skeptical, but if the reports were accurate, I saw the situation as favorable. I had been using steroids for two years. This meant that I had an excellent base of strength. If I never took another steroid in my life, it would be impossible to lose the advantage of muscle tone I had gained through steroid-assisted workouts. Still, there was an alternative.

I had heard about an aid to training called human growth hormone, extracted from the pituitary gland of cadavers. It is sometimes called GH or STH, for somatotrophic hormone. A magazine article described how scientists had recently achieved a breakthrough by manufacturing synthetic GH in a laboratory. Human growth hormone was developed for children born with a growth deficiency, like my great-aunt Enid. Athletes, especially weightlifters, had started to use it in place of steroids to build muscle because it has a very short half-life. This means that it passes through the system quickly. Human growth hormone is not detectable.

By the beginning of September, we found out that the athletes at Caracas had been caught for using injectable steroids. As I've mentioned, steroids like Deca-Durabolin are based in heavy oil that takes a long time to move through the system. Apparently, orals – steroids in pill form – could still be relied on to clear the system before testing. There was no new magic steroid detector after all. I made a note to carry on with my usual program of Dianabol the following spring.

The news that Dianabol was safe was good, but the article describing human growth hormone had piqued my curiosity. In the margin of my diary I scribbled the name of one of the doctors the writer mentioned: Robert Kerr. He had written a book called *The Practical Use of Anabolic Steroids with Athletes*. Dr. Kerr's philosophy was that athletes were going to take steroids anyway, so he might as well prescribe them and give the athletes proper counseling on their use. At last, a practical approach! Dr. Kerr said that in sixteen years of administering steroids to athletes, he had not seen any side effects.

Somehow, I got Dr. Kerr's address — he was in a suburb of Los Angeles — and wrote to him. He replied promptly, and by the third week of September I had an autographed copy of his book, a letter, and an appointment to see him on October 11.

In the meantime, I started my fall training schedule. The sit-ups that Dr. Klimper had recommended were to be done in three positions: at a thirty-degree angle, a forty-five degree angle, and straight up. I took to the job with my usual dedication, starting with two sets of ninety-one sit-ups. It's always been this way with me; I don't do things halfway. If you tell an athlete to take one pill, he'll decide two must be better; if you suggest a three-hour workout, the athlete will double it to six hours. It is obsessive behavior, but obsessiveness wins medals. Later in the season, I was doing up to seven hundred sit-ups a day. Naturally, I strained my quads.

Two weeks before my twenty-fifth birthday, in September 1983, I was at York during a workout when I fell to the track running a 300-metre drill. My legs were awkwardly splayed, and I could feel a pull in the area of the ischial tuberosity. Within days, I could barely warm up, much less do a workout. It was an infuriating setback, and I seemed to be suffering more pain in my pelvic area than before. I began to wonder again if my hormones were out of balance, which would mean an appointment with an endocrinologist. I decided to visit my old friend Dr. Koch.

Dr. Koch put me through a few tests for reflex and strength. I told him about Professor Klimper's diagnosis of sciatica and how the Polish doctor had backed him up. Dr. Koch was unconvinced. He agreed that the problem was in the area of the ischium, but he diagnosed it as chronic "ischial insert tendonitis." He suggested that I go back on anti-inflammatories. This time, I disagreed with Dr. Koch. I had suffered for nearly a year with a disorder that Canadian doctors told me was tendonitis. It took a European doctor five minutes to decide that it was not tendonitis and a single day to identify it as sciatica. I did not see Dr. Koch again until he entered the room at the Dubin Inquiry five and a half years later.

It became important at the inquiry to explain why I had turned away from Dr. Koch. I was still seeing other specialists, trying to find someone I could trust with my problems. I could hardly expect the average general practitioner to understand my commitment to a training program that I knew would hurt me and to drugs I refused to give up. I tried an acupuncturist. I went to an endocrinologist, and the tests showed there was nothing wrong with my hormones. I went back to Dr. Meschino, the chiropractor at the Columbus Centre. One day, he led me down the hall to a cubbyhole of an office to introduce me to a new doctor who had worked with athletes in the islands. He knew a lot about sports injuries and had some new techniques with the Diapulse machine I had been using.

"Maybe he can help you," said Dr. Meschino. The new doctor's name was Mario G. Astaphan. We learned to call him Jamie.

To focus Dubin's attention at the inquiry, Robert Armstrong, the commission counsel, dangled his glasses from the ends of his fingers and paused before speaking. It was his way of signaling that we were entering deep waters.

"When you went to see Dr. Astaphan first, in early October, it was in connection with this injury to your leg?" Armstrong asked.

"Yes, it was." (It was probably easier for him to say "leg" than "ischial tuberosity.")

"And at that time, Dr. Astaphan concluded that it was a sciatic nerve problem?"

"It was indeed a sciatic nerve problem."

"So, I take it from what you've said that by virtue of the fact that you were not prepared to accept what the other doctor had said about the diagnosis in relation to your leg, you were prepared to accept what Dr. Astaphan had to say, and that would have been an additional reason for your being attracted to Dr. Astaphan?"

"Yes, it was."

"All right. And Dr — " Armstrong shook his head and smiled at his mistake. "Freudian slip. *Mr.* Francis has said that you and other athletes had a great deal of confidence in Dr. Astaphan as a sports medicine physician knowledgable in treating injuries suffered typically by track and field athletes?"

"That's true."

"And you held that view as well?"

"Yes, I did."

I did, yes. Let me tell you why we had confidence in Jamie. He was from St. Kitts, one of the Leeward Islands in the Eastern West Indies. St. Kitts is only about one hundred square miles. It is a twin-island state with neighboring Nevis, which is tiny, only sixty-eight square miles. Together with a few even tinier dots of land sprinkled between the Atlantic Ocean and the Caribbean Sea, St. Kitts–Nevis was formerly a British colony. It gained independence in 1983, twenty-one years after Jamaica became independent. Jamie was one of us. It was a pleasant shock to hear his accent when Dr. Meschino introduced us. We laughed at the same things.

If there is one thing a champion athlete has to learn to live with, it is: train all you want, watch what you eat, take your medicine, take your vitamins, take your drugs, get the right amount of sleep, avoid sightseeing when traveling — do all this and more and *maybe* you'll win your race. Jamie exuded an air of certainty, of being in control of the uncontrollable. If the old saying is true that salespeople are the worst suckers for a sales pitch, then surely athletes must be the worst suckers for someone who appears to be in command. The first thing Jamie told me to do was stop taking the birth control pill.

"It has a catabolic effect," he said. "Directly opposite to the anabolic effect."

To this day, I have no idea whether this was good advice or whether his pronouncement had any real meaning. The dictionary does say that anabolism is constructive metabolism, that it is the synthesis in living organisms of more complex substances from simpler ones. And that catabolism is destructive metabolism, the breaking down of more complex substances into simpler ones. Whether this has anything to do with me and the birth control pill is a question that burns in my mind. On that day, however, it sounded like the most obvious thing in the world. Good Lord 'n' butter, who would have guessed that the birth control pill was catabolic? I stopped taking it immediately.

Jamie said a lot of things that day, mostly to do with the plans he had for re-structuring my diet. "The diet is key," he said.

I was extremely pleased with myself. At last, I had found a doctor who understood my special situation. Years later, it occurred to me that I had told him all the details about my sciatic nerve condition and that his agreement with the diagnosis was mimicry more than anything.

"I have a sciatic nerve problem," I told him.

"Indeed. A sciatic nerve problem," he said, nodding.

We hear what we want to hear, sometimes. To give credit where it is due, I should add that Tony Sharpe did not trust Jamie from the beginning for the precise reason the rest of us did: Tony didn't trust him *because* he was from the West Indies. As for Charlie, I believe that he, too, was charmed by Jamie Astaphan, at least at the start. Charlie's primary concern was training, and he could be noncommittal about details like doctors. Jamie said he would lend Charlie a Diapulse machine to keep in his apartment so we wouldn't have to worry about getting treatment at odd hours when the Columbus Centre was closed. Charlie saw this as a generous move, a cooperative thing to do. He began to take more of the Scarborough Optimist athletes to Jamie's little office.

The generous impulse flowed both ways. Before I left for my appointment with Dr. Robert Kerr in California, I dropped off my copy of his book for Jamie to read.

I flew into Los Angeles and when the secretary greeted me in Dr. Kerr's waiting room, she asked me if I was the 800-metre runner from Canada. No, I told her, I'm the sprinter. I wondered if her slip of the tongue meant I had a friend I didn't know about. My eyes were attracted to the dozens of photographs on the walls, framed pictures of Dr. Kerr posing with celebrities and successful people thankful for his assistance. Then the secretary led me into his office, and Dr. Kerr pushed a printed form across the desk for me to sign. The form became Exhibit Number 122 at the Dubin Inquiry. On a cold day in March 1989, in Toronto, Robert Armstrong read it into the record:

> The use of anabolic steroids or anabolic drugs is an endeavour not to be taken too lightly. With the use of these drugs, as with all medicines, side effects can and do occur. Before taking these drugs, you will want to carefully weigh the facts, and if you are aware of the possible side effects and choose to continue with the use of these medicines, then it is hoped that you will find it a successful endeavour.
>
> Side effects from the use of anabolic drugs could include such items as baldness, sterility, increased bone size and weight increase, liver toxicity and pathology as well as kidney pathology. A shrinking of the testes, acne, hypertension (high blood pressure), and gynacomastia [sic] (painful male nipple or nipples). Rashes could occur, and a personality change is always possible. The possibility of a decreased body immunity must be considered where an

increase in the incidence of colds and infections might occur.

Science has not yet established the long-term safety of these drugs. Though the anabolic drugs have been used for many years, the possibility of long-term ill effects must always be considered, as with any medicine. In regard to this, it must be asked, could the ill effects from these drugs affect you in the years to come? There is now no established record that would guarantee that the effect of these drugs will not affect your offspring. So this must also be considered by anyone considering the use of anabolic agents.

If you have pondered the above warnings and still feel that, dangerous side effects aside, the use of these medicines will enhance your needs, then sign and have witnessed this statement. If unsure, then don't take any medicine of which you are unsure!

Obviously, if you do decide to take the anabolic drugs and if signs and symptoms of any of the above or any other side effects or ill effects occur, please with haste contact Dr. Robert Kerr or his representative. Most side effects are curable when medication and therapy is instituted quickly. Some of the ill effects that I have mentioned above, I have personally seen as side effects in patients taking anabolic drugs. Most of the other incidences mentioned above have not been seen by me but have been reported in the gym gossip that we all hear from various training centres. And though personally unwitnessed, these dangers must be considered.

Again, before you sign, weigh all the known facts. Will these drugs give you your desired benefits, and, if so, is the risk of side effect worth the possible gains?

Obviously, the longer a drug is used, the greater the possibilities for many of the side effects occurring. So report any abnormal effect or symptom immediately.

At the bottom it was signed, "My best wishes for success, Robert Kerr, M.D."

Reading this letter now, I can see that Dr. Kerr had drafted a not-so-subtle bit of ass-covering that still managed to convey his belief that steroids, properly prescribed, are not harmful. How else to interpret the remark that most side effects are curable? Or that most side effects were really only "gym gossip"? I didn't have any such opinion on the letter when I signed it, however, because I hadn't bothered to read it. I already knew the possible side effects of anabolic steroids.

In Bob Goldman's book *Death in the Locker Room*, he makes mention of a now-famous survey taken by Dr. Gabe Mirkin, a runner himself. Mirkin polled more than a hundred top runners and asked the question, "If I could give you a pill that would make you an Olympic champion — and also kill you in a year — would you take it?" More than half responded that they would take the pill. Goldman writes that he was stunned by what he calls "this willingness to die" among athletes. He repeated the poll himself, asking 198 world-class athletes a similar question: "If I had a magic drug that was so fantastic that if you took it once you would win every competition you would enter for the next five years, but it had one minor drawback — it would kill you five years after you took it — would you still take the drug?" Again, over half, 103 athletes, said they would.

Part of Goldman's theory is that athletes become addicted to steroids, though they are considered a nonaddictive drug. Steroid-dependent would be a more accurate description of my state of mind by the time I met Dr. Kerr. Although I had endured rigorous training and learned to polish my running technique over the past three years, there never was a time when I did it entirely without steroids. It's not as though I had turned to steroids after finding I couldn't improve. I simply began steroids and began serious training at the same time. The truth is, I no longer knew if I could run without steroids, and if I was addicted to anything, I was addicted to winning.

I've thought about how I would respond to the survey about a magic drug that would guarantee winning but kill me later. Then, my answer would have been yes. Perhaps that is obvious, considering the way I pursued steroids as an aid to training. But I sincerely believed then, and I still believe, that taken in properly prescribed dosages, anabolic steroids are not harmful. As for the drug that would kill me — today, my answer would be no. I am a mother.

On that day in his office, Dr. Kerr and I discussed the drugs I had been using. I discovered, to my surprise, that he disliked Dianabol, especially for women athletes. In his book, he had described it as a drug for speed and power, which were precisely the properties I needed as a sprinter. He said he thought Dianabol was too androgenic, meaning it promoted male characteristics. Instead, he recommended Anavar, the same steroid I had tried once before in 1981. Dianabol is from the methandienone group of anabolic steroids; Anavar is from the oxandrolone group.

Dr. Kerr said the athletes he treated in the United States used Anavar or human growth hormone in combination with levodopa, often referred to as L-Dopa. L-Dopa is a drug used for the treatment of Parkinson's disease or for people who are unable to naturally produce dopamine, which helps to regulate movement and emotion. According to Dr. Kerr, the L-Dopa increased what he called the uptake of human growth hormone — that is, it helped the body absorb and make use of the GH. I liked the idea of Anavar. Dr. Kerr had said in his book that it was a "cutting up" drug, meaning it would make me leaner. I had been bothered by water retention with Dianabol.

Essentially, Dr. Kerr was recommending a different approach, called stacking, to taking performance enhancing drugs. I had tried hot-shotting without success and pyramiding with limited success. Perhaps stacking would release the genie from the bottle. Dr. Kerr took my blood pressure and then wrote out a prescription with specific instructions for taking Anavar, L-Dopa, and a human growth hormone from Sweden called Crescormon. I went next door to the pharmacy and had the prescription filled — Crescormon cost $90 U.S. per bottle — before catching a flight back to Toronto that afternoon. In total, I paid Dr. Kerr just over $1,000 U.S. in a combination of cash and traveler's cheques for the medication. He told me there was no fee for his consultation; his policy was to treat Olympic athletes for free.

A week later, I went to a scheduled appointment with Jamie to discuss the details of nutrition and diet that he recommended. I told him about my visit to Dr. Kerr and he listened closely. It was obvious that he'd read Dr. Kerr's book. Jamie said he disagreed with Dr. Kerr on the subject of Anavar. Anavar was too hard on the liver, he said. He preferred Winstrol, which I had experimented with during the summer of 1982. I told him I had sworn I would never take Winstrol again. As far as I was concerned, Winstrol was too powerful a drug, and it had caused me serious problems with stiffness in the muscles.

Jamie nodded. He said he'd be happy to monitor my drug program, including blood testing. He told me there was no need to spend $800 on return flights to California just to get a prescription from Dr. Kerr. Jamie could get whatever I wanted.

We had quite a time at the Dubin Inquiry, sorting out the drugs and their various names. At times, it seemed to me that Dubin's glasses came close to fogging over. Once, Robert Armstrong tried to clarify the references to human growth hormone.

"Now, you will be happy to know that I'm not going to ask you to read all of this, nor am I going to read it myself. I simply note that in brackets – opposite Crescormon – is the name somatropin, and indeed we're going to see other entries in your diary that refer to somatropin, and I take it that when that word or short form of it appears, you're referring to – "

I put him out of his convoluted misery and said, "Human growth hormone."

"Human growth hormone as original Crescormon?" Amstrong asked.

"Crescormon, yes."

"Okay," said Armstrong.

Dubin's eyes narrowed before he spoke. "This is the original? This is not synthetic at this stage?"

"This is the one from humans, yes."

"Yes," said Dubin.

Armstrong sensed, or thought he sensed, some lingering confusion on Dubin's part and referred to the brochure describing Crescormon that he had promised not to read.

"Indeed, sir, you will see, if you want to pause for a moment, the makeup of it. You'll see in the very – on the first page, on the third column over from the left, 'Crescormon is prepared only from human pituitary glands,' which indicates that this is a natural growth hormone."

Dubin looked grumpy. "I see it," he said.

"Oh, sorry." Armstrong fell silent.

Dubin tried again. "This is in a – does it come in a vial?"

"Yes," I said. "It did."

Armstrong brightened and said maybe I could help them a little further. "I hope I'm not wrong here, but I think you told me that it came in a little white powder with some distilled water?"

"To mix it with, yes," I said.

Armstrong must have felt he was close to a breakthrough. "All right. And so, it's obviously an injectable?"

I told him it was, yes.

"All right. Now, on the fourteenth of November [1983], presumably *somebody* would have had to mix up the powder and the distilled water and give you an injection of it?"

I told Armstrong I always mixed it myself.

He looked crestfallen for a moment, then the idea light bulb glowed over his head. "Who gave you the injection?"

"My husband did," I said, then added, "Or – I wasn't married yet."

The spectators got a laugh out of this, which confused Dubin. What could be funny about mixing an injectable?

"I didn't hear it?" he said sharply.

Mr. Armstrong waxed genial, laughing with the crowd. "It's all right," he said, waving his hand.

Dubin became fierce as an owl. "Well, let me in on it."

I stopped laughing myself and tried to explain. "It's the fall of 1983 –"

"Fall of 1983," said Armstong. "It was her good friend at the time, later to become her husband, is what she said."

"All right," said Dubin.

There was not a peep from the spectators. We continued our sober journey through the daily dosages and complicated formulas of my fall program of drugs.

I tried to put the disastrous season of 1983 behind me. I told myself that I had expected too much, that I had mistakenly assumed my progress would continue as it had during the first two years. I reviewed my diaries, searching out the secret in training that had produced my victories in 1982. Obviously, the misdiagnosis of tendonitis was a major setback, and I realized that my experiments with pyramiding had not helped. But I had done my homework, lined up new doctors and new drugs. This year would be different; I would show the world that I belonged at the top when I competed in the 1984 Olympics in Los Angeles.

In November, I started a two-month cycle of drugs in preparation for the indoor season. Every morning, I took one tablet of L-Dopa and two tablets of Anavar. I repeated the dosage in the afternoon. I stopped taking the Anavar after one month, as instructed. At noon every day, Tosha injected me with one cc of Crescormon. The only time I varied Dr. Kerr's strict formula was when I went to a winter training camp in Guadeloupe and the airline lost my baggage for two days. The L-Dopa and the Anavar tablets were in my suitcase. However, I still had the human growth hormone. It had to be refrigerated, so I had bought a Thermos in Toronto and packed ice around the vials.

I had taken a room at a school of athletics in Guadeloupe known as CREPS, which is a French acronym. The accommodation is like a dormitory with a cafeteria. It was a good thing I'd brought the Thermos because there were no refrigerators in the rooms. Tony wasn't in training at the time, so he planned to join me a week later for a holiday. In the meantime, Tony Sharpe did the injections. They are impossible to do yourself. You would have to twist around and try to get the needle properly angled into the top of your buttock.

By the first week in December, I weighed 143 pounds. I was hungry all the time. And I was weary. Some of this was because my Tony was with me. When he is on holiday, Tony's a night owl. I found it hard to resist midnight walks under the tossing palms and ragged clouds of the beach in Guadeloupe. But I began to realize that I got especially tired after each injection of Crescormon, and that the spot where Tony injected me became sore. It felt like my muscles were becoming dense. It took twice as long to warm them up before a workout.

By the time we returned home to Toronto in January, I was dopey and tired enough that I was sluggish pushing off from the starting blocks at York. I was so slow around the track that Charlie checked the timer to make sure it was working. This was bothersome, but it didn't much worry me. As I wrote in capital letters in my diary, the important thing was, "MY LEG DIDN'T HURT." When I finally reported to Jamie at the end of the month, I learned that I was suffering from too little glucose in my blood: hypoglycemia.

Hypoglycemia wasn't included in Dr. Kerr's list of side effects, but I suspected it was caused by the Crescormon. Dwarfs who get human growth hormone sometimes develop diabetes, and sometimes hypoglycemia. As far as Jamie was concerned, I wasn't getting enough protein. He told me to eat more red meat, then he gave me an injection of two cc of inosine, an anti-inflammatory he preferred over all the others. I couldn't find it in the *Compendium of Pharmaceuticals and Specialties* that Dr. Koch had given me. Every time I went to his office, Jamie gave me a routine injection of inosine, then we went to work on my hamstring and calves with the Diapulse.

Privately, I worried. I'd shown a tendency toward anemia at the beginning of my career, when I first visited Dr. Koch, and now this, another blood problem. I called Dr. Kerr, my steroid guru in California, and told him what had happened. I also told him that regardless of the hypoglycemia, I intended to carry out my program and go on another cycle in the spring for the outdoor season leading to the Olympics. He told me that if I was determined to use human growth hormone, I should use it only under a physician's care and only for a short period of time. When I passed Dr. Kerr's advice on to Jamie, he nodded and said he'd look after me. Meanwhile, he would go ahead and make arrangements to get another batch of human growth hormone.

I had an unremarkable indoor season in February 1984. I came second in the 50-yard dash at the Toronto Star Maple Leaf Indoor Games and hurt myself on the temporary running surface. The boards at Maple Leaf Gardens had too much play in them for the kind of muscle power I now applied during a race. My hamstrings went into spasm. Jamie thought I might also have a touch of flu and recommended that I take a combination of niacin, folic acid, and molasses. By the end of the season, at the Indoor Nationals, I managed to rally for a decent 6.18 in the 50-metres. Angela Bailey beat me, with 6.16.

I had made up my mind to return to Guadeloupe for an extended ten-week training session in the spring. I had always had trouble with the cold, wet springs of Toronto. Back then the York field house closed from May 1 to October 15 every year; they said it was warm enough to train outside. But there were times when it even snowed it was so cold and it prevented me from doing serious outdoor workouts. Besides, Sport Canada had set up a fund through the Canadian Track and Field Association, and athletes could draw expenses for special preparation for the Olympics. Tony Sharpe, Ben Johnson, and I prepared training charts and sent them in as evidence of special preparation, and before we knew it, we had the money for Guadeloupe. Ten weeks away from home wouldn't be so bad. No sacrifice could be too much in the year of the Olympics, I thought.

During the week before I left, I visited Jamie's office and gave him $1,200 for more human growth hormone. He told me he had found a new source in New Jersey. I was disappointed when he failed to get it before I left on the first Sunday in March. BJ and Tony Sharpe promised to bring it down the following weekend. And what a story that turned out to be.

I went to the airport to meet Ben and Sharpe when they arrived in Guadeloupe. I had already arranged for rooms at the CREPS for the two of them, and I leased an apartment for myself and Tosha, who would arrive later for a holiday. The apartment was important. I was planning to stay a long time, and it had a hot-water shower, unlike the dorms at CREPS, as well as a refrigerator. BJ, Sharpe, and I had agreed that I would keep the human growth hormone at the apartment. When I saw first BJ, then Sharpe, through the glass partition in the terminal, I gave a little wave. Ben waved back.

Then the unthinkable happened. Uniformed customs inspectors motioned BJ and Sharpe into a baggage inspection area. I could see Ben freeze. He had no choice but to put all of his bags, including a large cardboard box, on the table. Sharpe's eyes briefly met mine before he reached over and smoothly removed a squat foam Labatt's beer cooler out of the top of the box. He flashed a smile and shrugged at one of the inspectors. When they began to empty the box, I could see it was loaded with boxes and bottles of pills. The inspectors became agitated and called for a supervisor. BJ and Sharpe waited, rigid. For a time I stopped breathing.

I couldn't catch what was being said, though I could see that the supervisor was being extremely sharp with them. The inspectors spoke only a little English – Guadeloupe is a French-speaking country – but there was much flapping of arms and exasperated slaps on the tabletop. Finally, the supervisor waved BJ and Sharpe through the gate with their own luggage, but the box stayed behind.

No one spoke until we got outside. I was in a panic.

"What the hell are we going to do if they take the GH?" I tried to keep my voice calm.

"They're not going to take it," Sharpe said.

"D-d-d-don't joke, man." BJ was sweating.

"I'm not joking. I've got it right here." As we walked away, Sharpe hung the beer cooler in front of us, dangling it from his forefinger. I could have kissed him. In fact, I think I did. Ben howled with laughter.

Customs returned the box to us a few days later. It was packed with enough vitamins and minerals to stock a health food store. As for the beer cooler, it held a vial of new GH in one barrel and – surprise, surprise – a vial of aqueous testosterone in the other. It seemed that Jamie hadn't been able to get enough human growth hormone and we would have to supplement it near the end of the cycle with testosterone. I was not pleased, but I was in no position to argue, hundreds of miles from home and with the customs experience jangling in my mind. I would cross that bridge when I got to it.

In addition to the new anti-inflammatory, Jamie had altered other elements in the drug cycle recommended by Dr. Kerr. He was stubborn about his dislike of Anavar and supplied me with Dianabol instead. I still had some Anavar tablets from California, so I took the five milligrams of Dianabol every day but alternated it occasionally with Anavar. I had complained to Jamie about low back pain during the winter, and when I consulted "my bible," the *Compendium*, I saw that L-Dopa sometimes causes such pain. I told Jamie about it, and he switched me to a substitute "booster" for the human growth hormone, called Dixarit. I was to take two Dixarit tablets per day. Finally, there was the new GH itself, which I took to calling somatropin only to distinguish it from the Crescormon I had gotten through Dr. Kerr.

This somatropin came in a 100-milligram glass vial with metal casing in a seal around the top. The seal protected a rubber membrane that was meant to be pierced with a needle to withdraw the proper dosage. It was a different type of human growth hormone in that it was premixed; I didn't have to bother making the potion with distilled water. I noticed that there was no label of any kind on the vial, just a rubber band holding a piece of paper with Jamie's instructions written on it.

The instructions noted I was to continue on the cycle of Dianabol, Dixarit, and somatropin, with occasional injections of inosine until the end of March. At the beginning of April, I was to switch to a different cycle, using two cc of somatropin per day, along with twenty-five milligrams of aqueous testosterone. By the third week in April, I was to stop taking everything but the somatropin, with an anti-inflammatory only if I needed it. Jamie had also supplied a small vial of Norflex to use after the cycles were complete. Like most muscle relaxants, it is not on the banned or restricted list of drugs published by the Sport Medicine Council of Canada. We understood that the testosterone would make our muscles bulky and stiff for a time, which is why sprinters don't use it during competitions. The Norflex would loosen us up in time for a meet scheduled for April 27 on the neighboring island of Martinique.

Our training camp that winter of 1984 in Guadeloupe raised eyebrows at the Dubin Inquiry. Robert Armstrong was interested in the relationships I had with other members of the Scarborough Optimist Club. For one thing, several of us had made contributions to cover the expense of getting Mike Dincu – Super Mike, we called him – down to Guadeloupe with us. Mike is a chunky Romanian, a graduate sports therapist from the University of Bucharest. He defected from Romania, where he was the trainer for Star Bucharest, the national soccer team. He eventually traveled to Canada and found a job at the Fitness Institute in Willowdale as a therapeutic masseur. Charlie got him to come to the center at York a couple of times a week, and soon, we came to rely on his expert ability to get the knots and lactic acid out of our muscles. Super Mike had magic fingers.

But it was the others in Guadeloupe that Robert Armstrong wanted to know about. Late on my second day of testimony, he said: "You've told us that Tony Sharpe and Ben Johnson came down about a week after you. You've told us that you were there and also your now husband, Tony Issajenko, came down as well at a later point in time, did he?"

I nodded. How could I forget?

"And the group was joined also by Charlie Francis and I believe a runner by the name of Angela Phipps?"

I added that later Molly Killingbeck came down, as well as Ben's girlfriend. We were a big group. Then, Armstrong got to the point.

"When you were at the Guadeloupe training camp, did you inject any drugs into any of the Scarborough Optimist athletes?"

"Yes, I did." I had injected Tony Sharpe and BJ with a mixture of human growth hormone and aqueous testosterone.

Armstrong wanted to know how often I did it.

"Every time I had an injection, Tony and Ben had one as well," I said. "I must point out, though, that Tony Sharpe sometimes would be off doing something else so maybe he would miss one or two."

"What about Ben?" Armstrong asked. "Was he faithful in attendance?"

"Yes."

My mind wandered to the time I had seen Ben on TV, after Seoul, denying that he was aware of having taken steroids. Casting around, looking for someone like Charlie to pin it on. Playing the idiot role, dumb black boy.

"Did you know whether or not Ben Johnson knew in April of 1984 that you were injecting him with an anabolic steroid in Guadeloupe?"

Ben didn't trust anyone but me to give him needles. I had already injected him at home several times with vitamin B-12. I'm not sure why he trusted me, though at the time, I was the star of the Scarborough Optimist Club. Maybe he thought I could do no wrong. Even though some of the guys used to get peevish because of all the attention Charlie showered on me, it never upset Ben. Like me, he felt that his competitors were in Eastern Europe and the United States, not at home in the gym. We had a good relationship, and I suppose the trust grew from there.

I took a deep breath and answered: "I would not have given him drugs without him knowing."

I wondered sometimes, at the inquiry, what kind of image people had of the drug situation after listening to day after day of testimony. It seemed an endless incantation of unpronouncable and weird alchemies. Did they imagine us lying around some apartment in Guadeloupe like junkies, flies unbuttoned, spent needles glistening in the shag carpeting?

Our routine in Guadeloupe was to get up at 6:30 A.M. for the first workout of the day before it got too hot. We worked hard on speed drills and acceleration until eight, then broke for breakfast and physiotherapy sessions with Super Mike. Later, after the worst heat of the day, we'd go back to an active training session that sometimes lasted another three or four hours, until sundown. When everyone had showered and dressed, they would either go to the cafeteria at CREPS for dinner or drift over to my apartment. There was a little stall outside the front door of my building, nothing more than two sticks and a zinc roof, where a man sold the greatest barbecued fish and chicken in the world. We'd have our dinner outside, sitting around the stall, or take it back into the apartment. After dinner, those who needed shots stayed behind. They'd pull down the top of their shorts or jogging pants to bare the top of one buttock, get the injection, and leave.

The drama in Guadeloupe that year started after they left the apartment each evening. My adorable blond Tony had come down to stay with me, and, as usual, we were having problems meshing his holiday schedule with my Olympic preparations. Night after night, I was up far too late, and I began to resent the way it made me drag through my workouts the next day. I was jealous then, too, brooding about Tony lolling about at the beach all day. I'm sure the drugs were making me more aggressive. After a week, we were at one another's throats. Tony hit me so hard once that he broke my eardrum. It was getting ugly. And then I discovered I was pregnant. I had phoned Charlie when I missed my period; he had brought a pregnancy test kit with him when he came down, and that's how I found out.

I don't know if I'll ever come to terms with the concept of abortion. It's a question of responsibility. When I found out I was pregnant, my first instinct was to relinquish responsibility and offer it up to the father of the baby in return for – what? Some kind of metaphysical bonding that neither death nor divorce can break? To fight that instinct was to consider abortion and hold the icicle of responsibility close to my beating, frightened heart. I fought it with reason.

I made a list. One, I was in the middle of my career, on my way to the 1984 Olympics in August. A baby would end my career.

Two, if my career ended, how could I support myself? Or the baby? Or, for that matter, the baby's father?

Three, the drugs: *It must be asked, could the ill effects from these drugs affect you in the years to come? There is now no established record that would guarantee that the effect of these drugs will not affect your offspring.* I had not bothered to read Dr. Kerr's letter of release because I already knew. I had to do what was right. Taking a chance with my own body was one thing, taking a chance with my baby's body was another.

In Guadeloupe, Tony and I did not recover from the abortion. I refused to cry, and after he left for home, I wrote in my diary:

> The relationship is over. I shall not pick up another worthless son of a bitch ever again. He may be doing me a favor. I have to prepare for the Olympic Games and I don't need to be in an emotional uproar. I have two weeks on my own to sort out my feelings. I hope he does well on his examinations.
>
> I hate getting the inosine shots, because the area is always sore the next day.

And then, the tears came.

11

Mrs. Issajenko

All during the early summer of 1984, I compulsively kept track of my competitors. Page after page of my diary was filled with names and times and wind factors. If I were better organized I would have used a wall-sized map, like army generals. I'd have put colored pins, clustered throughout Europe, the U.S., and Jamaica, for each of the women sprinters I had to run against during the year. It became an obsession as we moved toward the Olympics at the end of July.

The American 100-metre sprint team was shaping up to be Evelyn Ashford, Alice Brown, and Jeanette Bolden. Ashford, I noted, had run an impressive 100-metres in 10.78. But then she hurt a hamstring, and I began to monitor her faltering race results: perhaps she wouldn't be running in Los Angeles. In the 200-metres, I expected my American competition would be Chandra Cheeseborough, Florence Griffith, and Valerie Brisco-Hooks. Brisco-Hooks seemed to have come out of nowhere, running it in 22.16 seconds. Griffith was sounding feisty, cocky — and she was faster than ever before. Must have been those painted toenails propelling her around the track.

I tracked the Eastern Europeans until it became apparent that, tit for tat, they would boycott Los Angeles as we had boycotted Moscow. A revenge boycott. The U.S. retaliated by refusing to buy Stolichnaya vodka. The free world had to be content with Moskovskaya, Polish vodka. The Communist boycott didn't bother me nearly as much as our boycott in 1980, probably for selfish reasons; their absence from the 1984 Games meant a better chance for Canadians to win Olympic medals in Los Angeles. At least the real steroid pros wouldn't be in the adjacent lanes.

We'd been hearing gossip that the Soviet athletes now used testosterone year-round. This was a worry even to those of us who were used to running risks. By now we all knew that to compete internationally we needed a couple of cycles of steroids and whatever else was at hand – but year-round? It upped the stakes considerably.

There were also rumors about track and field athletes from the United States. Stories persisted like flies at a summer picnic that U.S. athletes had tested positive at various meets. Some of them were prominent runners and throwers, men and women. Each time, it was alleged, positive results were hushed up and nothing ever came of them. We came to the conclusion that the cover-ups must be officially sanctioned.

There are powerful vested interests at work in U.S. track and field. The Athletics Congress, the governing body of track and field in the United States, took in $8-million in revenue in 1988 from various corporate sponsors and television contracts. These deals can burn up like magnesium paper when drug scandals hit. And money talks.

These rumors finally made the press in the March 1990 issue of *Saturday Night* magazine, when a story by Varda Burstyn noted that the International Olympic Committee confronted the U.S. delegation with the news that "a prominent American athlete" had tested positive for steroids at Seoul. The article said, "The Americans are said to have threatened to kill U.S. media coverage of Barcelona [site of the 1992 Olympics], and the $401-million payment that goes with it, if the information were made public. The information remained secret."

The rumors of American cover-ups took hold that summer and persisted right up to the Olympic Games at Seoul, four years later. On my last day in the witness box at the Dubin Inquiry, Thomas Barber, counsel for the Sport Medicine Council, questioned me about the rumors I had heard. He asked about an entry in my diary for June 26, 1985, the summer after Los Angeles.

"You made reference in your journal that there was a rumor that an athlete at the Bruce Jenner Classic had tested positive, but there was no penalty?" Barber asked.

I recalled that it was only one of many rumors.

"And in effect you took that to mean that it had been hushed up?"

"That's correct."

"And you said that there had been other rumors to the same effect?"

"There have been lots of rumors about positive cover-ups in the United States."

Barber was fishing. "My question is, have there ever been rumors to your knowledge of cover-ups in Canada with testing?"

I hesitated before answering, "I don't think Canadians in general have that attitude, no. That's why we have an inquiry. This would never happen in the United States."

The irony in my answer became apparent long after the Dubin Inquiry ended. The United States, open and free society that it is, might never launch a commission of inquiry into drug use among athletes. But it's possible that inquiries similar to the Dubin might begin to pop up like dandelions in the Eastern bloc countries as more and more coaches and athletes feel free to speak out about what really has been going on over there.

(In June, 1990, *The Toronto Star* published a series of articles on the "past, present and future" of East German sport, especially in light of the collapse of the Berlin Wall. At least one major figure, Professor Hermann Buhl, in charge of medical research at the renowned Leipzig Institute, has admitted publicly that the actual doping of GDR athletes was supervised by the leaders of East Germany's sports system. Research on anabolics came directly from the GDR's pharmaceutical industry.)

In the summer of 1984, however, the Berlin Wall was still in one piece, *perestroika* and *glasnost* were unheard of, and my life as an athlete was the same as those of hundreds of others who were preparing for the Olympic Games in Los Angeles.

I wanted to look good in Los Angeles. Millions of people would watch the televised events, and I wanted some of that Jack London "silk" to shine through on the tube. Charlie was on our backs to look sharp, too. I made an appointment to get my hair braided and suffered through a steamy, seven-hour session at a beauty salon. The braids turned out to be too tight; my hair looked like a haystack in a windstorm. I went back and had it done over again, and this time the braids came out in an attractive soft weave. I put little beads here and there, envisioning myself as a sleek, ebony Bo Derek in the starting blocks in Los Angeles.

It looked great for about two weeks. By the time my picture appeared on the cover of *Star Week* magazine, for the Olympic issue, I had pulled it to one side with a red bow in an attempt to get it to cooperate, but my hair had a mind of its own. Any woman will understand when I say that the braids weren't "me." Just before the Olympics, I got it all chopped off.

For the six-week period ending in the middle of July, I went on another short cycle of Dianabol, somatropin, and Dixarit. I had cut out injections of the anti-inflammatory inosine and promised myself not to use it again. I probably had been taking dosages that were too high. Inosine had the same muscle-stiffening effect on me as Winstrol, which was puzzling.

Other mysterious things had happened since my return from Guadeloupe. One afternoon Tony arrived at the door, his cheeks rosy. On the rare occasions when he is embarrassed, my Tosha blushes. He handed me a small blue velvet box, then stood back in the doorway, his arms crossed over his chest, studiously examining the door jamb. I opened the box, and there was a ring. Holy Moly!

I don't know if it's possible to laugh and cry at the same time, but that's what we did. I wonder sometimes if this is what domestic bliss is all about — tidal waves of conflicting emotions. Two weeks later, we went to a friend's place and got two kittens and named them Pasha and Musette. The morning I left for the Canadian Olympic trials in Winnipeg, I felt like I was leaving behind a family. Feelings of responsibility and delicious freedom washed over me, I was happy and sad, strong and independent, and lonely. All this is bad for the concentration, of course. I threw myself into a fierce workout an hour after landing.

The trials were at the new University of Manitoba track, and I realized, in the 100-metre heats, that it was soft, almost bouncy. I won the final, in 11.13 seconds, but my sciatic nerve sent up a warning flare. The next day, July 1, we ran the 200-metre final, which I won in 22.61, but I had definitely hurt myself the day before on that spongy track. My quads throbbed. I wasn't the only one troubled by the surface; Angela Bailey dropped out of the 200-metres.

Charlie made us watch our races on television, to analyze technique. I could clearly see that I had won the 100-metres in the last 30 metres of the race. The curse of the weak start was still with me.

And I didn't get my knees up in the 200-metres. There were at least a couple of pre-Olympic meets scheduled in California, but we had less than four weeks left to prepare for the Games. I kept my obsessive notes and took to timing even my rest periods.

By July 24, we were in Los Angeles, at the Olympic Village. I checked in for physiotherapy: interferential (a machine which generates an alternating current designed to reach deep tissues) and ultrasound treatment on my hamstrings, a chiropractor to crack my back, a massage, then heat packs and Hepathromb ointment on my hamstrings. I regretted my decision to stop taking inosine injections. It was, after all, a powerful anti-inflammatory, a safeguard. But there were other details to worry about, like my hair. I got it styled again for the opening ceremonies. Bo Derek herself might be watching from the stands; Mariel Hemingway might see my break from the blocks. We were measured and weighed, and fitted for our Canadian track uniforms. I checked in at 135 pounds. Only two pounds more than my weight in Brisbane when I ran to victory, and I knew it was solid muscle. This was it: showtime.

By August 3, it was certain that all the guys from the Scarborough Optimists – Mark McKoy, Desai Williams, Tony Sharpe, Ben Johnson – would make the semifinals. Canada had already collected four golds, three silvers, and one bronze. I spent the evening fussing over what I would wear to the 100-metre heats in the morning. My sciatic nerve was acting up, but this time all my nerves were jumpy. I went to bed early and lay there for a while. How I wanted to show these Americans! How I wanted a medal! I rolled over, reached for my diary on the bedside table, and scribbled: "Please help me dear God to run to the best of my abilities." A faint voice, from long ago, added, *Ayy-man*!

There were three heats in the 100-metres. I false-started on the first one, which was unusual for me, and my concentration suffered. I did only 11.23, but it was enough to get me to the semifinals the next day. Ben won the bronze in the men's 100-metres, behind Carl Lewis and Sam Graddy of the United States. Lewis won the gold, in 9.99 seconds.

I was up against Evelyn Ashford, Alice Brown, and Jeanette Bolden from the United States, and Merlene Ottey-Page and Grace Jackson of Jamaica in the semifinal. The five most powerful women sprinters in track and field outside the Eastern bloc. I composed another desperate plea and committed it to my trusty diary with a shaking hand: "I will have to run at 100 per cent. Please help me God."

When I awoke the next morning at seven o'clock, I immediately knew there was something wrong with my hamstring. I went for a heat wrap and a massage. I even took a half cc of inosine. One of the doctors put a heat plaster on my back. As I lay on the table, I repeated over and over, like a mantra, that all I had to do was run as I did in the heats: *Good start, good acceleration, and smooth . . . Good start, good acceleration, and smooth . . .*

I ran 11.36 in the semifinal of the 100-metres, good enough to make the final, but my right hamstring was giving out on me, sucking me into a pool of pain. Charlie hustled me to the medical tent behind the stadium, but I didn't follow him in right away. I needed to breathe air without fear, if only for a moment. Outside, listening to the billowing, surging swell of the crowd in the Coliseum, I was transported back to that afternoon long ago, in Jamaica, when I had stood entranced by the fluttery colors of thousands of people at the national stadium in Kingston. The sky was surprisingly clear that day, for Los Angeles. It was a bright, cloudless, Jamaican blue, and I wished for just a moment that I could take off my shoes and curl my toes into the grass.

Then Charlie was shouting. "Ange! Where the hell are you? Angella! Get in here!"

I lifted the flap of the tent, ducked inside, and a team of therapists laid me out to apply ice and ointments. They taped my leg with rolls of tensor bandage, and I swallowed a handful of Aspirins. Two hours before the final. It didn't look good.

Ashford won, setting an Olympic record of 10.97. Brown came second, in 11.13, and Ottey-Page came third, in 11.16. Angela Bailey finished sixth, in 11.40. I finished eighth, in 11.62. I had not been able to lift my right leg for at least the last 30 metres. I was transfixed after, watching the damning figures as they flashed across the electronic scoreboard. Suddenly, I couldn't stand it anymore and rushed from the stadium, past the noise and the heat and away from the shame. Charlie was there, waiting, as he always was. I pushed my face into his chest and cried my heart out.

Bailey informed one of the reporters that she felt sorry for me, but confided that she was pleased with her sixth-place finish. She said she hoped to win a medal at the 1988 Olympics in Seoul, being only twenty-two, you know.

I rallied, though I don't know how. There was no way I could run the 200-metres, but there was a chance that I might be able to perform in the women's four-by-100-metre relay, which would be held in six days. That gave me nearly a week to recover, and we laid on physiotherapy sessions to stretch my wretched, aching quads. It hurt, but by the morning of August 11, I was ready. We finished a respectable second behind the United States, in a time of 42.77 seconds.

We won a silver medal — an *Olympic* silver medal. On the Wall of Fame at York University, they put up plaques under my name and Angela Bailey's for it. I was bitterly disappointed that I had failed to get an individual medal. Bailey and I probably will be intertwined on the Wall of Fame till the end of time. Old chums that we are.

The Olympics were over.

A European tour was scheduled to begin in the middle of August, and, dispirited though I was, it was important to go so we could capitalize on our status as Canadian Olympic athletes. Even York University wanted to share in the glory. The Metropolitan Toronto Track and Field Centre, our home away from home, was declared a "high-performance center," in partnership with the Ontario Track and Field Association, Sport Canada, the Canadian Track and Field Association and the Ontario Ministry of Tourism and Recreation. The center was approved through the athletic department of York, and we heard grandiose promises of extra resources to back up Olympic-level training. In return, the Scarborough Optimist Track and Field Club changed its name to the York University Optimist Athletic Club.

After the stardust settled, it turned out that we got shared space in a tiny office at the center, with some secretarial support. As Elaine Dewar wrote in a story called "Unsportsmanlike Conduct" in *Toronto Life* magazine, York got instant sports prestige without having to stoop to the athletic scholarship.

A certain hostility toward many of the Olympic medal winners from the York Optimist Club began to surface later that fall. Athletes under promotional contract with adidas, worth $500 a month and more in bonuses to me personally, were abruptly informed that the company did not intend to renew support. Glenn

Bogue, athlete services manager for the Canadian Track and Field Association, sent us an interesting memo explaining adidas' decision. He said that while he understood adidas' decision to pull out was primarily a budgetary consideration, he was concerned that some athletes had been rude to adidas people at the Olympics. More seriously, he referred to athletes demanding payment for wearing adidas products when they already were under contract with the company.

I had, in fact, heard a story that one of the sprinters had tried to pull a fast one. He had been approached by a competing manufacturer with a cash offer to wear the company's shoes in Los Angeles. He must have asked an adidas representative if adidas could match or better the offer. We shrugged this off, putting it down to bad manners, and forgot about it. None of us saw the contractual ramifications at the time. As for the charge that athletes were rude to adidas people, I can only speak for myself, and I don't believe I gave anyone cause to criticize my behavior.

When I got Bogue's memo, I was astounded at what I saw as trumped-up charges. Surely one bad apple shouldn't spoil it for the bunch. I called adidas and asked for the names of athletes who had been rude. I wanted to know exactly which of the sprinters had acted so foolishly. adidas never backed up the accusations with any details.

The real reason for cutting us off could only be a calculated marketing decision. As Bogue wrote: "adidas pointed to the fact that our athletes, as well as all amateur athletes in general, failed to generate sufficient media exposure to justify adidas' expenditures of approximately $175,000 in cash to specific Athlete Reserve Fund accounts, as well as equipment and travel reimbursement."

He added: "I was personally disappointed that the athletes did not grasp the media opportunities that we had in order to promote both adidas and Sport Canada.

"I forward these comments in the hope of jarring you, the best athletes in the country, into the realization that far more than athletic ability and a lawyer is needed if you are to succeed in securing funding from the corporate sector for both yourselves and those athletes who aspire to your positions on the world list."

I have not shared this memo with you to criticize adidas for a marketing decision. Heinz Piotrowski, vice-president of marketing for adidas at the time, told Al Sokol of *The Toronto Star*, "The sole and only reason we came to this decision was to channel the required dollars into consumer advertising and promotions because of the horrendous change in the market place. Our marketing research shows that over 70 per cent of the people who buy sporting goods are not involved in sports. The market is now in leisure and active wear and these consumers do not relate to high-performance athletes."

Organizations like Sport Canada have a remarkably hypocritical attitude toward athletes. We are expected to be grateful rubes, in sport for the pure, unblemished love of it. We are also expected to be sophisticated ambassadors for Canada, able to "grasp media opportunities" for sponsors and the salaried organizers of sport. It is an uneasy alliance for most amateur athletes. Bogue's memo engendered cynicism rather than regret. It was mainly about money, and the complaints about our behavior were paternalistic and demeaning. One thing Bogue said that I couldn't argue with was that it takes far more than ability and a lawyer to be an athlete in this country.

Another bit of dirty linen, not properly aired in the aftermath of the 1984 Olympics, had to do with the Harry Jerome meet in Vancouver. In the past, the best of the Scarborough Optimists had taken part in this meet to support the organizers' stated goal to raise the level of public recognition for black athletes. The members of the silver-medal relay team in Los Angeles were me, Angela Bailey, Marita Payne, and France Gareau, a white woman from Verner, Ontario. Officials at the Harry Jerome meet wanted the Canadian Olympic relay team there, but they did not want France Gareau because she was white. It was as racist as that. I refused to attend. I doubt that Harry Jerome, a marvelous sprinter in his time and a big-spirited man, would have condoned their behavior.

I went to see Jamie before we left for Europe, and he did what he could to ease my aches and pains in time for competition. The drug had not been invented that could soothe my disappointment with the Olympics, and I continued to brood over my performance there. He nodded sympathetically when I said that I didn't like inosine.

Jamie recommended that I start a cycle of aqueous testosterone. It was clear to me by then that he had certain preferences with regard to steroids: he liked testosterone and he liked Winstrol. I told him that I was leery of testosterone, that I'd read it was a dangerous drug for women. He assured me that the abbreviated cycle he was recommending, and the dosage of only a half cc per injection, was nothing to fear. Furthermore, he would recommend an extensive list of vitamins and minerals and dietary guidelines to offset any side effects.

Jamie really did have talent as a holistic doctor, emphasizing vitamins and proper diet. He had put BJ, Desai, and Mark on the same drug and diet regime for the European tour. Over the years, I had become used to eating out at Swiss Chalet and other fast-food joints and I had developed bad eating habits. Too often I loaded up on junk food, forgetting to eat three balanced meals a day. I wasn't getting enough protein, and Jamie knew it. I never did have much of an appetite. I'd get too involved in my workouts, or whatever else I happened to be doing, and I'd forget about food until I suddenly became ravenous.

I began the cycle of aqueous testosterone, and when we arrived in Europe I noticed that I was retaining so much water that my face swelled up to a full moon. I made a note to reduce the dosage to a quarter cc per injection. Perhaps Jamie had meant to shock my system with new fire power.

The day after landing in Europe, I realized that I would not be able to take any of the anti-inflammatories I had been using. The anti-inflammatories were hard on my stomach, and I had to vary them or else the cumulative concentrated effect was like knives. Someone on the team suggested that I try Butazolidin, a powerful anti-inflammatory that is widely available in Europe, sold at just about every pharmacy. The recommended dosage is one pill a day for no more than ten days. As an injectable, doctors will give it to you only once a year. I took a pill and it seemed to help, but I didn't much like the idea of combining such powerful drugs. Butazolidin and aqueous testosterone seemed a long way from my old formula of Dianabol and Naprosyn.

Europeans love track and field athletes, which is why we liked to go there at least once a year. They treated us like celebrities. Middle-aged men and women and teenagers crowded hotel lobbies when we arrived, pushing papers and photographs of ourselves we'd never seen before under our noses for autographs. We were "the Canadian Olympic stars." It was a wonderful, heady experience.

Mysteriously, we all suffered injuries on the tour. I did not connect these to the too-high dosages of testosterone. At the time, it seemed obvious to us that the Olympics had been too unsettling and that we were exhausted.

The celebrity circuit resumed, Canadian-style, when we arrived home and were invited to appear at the second annual Lieutenant-Governor's Invitational Games for disabled youngsters at Variety Village in Toronto. I held some of those brave little kids in my arms that day. It stirred up feelings I didn't want to face. I'm not sure I was ready to face those feelings any better on January 5, 1985, when I learned that I was pregnant again.

Jamie sent me to see an obstetrician and gynecologist downstairs at the clinic. We discussed another abortion, but there wasn't enough time before I left for a meet in Japan. While I was in Japan, I realized I couldn't go through with another abortion. I wouldn't be able to live with myself.

In Osaka, I came second in a 60-metre race, in a time of 7.54 seconds. We went on to Paris. It was an eighteen-hour flight, and all I wanted to do was sleep. I managed to get four seats to myself so I could stretch out. By January 17, the day before the French meet, I was having trouble getting motivated enough even to warm up. I was starting to feel strange. I didn't make the final in the 60-metres, and I decided not to run in the 200-metres. It was upsetting because most of the big-name winners were there from the Los Angeles Olympics.

I was overcome by lethargy. I could barely make it twice around the track, which terrified me. I knew that since I intended to keep this baby, I would have to perform in at least three more meets because I needed the money. I scribbled columns of numbers on scraps of paper, trying to figure out if the card money and mother's allowance would get me through. We were scheduled to fly home on January 20.

When I told Tony I was going to keep the baby, he was shocked, then angry, then deliriously happy, in that order. Tony had turned twenty in November, had graduated from grade thirteen, and we agreed it was time for him to take his own track career seriously. He must have felt that just as his boyhood was ending, he would be taking on the demands of fatherhood. There would have to be major changes in our relationship, with less brother-sister camaraderie, more parental responsibility.

Tony's emotions were mercurial. My stoic Russian was having a hard time of it. One day he threw himself into choosing names for the baby. Then, a few days later, he left me. Late one afternoon he stormed out and moved all his clothes to a friend's apartment.

I was confused, and hurt, but Babushka Helen wasn't fooled for a minute. She called me, saying she desperately needed some help around the house. She called again to say she felt lonely and wanted company. I went over to her place to share some tea and she gave me Tony's baby booties. Eventually, Tony called and told me someone at the track had stolen his spikes, and could he please borrow mine? That's when I knew the storm had passed and we'd be all right. I remembered lending him my spikes when he was fourteen years old. I recalled it gave me a handy excuse to telephone him, too.

My career went into a tailspin. Day after day, I was striking out the meets in my diary: Toronto Star Games, OUT; Ontario Seniors' Meet, CANCELED; Winnipeg meet, OUT. I worked out at the track every day, but there were times when I snuck back to the apartment for a nap between drills. It was becoming obvious that soon I would not be able to compete at all. By the second week in February, I limited myself to workouts only, but they were pretty tame. On February 27, I noted in my diary: "100 + 100 + 100 + 100. Didn't feel very good, so I quit."

The doctor told me that I could expect to deliver about September 3. My private worry was to figure out how to get over the rickety bridge of slim finances and no training in preparation for the 1986 indoor season. My worst fear as a champion athlete was realized: I had lost control of my body. I felt very much alone.

I applied for a job at the Bathurst Heights Community Centre, but it turned out to be coaching basketball and we agreed that it wasn't the right job for me. A chartered bank wanted an Olympic athlete in an advertisement and offered me $350 for two hours worth of posing, so I took it. These humiliations were only a taste of what I would go through five years later, as I looked for a job when my career ended after the Dubin Inquiry.

We began to pin our hopes on Tony's career. On a slate-gray morning in early March, I packed him onto a bus headed for a winter training camp in Florida. I had a month to myself with just my worries for company. I was having a lot of trouble sleeping, sometimes I didn't fall asleep until five in the morning, and I had no appetite at all. Super Mike Dincu took me to lunch one day, but I had trouble keeping it down. I worried that I wasn't feeding the baby properly.

One way or another, though, I tried to keep up some basic training schedule, even if it was one lap around the track and three loads of laundry. I started doing stretch exercises in the laundry room – leg lifts during the wash, sit-ups during the rinse cycle. I saved my reading for when the clothes were tossing in the dryer. I'd been hanging around track people for so long, immersed in jockdom, that I'd forgotten the thrill of intellectual stimulation. I came across a copy of Dostoevsky's *Notes from the Underground*, which sparked an interest in Russian literature that continues to this day.

By April, Tony was back from Florida, and I went to the track with him one day to see how Charlie's group was doing. They looked strong and talented. Champions, even without me. Tony seemed to fly around the track, and his progress thrilled me. We shared a dream that he would get carded, at least provincially, and we would be able to travel to meets together. No more long months apart, no more lonely hotel rooms or cold beds in dormitories. Daydreaming kept me going. On April 11, I noted in my diary that I weighed 146 pounds, but I hastily added, "Not as big as it seems; my legs are so much smaller." Sometimes you see what you want to see.

That Easter, Tony and I went to Babushka Helen's for lunch, then he went on alone to visit his father's family near High Park. Tony's family is Russian Orthodox, so we get to celebrate Christmas, New Year's, and Easter on the Christian calendar, then each on the Gregorian calendar two weeks after. It was the first time he had gone to see his father and paternal grandparents in years. It was also the first time he would meet his father's girlfriend, Molly. I was encouraged by Tony's decision to visit. Having a baby put things in perspective, especially with regard to family. I began to consider a thaw in the relationship with my own mother, Olive.

Tony came home and told me we should consider moving down to the High Park neighborhood. Things had gone well with his dad. The next day, we saw the ultrasound image of our baby. It was an exciting, happy time, and I wished I didn't have to worry so much about money.

On the first day of May, three amazing things happened. I opened a letter that informed me I had been selected to receive the Order of Canada; the baby moved for the first time, at five months and two weeks; and Olive called. My mother had bought some clothes for the baby and wanted to know if she could come over to give them to me. Also, my weight had shot up to an amazing 156 pounds.

Once the news about the Order of Canada was announced, I began to get invitations to make appearances here and there — once for a tennis match, once for the City of North York's department of parks and recreation. The appearances paid $150 or $200, sometimes as much as $350, for which I was grateful, but I was still having trouble paying my bills.

I continued to make daily entries in my diary during 1985, recording Tony's progress on the track and my baby's progress toward birth. Our big hope was that Tony would make the Canada Games Team but he strained a tendon early in April and it bothered him through the summer. He couldn't train over longer distances. When the trials came, he looked great exploding from the blocks, but he couldn't sustain his speed. He didn't make the team.

Meanwhile, I could feel the baby's heartbeat and she had wriggled around to press against my ribs. The money situation worsened.

Timex, one of Ben Johnson's sponsors, asked me to step in for BJ to make a promotional appearance at a major trade show. Ben was on tour in Europe, and I jumped at the chance to make the estimable sum of $2,500 for two days' work. But Timex canceled the appearance when they found out I was pregnant and unmarried. They said their department store distributors objected to my appearance. Being an Olympic champion and named to the Order of Canada apparently wasn't good enough. I wondered what they would have done if they had discovered Ben wasn't a virgin. As it turned out, Timex decided to pay me *not* to appear.

Tony and I did what we had to, for practical purposes. I gave up my apartment and we moved into a one-bedroom flat on the ground floor of his father's house near High Park. It didn't take me long to fall in love with the neighborhood. It has an old, settled feeling: large, leafy shade trees, backyard fences, ivy crawling up stone walls, honeysuckle hedges, lovingly tended flower gardens, thick green lawns. The houses are different shapes and sizes, many with large, covered porches. It is a neighborhood for walking. I love the shops of Roncesvalles Avenue, the smell of bread cooking in the bakeries, the streetcars tocking by.

For the first time, I met Tony's paternal grandparents, Babushka Galia and Dadushka Grisha. During one of our long talks, I told Babushka Galia over tea that I was worried about Tony being such a young father. "If he's old enough to make babies," she told me, "he's old enough to get married."

Tony worked hard, painting and sanding and wallpapering, to get the flat ready for our move on the first of August. I had energy to burn and I enjoyed negotiating with the drapery and carpet installers, and, toughest of all, the movers.

Tony explored the idea of getting into the retail business. His father, Alex, owned a small building on Roncesvalles with apartments upstairs and stores below. We conducted a haphazard market survey and determined that there weren't many shoe stores in the neighborhood, so Tony made a presentation to his father, who let him lease one of the stores.

On a sunny summer day when the maple trees hung thick with leaves over the streets of High Park, Tony's father got married for the second time. It was an elegant service in the local Russian Orthodox church. I was entranced by the *a cappella* hymns sung in English and ancient Slavonic. Babushka Galia was there. She pressed her hand into mine and whispered her wish that Tony and I would get married, too. I had been considering the idea. My brush with Timex made me realize that the live-and-let-live Jamaican approach to marriage and motherhood might be a problem with other North American sponsors. A week later, Tony and I went to City Hall and got a marriage license.

Once the decision had been made, everyone flew into action. We must have unleashed all the unspoken worries about the baby being born out of wedlock. I was due to deliver on September 3, and by August 25, Tony and I were standing in front of the priest in the same old church where his father had married Molly. The church was magnificent with its intricately painted icons and baskets of fresh flowers. Tony had been to confession, so he could take communion before the service. His father gave us two rings for the ceremony.

Father George had politely told me that white would not be appropriate for my wedding dress. Tony and I spent a frantic day riding the escalators at the Eaton Centre, looking for an affordable nonwhite size-fourteen dress. I found a silky blue gown with a delicate pattern and a full, ankle-length skirt. Tony's cousin Tanya lent me a hat with a small veil. Even though I hadn't had time to carefully plan, I managed to get married in something old, something new, something borrowed, and something blue.

It was a lovely ceremony, and I treasure the pictures showing Tony with his long blond hair and the two of us signing the register. Tony has since cut his hair short and spiky, which makes him look more Russian than ever. With the baby coming and Tony's new shop, we couldn't afford a honeymoon. I doubt I would have wanted to go anywhere even if we had the money; the pains were becoming longer and more urgent.

After the wedding, we went out with Tony's family to Chung King Chop Suey House for garlic shrimp, fried rice, wonton – the works. Then Tony, his brother Peter, and I came home and sat on the couch in the living room and watched a movie while I folded laundry. I couldn't help peeking at my Tosha and he caught me doing it once or twice. For the first time in my life, I felt a bit giggly. From Marie Taylor to Angella Taylor to Angella Issajenko. It was hard to believe we were married.

Tony used the money we got as wedding presents to start up the store. He also managed to negotiate a Youth Venture capital loan of $5,000. He persuaded a supplier to advance him $25,000 worth of Italian leather shoes on credit – we were in business! He set to work again, papering and painting, buying display shelves. Ross Earl lent us some antiques to furnish the store. But we knew the shop was a gamble: Tony had to repay $2,500 a month for the stock, the rent was $750 a month, and there were other operating expenses.

Exactly a week to the day after the ceremony, on September 1 at four o'clock in the morning, my daughter Alexandra was born at Central Hospital, the same hospital where Tony's mother had given birth to him. Sasha weighed six pounds, nine and three-quarter ounces.

They had to put me under and use forceps. I made up my mind I would never have another baby. It hurt too much, and the stitches itched. But little Sasha was beautiful, with jet black hair and big blue eyes that eventually changed to chocolate brown. Her skin was surprisingly light, like a baby with a soft suntan. I was in the hospital for nearly a week, and the nurses taught me how to breastfeed. I realized I didn't know anything at all about taking care of a baby.

Tony's father came to the hospital and picked us up and took us home. That night, Tony and I lay with Sasha on our bed, fascinated by her every breath, until she fell asleep.

I had trouble falling to sleep myself, though, and I noticed Tony was restless in his dreams. Late in the still, still night, I wrote in my diary, "Please help us dear God."

12

"Foot hurt, mon."

With all my appeals to God, during the Olympics in Los Angeles, then with the baby, I noticed that He seemed to need an awful lot of help from me to get things going. God helps those who help themselves, I guess. During the near-sleepless nights of September, when Sasha wanted to be fed every three hours, I pored over my diaries. I was looking for the connection between training and winning races.

I came to the conclusion that I had been training too hard. My excellent performance in 1982 had made me vow to "work harder than ever," but my career had faltered since. I had reached the point where I was afraid of my workouts and I didn't believe I could get through them without several cycles of steroids and various painkillers. There were days when I nearly crawled off the track. This time, I intended to follow the less strenuous 1982 training schedule closely when I prepared for the 1986 indoor season. My return date would be October 1.

One of the first lessons I learned as a parent was that I could make all the plans I wanted, but the baby had a schedule of her own. Sasha took to sleeping all day and playing all night. She spat out the formula I tried to feed her. She must have known I was trying to wean her and get back to work because she took to smiling only at Tony. Tony told me not to take it personally; Sasha must have decided I was merely the restaurant. Charlie came back from a meet in Australia and gave her a giant koala teddy bear, which fascinated her. I told her this was the sort of perk she could expect as the daughter of a world champion athlete, and could I, please, now, get back to training?

On October 30, Tony and I drove with Sasha to Ottawa, where I was to be presented with the Order of Canada. The formality of the occasion made my hands shake with nerves, but years of performing in front of spectators and cameras stood me in good stead and I managed to take the scroll and the medal without dropping them. Jeanne Sauvé, the governor-general, seemed genuinely interested in each of us, and I found her pleasant manner calming. The new prime minister, Brian Mulroney, shook my hand, but the man who stole my heart was Pierre Trudeau. He, too, was receiving the Order of Canada, and after the ceremony, he gave me the Gallic kiss on each cheek and we talked about our children, both of them nicknamed Sasha. I didn't want to wash my face ever again, and I didn't for two days, though it played hell with my complexion.

By the time she reached ten pounds, Sasha seemed to think the time was right, and the day after we got back from Ottawa I took her to the track for my first decent workout of the year. I gained a new appreciation for the guys at the track, people like George van Zeyl, an assistant coach. They fussed with Sasha and sometimes picked her up to soothe her so I could get through the routines. George actually stood with Sasha on one hip, while he barked orders. The warm-up and the drills went well, but by the end of my second 60-metre run, I realized the comeback would be a lot more gradual than I had thought. I felt an odd pain in my left heel and called it quits for the day. It was a start, barely.

By Christmas, I was back up to full workouts, and I'd battled my weight down to 139 pounds. Sasha was still breastfeeding, which made for some interesting Rorschach patterns on my T-shirts. Finally, by the middle of January I felt she was ready to be weaned.

The York Optimists, especially Ben, were heading into what promised to be an exceptionally good season. BJ ran 10 seconds flat in October to win the 100-metres at the World Cup in Canberra, Australia. He set four records in that one race for the World Cup, Commonwealth, Canadian, and Australian opens. Then, in January 1986, he set the world indoor record in the 60-metres with 6.50 seconds in Osaka. Ben's rivalry with Carl Lewis was heating up. Lewis still smarted from a meet in Zurich, when Ben had beat him in the 100-metres.

Ben and I became a little closer that winter. We weren't bosom buddies, but we had been working together for five years and, while I had been the darling of the club at the start, his star was now rising.

I imagine he began to sympathize with some of the pressure to perform that I had been under when I had been at the top of our little circle. He began to take an interest in my training.

Charlie and I in turn studied Ben's training techniques because he had perfected that part of the sprint that was my weakest: the starts, the break from the blocks. BJ seemed to propel himself out of the blocks with both feet, so that he was actually flying. At the crack of the pistol, he was unbeatable. He seemed to defy gravity.

The funny thing is, Ben had formulated his perfect start because the guy was bone lazy. All those years, he had managed to avoid doing the longer endurance runs that we hated as sprinters. Charlie forced us to the limit in the belief that it would help us develop the ability to maintain speed. Ben would come up with an excuse nearly every Wednesday to avoid the special endurance runs. It became a joke around the track. Sometimes, he just failed to show. Most of the time, he'd fake a hobble and turn those big eyes on Charlie.

"Foot hurt, mon. Foot hurt," he'd moan.

Of course, this made us laugh our heads off. After a while, whenever someone wanted to get out of doing something, we'd imitate BJ. Want help to move some equipment? Foot hurt, mon! Want someone to pick up pizza for the gang? Foot hurt, mon!

As a result of his laziness, Ben did nothing but starts and short spurts of 50 and 60 metres. Over and over and over. This was his big secret, and the way he became the fastest man alive. Gradually, we stopped joking about it. During the winter of 1986, I worked to adopt BJ's training methods. Again and again, I did standing starts, running starts, block starts, then only 30-metres or, at most, 60-metres. I mixed the work on starts with endless sit-ups, again, to strengthen my stomach muscles. And I began serious weightlifting to increase my upper body strength. In addition to his superhuman starts, BJ was able to propel himself at astounding speeds by pumping his arms like pistons. I began to do the same. However, with each day of training, the pain in my heel became progressively worse. Jamie finally concluded that it was bursitis.

Bursitis is a fairly common condition. It is the inflammation of a little sac called a bursa, which is filled with lubricating liquid to ease friction between tissues like a muscle and a tendon. In my case, I'd let the condition go on too long and it had become chronic. Jamie recommended an anti-inflammatory, which is the standard treatment, but I wanted to be sure I was finished nursing Sasha, so I let it get worse than I should have. By the second week in January, I couldn't stand the pain any longer and I put my little Sasha on formula. The next day, I started on Butazolidin.

During 1985, when I was pregnant and off the track, Jamie had been dispensing water-based Dianabol to the athletes. I'm not sure if he couldn't get it anymore or if he had decided the clearance time of twenty-eight days for Dianabol was too long, but in 1986 he switched us to a new drug that was something of a mystery.

Jamie told us that he'd found a drug the East Germans were using. The story was that he had been assisting with the training of a young German athlete, a potential superstar, who had been living in Canada when his parents died. This kid's relatives had shipped him back to East Germany to live with his grandparents until he graduated from high school. In the meantime, he traveled back and forth for training sessions. Each time he returned to Canada, he brought more of this new drug with him. At least, that's the story we heard.

We had our doubts. It seemed strange that this unnamed young athlete, whom we never met, was able to travel so freely. He appeared to pass through the iron curtain as regularly as Canadians from Niagara Falls slip over the Rainbow Bridge for a case of Coors. But we didn't dwell on the details. As far as we were concerned, our little group shared a powerful advantage with the East Germans. We lusted for the chance to meet them on what we liked to call "a level playing field."

I eventually got a name for the drug out of Jamie. He called it estragol, but we came to know it as "the white stuff." It came in glass bottles without labels, but I was used to that by now. Usually only the injectable vitamin B-12 compounds had labels. Jamie instructed us to visit his office three times a week, every Monday, Wednesday, and Friday, for an injection. He charged us $50 per 100-milligram bottle, though it went a long way at three cc a week. Whatever else I came to think of Jamie, I don't believe he tried to make a profit from the drugs he sold us.

My immediate goal in 1986 was to try for a decent showing at the Canadian Nationals in Ottawa the third week in June. The Nationals were to serve as the trial meet for the Commonwealth Games in Edinburgh in July. I saw the Commonwealth Games as crucial to my plans for a triumphant comeback after having Sasha.

Jamie recommended that I stay on the cycle of estragol until May 8, to give my system plenty of time to clear for the Nationals. We were being extraordinarily careful; Jamie said the actual clearance time was about fifteen days. In the meantime, he regularly injected me with Butazolidin and gave me some corticosteroidal cream to massage into my bursitic heel and Achilles tendon.

While I had been away from the track, Charlie had arranged for a full-time physiotherapist named Waldemar Matuszewski to assist the York Optimists. Matuszewski had been a masseur with the Polish national track and field team and head of the country's rehabilitation medicine program. He had defected from Poland, so it was understood that he couldn't travel with us to Eastern bloc countries. I became increasingly dependent on Waldemar's massage techniques – they erased the aches and pains from training before they had a chance to grow – and we were pleased to learn that he would accompany us to a two-week winter training camp in Florida in March.

Just before we left, Bio-Med Systems Corporation came through with a generous offer to sponsor me for $500 a month through to the 1988 Olympics and six months beyond. Bio-Med was the distribution company for a sophisticated electronic muscle stimulator called Powerstim 16. The people at Bio-Med knew I favored electronic muscle stimulation as part of my training, and they gave me a fancy new machine along with the sponsorship money. They called a press conference, and Otto Jelinek, the minister of sport, flew in from Ottawa to attend. I was most grateful for the support: my year off had cost me a world rating, and I no longer received card money from Sport Canada.

I had been taking Sasha to the track every day with me and I saw no reason to leave her behind when I went to Florida. Tony wouldn't be able to watch over her while he ran the store, so I bundled her on the plane and off we went, track shoes, shorts, diapers, bottles, baby food, and all. Most days, I was lucky enough to find someone to watch her while I trained. Other days, I took her along to the field house and did my thing, watching her out of a corner of my eye. The day before we left for home, the poor little gal got sick and I had to take her to the hospital. It turned out to be a mild stomach flu.

I can laugh now about some of the things I went through in 1986, trying to balance my return to track with a new baby. I adored

Sasha's company and her sweet little face. I felt calmer than ever before, and I didn't push myself so hard in training. If I felt an injury flare up, I packed it in for the day. As I mentioned, it seemed silly to think of the two us of spilling tears at the track. Sasha gave a richer dimension to my life, and I no longer felt I lived or died for track alone. This doesn't mean that my ambition waned — I still wanted to be number one in the world — but Sasha brought perspective to my goal. There were other things in life.

Every once in a while, though, the perverse demands of track pressed in on me. When we returned from Florida, I spent a lovely early spring day raking the leaves in the yard. Sasha gurgled at me from her stroller. The next day, my back was killing me, and I made a note in my diary to never again rake soggy leaves as long as I was in athletics.

In April, Sasha and I were off again, this time to Guadeloupe, then a meet in Trinidad. It would be my first competition in sixteen months. I thought at first that Merlene Ottey would be entered, but she backed out because of an injury. Funny how things change — I was dismayed to discover it was a grass track. At this stage in my career, I knew enough to fear an uneven surface, and, sure enough, the race did cause my sciatic nerve to flare. In the 100-metres, I came second, in 11.15 seconds. That's what they told me, but I knew the time had to be wrong. It was hand-timed, and I had not run that well. I added the standard 0.24 seconds to bring the time to a probable, electronically timed 11.39. Not bad at this stage of my comeback.

There was a 200-metre race scheduled in Trinidad, but I decided not to enter it. I didn't feel ready. Sasha was only seven months old, and she had spent most of her life at the track already. I'd had enough. We flew home.

Charlie had arranged for me to travel to Martinique for the annual Marie Perrine meet that I had run in other years. The day before I was to leave, we ran into trouble with the meet promoter. He was refusing to pay appearance money. Charlie phoned Gerard Mach, looking for advice. Gerard told Charlie to bill half the cost of the airline tickets to the Canadian Track and Field Association.

I managed to come third with the sluggish time of 11.50 in the 100-metres in Martinique. Sasha and I were to travel home via Antigua, but the airline canceled our flight, so we had to stay in a hotel for an extra night. I began to wonder if I wasn't putting too much pressure on myself by entering competitions this early. Sasha was a little trooper, though. I took her to the beach and strolled her around the hotel grounds the next morning.

At the end of May, a story by Jean Sonmor appeared in the Toronto *Sun*. It was the first time Sonmor had interviewed me, and her research was impressive. Little could I know, of course, that later she would write the fateful "TIME BOMB" story when I tore a strip off Ben in October 1988. This time, Sonmor was writing about the effect of pregnancy on athletic performance. She cited instances when it appeared that some athletes had performed better after having given birth. Debbie Brill, for example, broke the world indoor high-jump record a few months after delivering her baby, and Valerie Brisco-Hooks won three gold medals at the 1984 Olympics in Los Angeles, then loped over to the stands to pick up her baby.

Sonmor quoted several experts on why pregnancy might improve performance. An endocrinologist said the high level of testosterone in a woman's body during pregnancy probably would build muscle strength. (We'd heard this before, from the Russians.) A professor of gynecology said the extra weight and blood volume of a pregnant woman's body has a natural training effect in that the body does more work even while at rest. An anatomy professor said she was not surprised that some women seem to get stronger after pregnancy because it was like training with an extra twenty pounds on your back, then taking it off to run a race.

Sonmor's story went on to point out that Evelyn Ashford, my longtime American rival, had given birth only a few months before I had had Sasha. Already, she was only one-tenth of a second off her Olympic record of 10.97 in the 100-metres at Los Angeles.

The story brought to mind a nasty rumor that had circulated around the track when I announced that I was pregnant with Sasha. Some people said that I had shown already that I would stop at nothing to achieve my goal of becoming the fastest woman sprinter in the world. They whispered that I'd probably gotten pregnant to try out the Soviet theory of natural testosterone generation. It was a hurtful rumor. How little they knew that if I'd coldly wanted to experiment with natural testosterone, I would have prolonged the first pregnancy, in Guadeloupe, so I would be better prepared for the 1984 Olympics in Los Angeles.

There was no doubt that my performance did change after I had Sasha. I knew I was stronger; I could feel it. But I didn't know if it was because of Jamie's new mystery drug, estragol, or my imitation of BJ's workouts. My starts had begun to improve dramatically, though now my endurance was suffering. I had reversed my previous problems; now, I had a great start and a lousy finish. I began to think I should concentrate on competing only at the shorter distances of 50-, 60-, and 100-metres. The 200-metres could wait until I was a little older, with less strength and speed but a more seasoned technique. For now, the main benefit from having Sasha was her sweet disposition. She soothed me.

I went ahead and entered whatever competitions I could, building toward the 1986 Nationals. Because I had taken the year off, I didn't have enough merit points to enter anything big, like the European meets. I ran against some junior boys in a high school meet at Centennial Park in Etobicoke and came fifth with 11.36 in the 100-metres. I toted Sasha along to a meet at Brigham Young University in Provo, Utah, and improved my time to 11.19 or 11.20. I'll never know exactly because the timer conked out on us. In the meantime, BJ entered the Bruce Jenner Classic in the U.S. and trashed everybody with 10.01 in the 100-metres. Carl Lewis trailed behind at 10.18. Ben was on his way.

At last, the Nationals arrived. On a crystal clear June morning, I loaded Sasha and all her gear into Charlie's car and off we went. I was so nervous, I couldn't eat, and Sasha must have picked up on my nerves because she got fussy. But I was ready. I'd worked hard on my comeback and it showed. I came first in the 100-metres with 11.08, though it was wind-assisted, and I finished first in the 200-metres, in 22.88. I was on my way to the Commonwealth Games in Edinburgh; I was back in the game. On the way home, Charlie and I sang along with some old songs on the radio with the breeze in our hair, and Sasha clapped her hands — for the first time!

I found out later that three athletes had been caught in doping controls at the Nationals. "Well, the shit will surely hit the fan," I wrote in my diary. But it didn't. Not yet.

I have fond memories of the season surrounding the 1986 Commonwealth Games. I was pleased by my re-entry into the international circuit, and it began to pay immediate dividends. New

Balance, a company that makes athletic footwear, approached me with an interest in sponsorship the following season. In the short term, they were willing to pay me bonuses for wearing their shoes at the Commonwealth Games. Here follows the kind of inspiration amateur athletes like to add to their pure love of the sport: $2,500 for a gold medal, $1,000 for a silver medal, $750 for a bronze medal, $5,000 for a new world record, $2,500 for a new Commonwealth record, $1,000 for a new Canadian record.

But the real reason for my happiness that July had little to do with money or my career. As soon as I found out I would be going to Edinburgh, with a warm-up meet scheduled for Birmingham, I called Grandmother Vasthie. I had not seen her since that unfortunate visit when I was still a teenager and Olive and I were throwing dishes at one another. Grandmother Vasthie lives with her husband, Byron Harris, in Birmingham, an industrial city in central England. She invited me to bring Sasha for a month-long stay while I attended the Commonwealth Games and the meets scheduled in Europe. I took a deep breath and called my mother to ask her if she'd like to help care for Sasha and stay with Vasthie, too. She could return home with Sasha, leaving me to be flexible with any last-minute invitations to compete. Olive was delighted; she had never been overseas.

On July 6, I packed up Sasha and we left for Europe. I had found some dry packets of baby food made by Heinz that were lightweight, and I planned to buy a collapsible stroller when I got there. I worried about the five-and-a-half hour layover in London, on our way to East Berlin, but Sasha was good as gold. Ben and Charlie had left a few days before to attend the Goodwill Games in Moscow put together by Ted Turner, the Atlanta media magnate. The first bit of news I got when we arrived in Berlin was that BJ had won the 100-metres with 9.95, the fastest time ever recorded at sea level. Outrageous! That made him *numero uno* in the world, for sure.

I had been entered in a meet in East Berlin and did reasonably well with a first-place finish in the 100-metres, in 11.28 seconds. Traveling with Sasha made me less the loner I had always been on these trips, and I took her for a stroll-about downtown. For the first time, I realized how frightened the locals were of making contact with foreigners. One shopkeeper told me that East Berlin residents risked a $1,000 fine if they were caught visiting a foreigner in a hotel room. I wondered how on earth people could live like that, with those silly, Draconian curbs on their freedom. I got my answer, along with everyone else in the world, three years later: they couldn't.

I called Grandmother Vasthie as soon as we reached the athletes' dormitory in Birmingham. Sasha and I jumped into a taxi, and soon enough, we were standing at her front door. My grandmother and her husband live in a tidy little townhouse, typical to the area, with a gate that opens directly onto the street. They both were ailing a bit, Vasthie with diabetes and Byron with arthritis, but Byron loved to take Sasha along for his daily morning walks.

My mother arrived a few days later, and for the first time in her life, Sasha got to see her mother, her grandmother, and her great-grandmother under the same roof. Before I left, Grandmother Vasthie gave me her wedding ring as a keepsake, and I have worn it ever since. We didn't do much, really, besides talk and make a visit to Vasthie's brother's house. I found out that during all those years when she sent me dresses in Jamaica and presents in Canada, she had bought them with money she had scrimped from her job at a local nursing home. There was a great deal of love in the air in that little townhouse in Birmingham.

I did well at the Commonwealth Games, winning a gold medal in the 200-metres, a bronze in the 100-metres, and silver in the four-by-100-metre relay. My times still were slow, for me, but I was pleasantly surprised by my stamina in the 200-metres. The meet invitations began to arrive – Gateshead, London, Zurich, Berlin – then, later in the summer, Lausanne, Brussels, and London again. The recovery from my year off was complete.

There had been a major change in the way the top athletes in York Optimists had their competition schedules organized. Early in 1986, Charlie had received a call from a man named Larry Heidebrecht, who had worked as an agent for International Management Group, a major American sport agent and event-organizing firm. Heidebrecht had joined a new competing agency called Heritage Sports, and he wanted to drum up business. He was interested in becoming BJ's agent. Charlie told him to consider taking on me and Charmaine Crooks as well. He had confidence that the two of us were heading for a good year.

In 1985, the International Amateur Athletic Federation ruled that corporations could sponsor various track clubs so long as certain rules were followed. For example, in Canada, all the sponsorship money, even if directed at individual athletes, had to be paid into the Athletic Reserve Fund.

The fund kept an account in each member athlete's name and issued a monthly cheque to the individual for up to $1,000, depending on how much had been deposited into the account. In order to get access to more than the monthly minimum, we had to submit invoices or receipts. As the deposits got larger and athletes acquired costly monthly payments such as mortgages, the monthly maximum was raised to $3,000. Periodically, we'd get a statement showing our debits and credits. In theory, the system worked smoothly, but in practice, because the fund made its payments in the middle of the month and most bills were due before that, we often had to borrow money from our track club, via Ross Earl, to make ends meet.

Heidebrecht was confident that he could get sponsorship funding from the huge multinational firm of Mazda Corporation of Japan. In return Mazda wanted us to adhere to certain performance schedules, wear clothing with the Mazda logo displayed, and be available for promotional appearances.

Heidebrecht managed to strike a deal with Mazda that was worth $1,000 a month to me. Ben got more. As a result, the three of us became known as the Mazda Optimists when we performed outside Canada on the international circuit. During the summer of 1986, Ben's times got to be so fantastic that he became a superstar in Japan, and Heidebrecht renegotiated the deal with Mazda to tie it more closely to his world rankings. As well, Tony Sharpe, Desai Williams, Molly Killingbeck, and Mark McKoy joined our elite group. We were to pay Heritage 10 per cent of our income from the Mazda sponsorship and any appearance fees Heidebrecht negotiated. I didn't know it at the time, but the Canadian Track and Field Association also took a $10,000 flat fee and 10 per cent of the total interest earned by the Athletic Reserve Fund every year. I guess they reasoned that it was a big pie, so why not stick a finger in it?

After the Commonwealth Games, I became one of Mazda's official ambassadors, and Heidebrecht had plenty of inspiration to load on a schedule of meets. The immediate effect of all these high-powered negotiations seemed innocuous enough: I scribbled down the appearance fees next to each race, mostly because I had to remember to calculate a 10 per cent commission for Heidebrecht.

But the long-term effect had begun to develop an ugly face already. We found out at the Dubin Inquiry that Desai Williams had turned informer by calling Glenn Bogue, the athlete services representative at the Athletic Reserve Fund, with news of our steroid use. As far as we could tell, Desai did it in a fit of jealousy when Mazda signed up Ben, Charmaine, and me, though as far as I knew Charmaine never used steroids. I'd love to know some day how Desai back-pedaled with Bogue when Mazda signed him on, too. Maybe he didn't have to; Bogue quit shortly after.

Our deal with Mazda turned other eyes green with jealousy, too. Angela Bailey began to openly accuse the Mazda sprinters of steroid use, but I'm convinced her real beef had to do with money. She complained that she was being overlooked by sponsors. In an interview with Beverley Smith of *The Globe and Mail* on August 3, 1987, Bailey said: "I have no sponsors. Angella gets thousands of dollars and I get nothing. I'm not part of the Mazda team or Timex. They consider me nothing."

To give her credit, Bailey might have had a legitimate complaint regarding the Canadian Grand Prix circuit, which included the Harry Jerome meet in Vancouver. Apparently, the meet director told Bailey that he didn't need her to enter because he already had "the other Angella." Bailey called the Canadian Track and Field Association about it, but they said they couldn't help her. Incidents like this, usually based on envy, began to make people look for a way to bring the Mazda group down. By the time BJ tested positive at Seoul, we had all become paranoid over the back-stabbing that had gone on. Sabotage didn't seem out of the question at all.

By my twenty-eighth birthday, on September 28, 1986, I had earned my way back to a B-card, and I began to dream of buying a house for my little family. The only cloud on the horizon was Jamie's abrupt decision to leave Toronto and return to St. Kitts. It was a strange move, and the circumstances surrounding it were mysterious. A couple of us walked into his office one day to find the place demolished. Files everywhere, on the floor, thrown about. A lot of them had been damaged with water beyond reading. The funny thing was, several records remained intact. When we went to his house, Jamie pulled out my file and BJ's file and said, don't worry.

And then, he was gone.

At the end of 1986, I received my annual amateur athlete agreement with the Canadian Track and Field Association. My victories meant that I would be representing Canada again, and the contract was a necessary bit of paperwork. The agreement became an item of interest at the Dubin Inquiry when Robert Armstrong brought it out as Exhibit Number 127.

He took a sip of water before plunging in.

"I wanted to direct your attention to page four of this contract where the athlete's obligations are set out," Armstrong began. "It says, 'To avoid use of banned drugs in contravention of the IAAF rules set out in Appendix F and submit to dope control tests at competition.' "

Armstrong paused. I could see he wanted to highlight something for Dubin. "And then the following words are stroked out: 'Or, upon random request by CTFA, CTFA appointee or Sport Medicine Council of Canada during the competitive and/or non-competitive season.' And all those words that I've just read are stricken out," Armstrong said, looking directly at me. "When you signed the contract, did you strike out those words in relation to random doping control?"

I had, of course. Charlie told all his athletes to strike them out.

"And presumably you sent this contract in to the Canadian Track and Field Association?"

"Yes."

"Did you ever receive any complaint back from the Canadian Track and Field Association that you had removed from the athlete's obligations clause the random doping control requirement?"

"No."

This opened a can of worms at the inquiry, and one of my lawyers, Dennis O'Connor, grilled me about the contract again, on the third day of testimony.

"So I take it that what you are suggesting is that the silence from the CTFA, certainly as far as you were concerned, was a message — was a signal, when you crossed it out, that there would be a problem with in-training random testing, and their silence about that was an indicator to you that they must have suspected that you would have a problem with that?"

O'Connor's question was long and obviously composed for the record, but I was bursting with the answer. I'd been dying to get to this point for two days.

"That's correct," I said. "It also struck me as strange that there were always reports and accusations in the newspapers that the Mazda group were on anabolics. And if other athletes can figure that out and speak out in the newspapers, then certainly the CTFA, they read the newspapers, they must suspect that something was going on, but at no point did they decide that they would lead an investigation into these allegations."

At about the same time the CTFA contract arrived in the mail, Charlie passed on the astounding bit of gossip that a well-known thrower might be put in charge of random doping control in Canada. You can imagine our mirth. It was like inviting the fox in to play with the chickens. One way or another, though, between rumors of random doping controls being considered, and the pointed, if ignored, reference in our contracts, we had to come to terms with the fact that Canada might be considering a clampdown on steroid use during training.

Bourque, the lawyer for the CTFA and a testy man who did his best to make me look bad on the stand, addressed this and a few other things at the inquiry.

When he started, Bourque was ramrod stiff. "There is an entry in your diary, and you needn't refer to it. It's September 16, 1986. It's an entry that you had learned of the CTFA decision on out-of-competition testing was postponed to December first, 1986. Do you recall that?"

"Yes."

"And I believe it was at this point in your evidence that you spoke of a plan to train out of the country once the out-of-competition testing program had been implemented in Canada?"

"That's correct."

"Well, was this a plan that you were considering along with Mr. Francis?"

"That's correct."

"And to your knowledge were other athletes in on this discussion?"

"That's correct."

"Who were they?"

"The people in my group that were on anabolics that were going to St. Kitts. Mind you, I must also say that there were a couple of other athletes in that group that were not using steroids."

The fact is, Jamie had been successful in luring us down to a winter training camp on his own turf in St. Kitts. The conditions were abysmal, what with the heat, the mosquitos, and the rutted grass track. He seemed to have some wild idea that he could be a coach as well as a doctor.

"Right," Bourque said. "And just how definite was this plan at this stage in the fall of 1986?"

"I would say very definite."

"Was it definite enough that foreign training sites had been selected by you for various training periods in the year?"

"This was the first one, yes. If random doping control was instituted, we would, indeed, go away. But as you can see, random doping control was not instituted, but we went anyways."

"Right. And I believe you mentioned St. Kitts in what would be the winter months in Canada. Was it your intention under this plan, if it were carried out, to conduct your training and your steroid use in St. Kitts?"

"Well, training camps are not only for steroid use. As Charlie pointed out, we also needed to work out on grass."

"I will ask the question again, Ms Issajenko. Please pay attention."

Dubin was startled. "I think she's paying attention," he said.

"Well, don't get upset at me," I said to Bourque. I couldn't believe what I'd heard.

"She is not at all responsive, Mr. Commissioner," Bourque snapped.

Dubin pulled on his earlobe and eyed Bourque. "I thought she was," he said.

"No, she is not," said Bourque. "Let me ask you again . . ."

And so it went. I suppose Bourque might have wanted it on record that I was being uncooperative in some way. It was a dirty tactic, considering I had been the one to offer my testimony to the inquiry. I decided if I was going to fink on my friends, unlike Desai Williams the least I could do was do it publicly.

Then again, Bourque had a difficult task on his hands, trying to protect the credibility of the CTFA. He had a particularly hard time with the conduct of the CTFA director-general, Don Fletcher, and the CTFA chairman of the board of directors, Jean-Guy Ouellette. Fletcher had tipped Charlie off at least once before about whether the foreign meets were slated for testing. Ouellette was the organizer of the annual Sherbrooke meet in Quebec, and in return for his favors we collected only half the appearance money we were usually paid elsewhere. Ouellette kept Charlie informed about the status of plans to introduce in-training doping controls in Canada.

Bourque did his best to discredit my testimony:

"You have testified that Mr. Francis told you in June 1982 that he had called, as you put it this morning, a CTFA official and been advised that an upcoming meet in Yugoslavia was not going to be tested. Is that correct?"

"That's correct."

"Do you remember the official's name?"

"Mr. Don Fletcher."

"Now you also testified that every time Mr. Francis put a call through to Mr. Ouellette, you would hear about it because it affected you?"

"Regarding the problem of doping, yes."

"I am just asking you to confirm what you said this morning," said Bourque tersely. "So where Mr. Francis spoke to one of these CTFA officers, whenever he did that, he would then report on the conversation to you?"

"If it regarded doping, yes."

Dubin appeared to be impatient with Bourque. He looked down at Bourque standing at the lectern and said, "Which you would assume he would."

Dubin's interruption seemed to upset Bourque.

"I'm sorry?" Bourque said. I didn't think he was sorry at all.

"She would *assume*. She assumed he did," Dubin repeated.

"Yes," said Bourque, clearly peeved.

My lawyer, Dennis O'Connor, spoke up from his seat behind Bourque. "I think my question [earlier], in fairness, was that the [calls] Mr. Francis had testified to, and she said she had heard . . . it was those specific ones. I didn't say it could be every time because as you point out, she might not have known."

Bourque's voice became icy. "Let me ask you then, is that true with respect to all such conversations — "

Dubin cut him off again. "Why don't you ask her what specific conversation you're speaking about, Mr. Bourque?"

The point Bourque was trying to make, of course, was that I had heard about the tip-offs only through Charlie and that I had never spoken directly to either CTFA official. Perhaps he hoped it would make my testimony less believable. Bourque said he just wanted to clarify that I was not a party to these conversations. Dubin could not resist taking a poke at Bourque for his line of questioning.

"Nobody was quite clear, but I'm glad you're clearing it up."

Bourque was clear, all right. Transparent.

I began to train for the 1987 season in the first week of October 1986. There was a new policy in place up at York — I was no longer allowed to bring Sasha to the track. It was just as well. At one year old, she was getting to be a sprinter on all fours and much harder to keep an eye on. I took her to a baby-sitter for the first time in her life, though I missed her constantly. My little traveling companion had to stay behind.

I began to read voraciously again, mostly to pass the time on the long bus trip from High Park to York University in Downsview. Lucky for me, Tony's dad, Alex, was a retired professor of Russian literature, and I found a massive cache of good books stacked high on the shelves of the laundry room. I went through *The Gambler* and *Poor People* by Dostoyevsky, *Dead Souls* and *The Inspector General* by Nikolai Gogol, *The Stone Guest* by Pushkin, *The Power of Darkness* by Tolstoy, and others.

Perhaps food for the mind is good for the body, because 1987 turned out to be the pinnacle of my career. I flew among the stars in 1987, though no star would be as high as Ben's that year. And I reveled in my good fortune; I had money, I had talent, I had a family, and I had good friends. Charlie, generous as always, bought me a microwave oven for Christmas. On New Year's Eve, I wrote in my diary of Charlie: "I will repay him someday."

13

Me and Flo-Jo

The seeds of our destruction in Seoul were sowed in the charmed lives we led in 1987. If ever there was a time when Mr. Justice Charles Dubin's assertion was true, that we led "nice" lives as gallivanters of the world, it was 1987. It was the year Ben bought a $25,000 solid gold Cartier watch; the year the Japanese held banquets in our honor; the year we stayed in hotels furnished with antiques, ceiling murals, and soft, thick carpets.

On the track I set world records which made me the fastest woman on the planet over the distances of 50 metres and 50 yards, indoors. I also broke my own Canadian record in the 100-metres five times over. And on one memorable afternoon, Florence Griffith-Joyner, beautiful Flo-Jo as she would soon be known throughout the world, danced with me in a joyous circle in Cologne, West Germany.

But the details will have to wait because I have a confession to make.

I have no rational explanation for my visions. It's as though I can't shake the voodoo and obeah I absorbed with the heat and dust of Jamaica in my girlhood. I am a modern woman, skeptical of dogma and superstition. Usually I scorn talk of ghosts and apparitions, except, perhaps, as figures in literature. But these visions haunt me and are as real as the ghost I saw through my bedsheet after my great-grandmother died. Perhaps if I share the visions with you, I will drive them away. I want to. They frighten me.

It first happened soon after Sasha was born, when we lived in the one-bedroom apartment at Tony's father's house. I had gone to bed and Tony was watching television in the living room, stretched out on the couch. Tony often falls asleep in front of the TV; he's a great fan of old movies. I was lying there and I can't tell you if I was awake or asleep, but a face appeared and floated directly over mine. It was the face of an old man with wispy white hair to his shoulders. I tried to scream for help, but no sound would come out.

It happened again, in March of 1987, as I lay in my hotel room in Osaka.

I would like to think that it was because I had just come off a busy if highly successful indoor season, starting in Perth, Australia. At the Swan Premium Challenge, I had run 11.21 in the 100-metres, for first place; two days later, I ran a wind-aided 10.8 in the 100-metres to win an international meet.

BJ was there, rated the world's fastest human after his victory over Carl Lewis at the Goodwill Games in Moscow the summer before. Early in January, in Japan, Ben set a world record of 6.44 seconds for the 60-metre indoor dash. In Perth, he ran the 100-metres in the sizzling, wind-aided time of 9.7 seconds. Neither of us could register our breakthrough times with the International Amateur Athletic Federation because of the wind and because the races were hand-timed. But we were the darlings of the circuit; we nearly convinced the authorities to set up a 100-metre race between the two of us, giving me a handicap. I told BJ I wouldn't need much of a handicap to beat him.

BJ and I were flying. When we got home, we went to the Winter National Games in Ottawa, at the end of January, and I set the world record in the 50-metres with a time of 6.06 seconds, beating the old record of 6.11, set by Marita Koch in September 1983 in East Germany. This achievement became the second of three plaques under my name on the Wall of Fame at York University. The crowd of 7,400 at the Ottawa Civic Centre had come to see if Ben could set another world record in the 50-metres, which was a rarely run distance for the men. He did just that, with a time of 5.44 seconds. I went on to the annual meet in Sherbrooke, to set a Canadian record of 7.15 seconds in the 60-metre sprint.

And so it went that winter, with a succession of wins for BJ and me, and a growing fanaticism about Ben's world status. The newspapers began to stage promotional sprints, with BJ lined up against roly-poly reporters, and against schoolchildren for the "thrill of a lifetime." At the National Indoor Championships in Edmonton at the end of February, BJ equaled his world record of 6.44 seconds in the 60-metres, and I broke my own Canadian record in the 60-metres with a time of 7.13 seconds.

Just before we left for Osaka, BJ and I attended the World Indoor Championships in Indianapolis. BJ broke his own world record with 6.41 seconds in the 60-metres. The officials had to inspect taped reruns of the start because they thought Ben had anticipated the gun. He ran the race so fast, he couldn't stop in the distance available at the Hoosier Dome and flipped over a chest-high barrier at the end of the track. BJ landed flat on his back on a cement floor seven feet below, but he jumped up – RoboCop-style – and shook hands with Carl Lewis. Lewis had not qualified for the race and was simply there to see BJ run.

As for my performance in Indianapolis, I tied for first place with Nelli Cooman-Fiere of the Netherlands with 7.08 in the 60-metre sprint, again breaking my own Canadian record. But the judges gave her first place after inspecting a photo that showed Cooman-Fiere's shoulder was one one-thousandth of a second ahead of my chest. It was a shock because I had been acknowledged the winner and I was surrounded by reporters, giving my victory speech, when the new decision came through. I was given a silver medal, and this achievement became the third and final plaque under my name on the Wall of Fame at York.

Even Mark McKoy had problems in Indianapolis. His were more spectacular than either mine or Ben's. The next day, the papers were full of photos showing him crashing to the ground with Greg Foster of the U.S. in the 60-metre hurdle final. They had drifted into one another and Mark ended up with a badly bruised hip and spike gouges up and down his legs. We Canadians had a time at the Hoosier!

We left for Japan on March 11. Our itinerary took us on flights to Toronto, through San Francisco to Osaka, then a one-hour drive to a seaport just outside Osaka called Kobe. It took us nearly twenty hours, and we were traveling forward in time zones thirteen hours, so I may have been suffering from exhaustion and jet lag. My sciatica flared after the hours of sitting strapped in a cramped airplane seat.

I am looking for rational explanations, but I'm not sure there are any. I had drawn shut all the blinds in my hotel room, hoping to recuperate with a good night's sleep. In the early morning hours, just before dawn, the face appeared again, though I couldn't see it clearly this time. It hovered just beyond my reach, not that I would have or could have touched it. My body felt numb, paralyzed; I tried to move but I couldn't. It was as though an invisible force pinned me down. Again, I tried to say something, but no words came. I felt very strongly that this vision meant me harm. My only defence, I thought, was to stay awake, so it couldn't creep in again and hurt me. I was frozen in my bed until morning when the maid came with tea and hot towels. She opened the curtains, then turned to me, smiling, and said, "You go big banquet tonight, Miss?"

My third vision happened a year later, in 1988, when we were in West Germany. This time, the old man with the flowing white hair slapped me, hard, across the face. My life had become very complicated by then. Visions weren't the only things threatening me.

Those of us who followed Jamie's advice continued on our cycles of estragol injections, mixed with megadoses of calcium, minerals, and vitamins. I wasn't always faithful about taking the supplements, though not for any particular reason. I paid for it by feeling lousy most of the time. I was perpetually tired and in more or less constant pain of one kind or another. The bursitis in my feet meant that I was always trying some new brand of anti-inflammatory, and I tried to take suppositories to soothe my stomach. My face was breaking out because of the estragol, and occasionally I resorted to antibiotics to clear it up. I also tried every product available through cosmetic companies to improve my complexion, but none of them helped.

One winter day in 1987, I ate a piece of rotten tomato and felt sick to my stomach. At least, I think it was the tomato. It might also have been my daily mixture of Aspirins, vitamins, anti-inflammatories, estragol — or forgetting to take my birth control pill one day and doubling up the next. Then again, I was feeling raw after a treatment at seven in the morning at the chiropractor's clinic for my sciatic nerve. And after my workout that morning, Waldemar had given me a thorough stretch, massage and interferential session. Maybe it was the tomato, maybe it wasn't. The estragol had puffed me up to 153 pounds, and I felt heavy and water-logged.

I had tried, without success, to replace Jamie with a doctor he recommended before he left so suddenly for St. Kitts. I needed a doctor for me and for Sasha. I got along with Jamie's friend reasonably well, but he said he disliked estragol because it was too androgenic. He favored testosterone. I still feared testosterone and I didn't want to switch, so I stopped seeing him. It became obvious that Charlie could still get estragol if we needed it, through Jamie, and I switched to a local general practitioner for day-to-day health matters. The fact is, Jamie had left us a huge supply of estragol when he fled to St. Kitts. Charlie had about twenty bottles in a briefcase that he kept in his bedroom at home. Later, we moved the briefcase to my house.

We thought it was stupid of Jamie to have left the estragol. We had begun to suspect that he was interested in making us dependent on him – that's why there were no labels on the bottles, so we couldn't find a supplier of our own. And he used to mix what he called a "concoction" of estragol with a vitamin B-12 compound. But then he went and left enough pure estragol that we might never need him again. He also sold Charlie a supply of the anti-inflammatory inosine.

We were still following Jamie's recommendations after he left Canada, and he had started us off in the fall of 1986 by prescribing Winstrol in pill form. I didn't want to take Winstrol, so I replaced it with Dianabol. The idea was to lay a kind of "base" in our systems for about ten days, to prepare for the injections of estragol that started in January. We followed the same plan in the fall of 1987. With Jamie gone, it fell to my Tosha to give me the injections of both estragol and inosine. Tony wasn't crazy about the idea, but it was hard to argue with the success I had during that indoor season.

I continued with my regimen of food for the mind that winter. I really had begun to suffer for lack of intellectual stimulation, and I cut a wide swath through Alex's books in the laundry room. In January alone, I read *Mother* by Maxim Gorky, *Wicked Angel* by Taylor Caldwell, and *Candide* by Voltaire. Alex gave me a list of other novels by Gorky and I read my way through them, back and forth on the bus to York.

As I have mentioned, I have an obsessive personality. It is what kept me going in track, what made me win. The winter of 1987, I was obsessed by reading. After Gorky, I went on to short novel masterpieces, also recommended by Alex: *The Childhood of Zhenya Luvens* by Pasternak, *Father Sergius* by Tolstoy, *Ward 6* by Chekhov, *The Story of How Ivan Ivanovich Quarrelled with Ivan Nikiforovich* by Gogol, and *A Dilemma* by Leonid Andreyev.

At the beginning of May 1987, I was entered in a meet at York University when my sciatic nerve acted up so badly I had to withdraw from a race. In the haze of pain, I suddenly realized that I must have been overdoing the estragol, that my weight was too high and it was causing the imbalance in my posture again. One morning at the track, Charlie told me that I looked much bigger. I'd also been suffering from extreme stiffness. Again, I identified my reaction to estragol as remarkably similar to my reaction to Winstrol, but it was no more than a passing thought. I immediately cut my injections down from one cc to a quarter cc, and I asked Charlie to try to find out something more on the composition of estragol. Any information would be satisfactory; I had not been able to find reference to it in my copy of the *Compendium* or anywhere else.

We traveled the world during June and July, shooting over to Italy and England, then back to Utah and over to Spain, then home and off again to Athens, where Ben bought his solid gold watch, then Fürth and Florence. One organizer flew us to a meet in a helicopter, another offered a private jet. I won every race I ran, except for a meet in Seville, when I finished second. An odd thing happened in Seville, just at the point I thought I'd seen it all when it came to steroids. An American sprinter, a woman, had arrived to compete not knowing there were doping controls in place. She won her race and realized she would be tested. We were mystified when someone got her a bottle of vinegar and she drank it on the spot. Either it worked, or the meet organizers didn't bother publicizing the positive results, because I didn't hear anything about her being caught. It certainly caused a buzz among the athletes. I don't know which one of us passed on the information to Jamie.

For all my success in Europe, I wasn't happy with my times. It didn't seem to matter if I ran 11.24 or 11.61, I still won, but I had my sights fixed on knocking off Evelyn Ashford's 10.87 world record in the 100-metres. I was determined to get under 11 and have it officially recognized. Then, at a meet in Budapest on July 7, that I had not entered, Angela Bailey hit 10.98 in the 100-metres, setting a new Canadian record. "The Midget" (as I called her in my diary) had struck again!

I told the reporter that the conditions must have been tremendously favorable in Budapest for Bailey to have run that fast. Then I made the colossal error of saying, "Obviously, if I had been in Budapest I would have run faster than 10.98." Almost every sprinter in that meet set personal-best times, and most of them never came close to those times again. I said that I wished I had been there, because I would have run under 11 seconds as well and I would have benefited from the conditions, too. The reporter asked if I meant to say I would have beaten Bailey and I replied, "Of course." Well! The feathers flew. I swear I could hear the Midget's teeth gnashing from across the Atlantic.

Things once again came to a head between us at the National Outdoor Championships in Ottawa on the first weekend of August. The championships, which were also the Olympic trials, were held at the new Terry Fox Centre. Bailey's coach told someone that in his opinion I was "history." I made a little note in my diary: "Oh well, one needs an idiot like that, for motivation." Then, I heard that Bailey had told a reporter that she did not care for me.

"Well, fuck her," I wrote.

The next day, I blasted down the track in the 100-metres to win with a time of 11.08, leaving Bailey to eat my dust, a distant second at 11.27. It was my seventh Canadian championship in ten years. Bailey refused to come up on the stand and accept her silver medal during the award ceremonies. She told a reporter that she was devastated, that maybe an antibiotic she had been taking for a bout of bronchitis had affected her performance. As for me, I opened my fat mouth and said the obvious: "It was not a question of whether I was going to win or lose, but how much I was going to win by." My casual remarks must have sounded insufferably patronizing and probably sent Bailey into paroxysms of rage, but, you know, we all played head games from time to time. Why did she tell a reporter, just before the meet, that she didn't like me? She probably thought it would throw me. The next day, I blasted down the track again in the 200-metres and won in 22.90. Bailey came second again, in 23.28.

The world press had come to Ottawa *en masse* to see Ben, to check on how he had recovered, if he had recovered, from his injuries earlier in the year. In St. Kitts, Jamie made Ben run forward and backward in seawater, 3,000 metres a day, to exercise his muscles without straining them. Thoroughbred race horses sometimes are put through the same regimen. Ben looked fine. Charlie hand-timed him over 100 metres in 9.28, which he said would be about 9.90 electronically timed.

After the Nationals, we took off again for Europe, and I came out of the blocks with a couple of first-place finishes ahead of Flo-Jo, who was touring with the U.S. team. Florence Griffith-Joyner was not yet the glamour girl she became at the 1988 Olympics in Seoul, but she had always been exotic-looking, and a free spirit. I liked her in a lot of ways. She was never petty the way some other sprinters could be, never precious. Flo-Jo had her sights set on being number one in the world, just like Ben, just like me, and it made her a fine competitor. And she really was pretty, though I never saw her flaunt it.

Flo-Jo and I talked in Switzerland, and again on the trip to Cologne. Cologne was shaping up to be one of the more important meets on the 1987 European tour, with Merlene Ottey among the competitors. As it turned out, both Flo-Jo and I were lusting after an official time under 11 seconds flat. And, my God, we did it! The track conditions were tremendous. Ottey ran 10.93 in the 100-metres. Flo-Jo came second with 10.96, and I came third with 10.97. At the finish line, we seized one another in a big bear hug and danced round and round, laughing, howling. Ottey must have thought we were nuts.

It had taken Bailey five years to break my 100-metres Canadian record, with her sensational 10.98 sprint in Budapest. But a mere three weeks later, I ran the distance in 10.97 and regained the title as the fastest woman in Canada. Bailey has never really spoken to me again.

By the World Outdoor Championships in Rome, scheduled for the last weekend in August 1987, I was missing my little family badly. Sasha would be two years old on September first. I'd been on the road since August 5, and Larry Heidebrecht had us booked from here to kingdom come – sometime at the end of September. The last time I had seen Sasha, her worried dark eyes had followed me every minute, and I'm sure she was afraid I'd drop out of sight again. Tony hired someone to work at the store each morning so he could spend more time with her. I sent for Tony and Sasha and they came to Rome, along with Olive, who said she'd be happy to help out with baby-sitting again.

We checked into the Hotel Turner, an elegant place in the center of Rome, with marble floors and exquisite antiques. By now, Larry was selling our appearances as a package deal, with BJ as the centerpiece, and there were plenty of perks as a result. Management at the Hotel Turner gave us a half-price rate for single rooms, at $70. If Ben won at the Championships, the rooms would be free.

No one doubted Ben would win. The mood of the Mazda athletes had changed dramatically from those early days when we set him up for practical jokes.

I reveled in having my little girl with me again, just like the days when she was a baby and I lugged around diapers and a bottle. Olive seemed to enjoy herself, and Tosha looked terrific in some new clothes we bought. On September 1, we celebrated Sasha's second birthday, and she got cards and gifts and streamers from everybody on the team. My family's presence didn't do my concentration any favors, though. I went through two heats in the 100-metres at the Championships, and flew with 10.99 for second in the semifinal. By the final, however, I dropped to fifth, in a time of 11.09. BJ, on the other hand, trounced Carl Lewis in the men's 100-metres final. Lewis came second, in 9.93 seconds, but Ben ran a phenomenal 9.83, for a world record.

Free rooms!

Before they even got on the plane for home, a week later, I knew that I couldn't put the blame entirely on my family for my lack of focus. The real reason I couldn't see my way to a first-place finish was because dollar signs clouded my vision. Before I reached the track for my warm-ups, I was calculating what I would make from each race for appearance, placement, any records I set, as well as the sponsorship money.

Just before we left for Rome, I made the most money from a single race in my career at a meet in Zurich: $3,250 in appearance money, another $5,000 for winning the 100-metres in 11.03. This was peanuts compared to what BJ and Carl Lewis were getting — $20,000 . . . $25,000. In my diary I wrote that the money Ben was pulling in was "mind boggling." I also noted that the money was hurting my concentration. Figures kept running through my head, but they were the wrong kind of figures. Where once I took aim at seconds and hundredths of seconds, now I toted up columns of figures, all of them with dollar signs.

Running had become a business. We'd always suffered the pressure of wanting to control our bodies and meet conditions so that we could perform at our best, but now more people depended on us, and our dreams were more elaborate. Now, we went as an entourage, like rock stars, with Waldemar the masseur, Charlie the coach, and Larry the agent. To our surprise, even Jamie the doctor showed up in Rome in 1987. We heard later that he was circulating among the European athletes, emphasizing his relationship with us, and especially Ben, the star performer. We found out that he was offering to help them, for a 10 per cent cut, with steroids and his holistic approach to vitamins and minerals.

Other people were counting on us, too. Just as he had worked with me when I joined the Scarborough Optimists, Charlie continued to attract younger athletes into the club and bring them along. He pressed Larry to negotiate package deals with meet promoters and Mazda that would allow for a little extra money for these newcomers. Charlie suggested $300 each, so they could attend meets in Europe and gain international experience. I was sympathetic to his goals; I remembered how good he had been to me when I was raw. BJ got upset about it, though. Soon he was grumbling about all these "hangers-on." I thought he was being selfish, considering the money he was making.

At the end of 1987, however, BJ got a little generous and paid Charlie a $20,000 bonus. He also gave Waldemar a $5,000 bonus. Larry Heidebrecht renegotiated our contract with Heritage Sports. Ben's fees would go up in 1988 if he significantly improved his world rankings. As a result, we all would make more money. Heidebrecht's commission would rise to 20 per cent of contracts and 10 per cent of meets.

As far as we knew, Charlie was getting only his salary as a paid coach of the Canadian Track and Field Association, plus a small percentage, 1 or 2 per cent, of the contracts. Charlie never got greedy like the rest of them.

We were in no hurry to shut the business down, as we normally would have done after the World Championships in Rome. Larry had booked us straight through to the end of September. *Track & Field* magazine had just come out, with Ben ranked first in the world in the men's 100-metres, and me ranked fourth in the women's 100-metres. When we set off for London, I didn't care how I finished in the race, or what time I ran. I just wanted my appearance money. I finished third, in 11.34 seconds. I had decided that this was my chance to start preparing for a future after my career in track.

We went on to Lausanne, where I came third again, then to Sardinia, where we arrived three hours before the race. I ran the 200-metres in 23.47, but I didn't bother to note the headwind. "Don't know, don't care," I wrote in my diary. Then, on to Monte Carlo, where I came fourth with 11.37. Monte Carlo is a beautiful place, I'm told, but I didn't see much of it. Ben, Desai, and Tony Sharpe went off to the casino, though, to try their luck. Tony used his own system because he didn't think the others knew what they were doing, but Desai followed Ben's advice and won $5,000. We flew out immediately for Japan in a killing itinerary, hopping from Nice to Paris to London to Tokyo. In Tokyo, I managed to come second in the 100-metres with 11.36. I was exhausted.

I lashed out at Charlie, blaming him for poor training, and I said he was the reason I wasn't first in the world, like Ben. One day I shouted at him, "I hate you! What makes you think you're so smart, all of a sudden, with Ben? Did you get a brain transplant?"

We were all exhausted, strung-out. Desai and Mark got into some other fight, I forget what it was about. And on the plane returning from Tokyo, Gerard Mach sat with us and started to cry because he had read some newspaper reporter's harsh assessment of his skills as a coach. I wrote in my diary, in furious handwriting: "My God, I have deteriorated so fast."

And then we were home. As we circled Toronto in the night sky I looked down on the lights of the city, thinking of Tony and Sasha, and calculating my figures again. I could not even rally to celebrate my birthday on September 28. I turned twenty-nine, but I felt much older.

In all the years I had been in track, Charlie always made me take two weeks off at the end of every season. Usually, at the end of the first week, I got bored and started hanging around the track again. Not this time; in the fall of 1987, I took thirty-two days off. I could feel my muscles become disgustingly soft. I was chosen to help bear the Olympic flame in Toronto as it made its way across the country to light the torch in Calgary at the upcoming Winter Games. I don't know how I was able to carry it off. I had so many other things on my mind.

For one thing, we bought a house. Regardless of the money I made as the tail of Ben's comet, it was still an enormous risk. I took on a $250,000 mortgage, based on the income I would make from tenants already living there. The house was a "fixer-upper," but Tony's maternal grandfather, Dadushka Misha, had come to Canada with skills as a painter and plasterer, and he promised to help. I put every penny I owned into the house and still had to resort to taking out a $30,000 second mortgage. Tony's dad let him temporarily suspend payments on an outstanding loan we had needed for the store. I borrowed money from friends, and Grandmother Vasthie, bless her, sent us a contribution to the downpayment, all saved from what she earned working at the nursing home in England. I spent sleepless nights juggling figures in my head.

My life as the owner of a house, landlady, mother, wife, and athlete had become bewilderingly complicated. Amateur athletics is a selfish master. With all the distraction and worry, I found it hard to return to training in the fall of 1987. Every day, a new crisis popped up: a tenant moved out, the basement flooded, Sasha developed croup, Tony had to renegotiate a loan, we had to haul furniture through a second-floor window, Olive and I had another noisy fight, Charlie's dad died. It was just life, of course, the ordinary ebb and flow of living. But track and field had never allowed me a normal life. I had no experience with normal life. I looked back longingly to when I had lived in my little apartment near the university, the one on the "penthouse" floor, when I had no one to worry about but myself.

By November 16, Tony's twenty-third birthday, my nerves were so bad that my sciatica erupted again, and I made an appointment to see Morris Zubkewych, the chiropractor. This time, he stuck a pin in my ear, using acupuncture to bring me some relief. We never did get around to celebrating Tony's birthday.

I paid for my stressful fall with a poor indoor season in the winter of 1987–88. I had to start taking injectable anti-inflammatories for my bursitis, which seemed worse than ever. According to plan, several of us went on Astaphan's regimen of building a base with Dianabol – the others took Winstrol – then switched to injections of estragol. I kept to the lower dosage of a quarter cc per injection. But my body was not responding well. I was constantly tired.

Complicated as life was at home, it became equally complicated at the track. It was no longer good enough just to do the workouts. BJ was a star, the fastest man on earth, and it was important that the chorus line kicked in. During a single week in January, we attended two press conferences, a television taping, a meet in Hamilton, and a meet in Vancouver, along with the grueling daily workouts. I ran badly in both meets and wrote in my diary: "My God, I stink."

By mid-January, I had run in two more meets – Sherbrooke and the Winter Nationals in Ottawa – but I still was dragging around with poor times and second- and third-place finishes. Charlie lit into me one day, told me I was out of shape and weak-minded. I was infuriated, but there was some truth in his accusations. I began to study BJ closely, not for his physical training secret but for his mental weaponry.

We had discovered that the formerly skinny little guy with a shy stutter had a will of iron. Ben believed with every fiber of his being that he would win any race he entered. We had chided him, when he was still running in the 10.20s, when he announced that he would beat Carl Lewis by the next year. Most athletes are pretty cocky, if only to keep themselves motivated, psyched up, but Ben *believed* it, and it happened. If you mentioned something to him like "improving on performance" or "seeing how a race would go," he would fix you with a blank, uncomprehending stare as though you were speaking a foreign language. BJ would win, end of discussion. I began to concentrate more on my own positive mental attitude.

I got help with my mental conditioning from Sue Wilson, a sport psychology consultant who had been hired by York University. A lot of the guys thought her approach was kind of silly, and at first I was skeptical, yet my sessions with her helped. Sue made me concentrate on a particular muscle group, then guided me through the exercise of mentally "visualizing" the blood flowing from my heart, through my veins and the tiny capillaries to the injured area. She coaxed me to close my eyes and imagine the lactic acid and tightness leaving my muscles, washed away and replenished by rich, red blood. She said it would help me recuperate faster, and the muscles would regenerate. I found it relaxing.

After my sessions with Sue, Charlie told me to get my ass in gear. "You can have the greatest head in the world," he said, "but if you're not prepared from the neck down you're not going to do shit."

Neither head work nor body work could shake my lethargy, though, and I continued to drag through my workouts. I went to our family doctor for tests, thinking perhaps my trouble with anemia had returned. Waldemar suggested that I try eating steak tartare for a hit of pure protein. Steak tartare is a fancy word for raw meat, served in a hideous red mound in the middle of your plate. I found it repulsive. I wasn't a vegetarian, but I never did eat much meat. If a chef knows how to spice steak tartare properly, it can be almost palatable, but the texture, like mud through your toes, turns me off. And it's always the most expensive thing on the menu. I tried it once and thanked Waldemar for his advice: thanks, but no thanks.

To our great sorrow, on January 28, Tony's grandfather, Dadushka Grisha, passed away. Tony fell into quiet mourning, and I had to ask Charlie to pick me up and drive me to the track or I wouldn't have been able to force myself to go.

I was surprised to see Jamie Astaphan there. He did, occasionally, show up in Toronto, but we usually knew when to expect him. We chatted for a while and I explained some of my troubles. After I'd done some warm-up exercises, Jamie reached over and grasped my lower thigh with his thumb and forefingers.

"Your synapse is not firing," he said.

I didn't know what he was talking about, but I didn't say anything. I'd heard it all by now — imagining blood in my veins, eating raw meat, conjuring a positive mental attitude. Why not this? Jamie said he would bring around some vitamins that would fix me up. Sure. I went on with my workout.

I had become wary of Jamie, though I did not share these feelings with anyone. When I had asked Charlie to find out what he could about estragol, he had come back with a strange answer. I had been puzzling over it ever since. Charlie said the only reference he could find to estragol was that it was a cleansing agent, perhaps like *DMSO*.

He also told me that a Bulgarian athlete had mentioned how Jamie offered his services to European athletes in Rome in the summer of 1987. According to this Bulgarian, Jamie told them his combination of vitamins, minerals — and Winstrol — worked wonders. Charlie wasn't sure that the Bulgarian fully understood what Jamie had said.

What we didn't know, and didn't find out until it came out at the Dubin Inquiry, was that Jamie had begun to tape our telephone calls with him. It was natural for him to ask about the supply of estragol and natural for us to respond to his questions. It is interesting to speculate what Jamie might have done with the tapes if the inquiry hadn't been called.

It would have been impossible to openly reveal my growing suspicions about Jamie. To criticize Jamie would have been to criticize his medicinal concoctions: a key to BJ's success. Who could argue with that? What was good for BJ was good for all of us, and there was no better reminder than the sponsorship packages and group promotions that Larry kept digging up. I say a lot of this in retrospect because at the time I believed much of this myself. It did not occur to me that the brutal workouts and heavy drug dosages were perfectly tailored to BJ's physique and nobody else's. I had not even told anyone about cutting back my estragol injections to a quarter cc for fear of stepping out of the party line. BJ was winning; ergo, BJ's regimen must be right.

The next day, Jamie showed up at the track again, this time with a bag full of vitamins and instructions on how to take them. He had calcium tablets, zinc and enzyme tablets, and something called D.M.G. (to be taken one hour before a race). He also had carnitine (an amino acid), folic acid, vitamin E, iron, and multivitamin tablets. Jamie wanted me to take some with breakfast, some after training, and some at different times of the day. As well, he handed me a bottle of the biggest vitamin B pills I'd ever seen in my life. They looked like they were made for horses. Jamie told me to take two of them every day. I carefully wrote down this new concoction at the front of my diary.

Two days later, I won the first race of the indoor season, at the Toronto Sun Maple Leaf Indoor Games, with 5.82 in the 50-yard dash. It felt like every muscle in my body tingled. My synapse, or whatever, was firing on all cylinders. I looked it up and found that the word synapse is a verb, though Jamie had used it as a noun. To synapse means to transmit a nerve impulse; perhaps he meant that my synaptic cleft, where the transmission and reception of impulses between nerves takes place, wasn't firing. At least the word was in a dictionary. Maybe Jamie did know what he was talking about.

On the snowy morning of January 30, 1988, before I left for Europe later that day, Tony and I went to see Dadushka Grisha laid out at the funeral home. It didn't bother me to look at him, his head resting on the white silk pillow in the casket. I was not afraid. Dadushka looked peaceful to me, as though the cares of the world had fallen away to reveal the inner man, a man who knew he was loved.

It reminded me of my great-grandfather, Jacob the fisherman. I had felt no fear gazing at him, either, lying on his bed of ice.

14

Running on Empty

We had been in Spain barely a day when BJ, Desai, Mark, and I arrived back at the hotel after dinner and the desk clerk waved us over. He handed us a sheaf of telephone messages, all from Waldemar Matuszewski. This was odd, considering Waldemar was traveling with us. The message was that he wanted us to meet him in his room that evening at ten o'clock sharp.

When we arrived, Charlie was already there, looking frosty, and Larry was slouched in a chair by the TV. Waldemar got us all seated and launched into what sounded like a prepared speech. It became obvious what he was after: 5 to 10 per cent of our earnings, preferably 10. No one spoke for at least a minute. We were shocked.

We estimated that Waldemar must be making about $78,000 per year, between his salary from the Canadian Track and Field Association and his separate deal with Mazda. And BJ had given him a $5,000 bonus the year before. That's a lot of money for a masseur, no matter how good he is. We all started talking at once, angry at this display of greed. I pointed out that if we gave Larry 20 per cent, and Waldemar 10 per cent, surely Charlie was worth 15 per cent. Someone else said that Astaphan had been pitching for a percentage, too, which was news to my ears. "Pretty soon, no p-p-per cent left," Ben said.

We eventually worked out a deal whereby Waldemar would get $350 per meet, to be taken out of our combined earnings. Waldemar accepted it, grudgingly. During the entire exchange, Charlie said nothing. Later he told me that BJ cut Larry's percentage down to 17, in light of the new developments. I saw a hard look in Ben's eyes that I hadn't noticed before.

The next day, we left for West Germany, and it was there, during one of my restless nights, that the vision appeared for the third time. It was shortly after midnight. I wanted to shout, to scream, to frighten it away, but it hovered above me, closer than ever before with hateful eyes fixed in a gaunt face. I struggled with my invisible bonds. And then, a shadowy hand rose up and slapped me, hard, across the face. The vision instantly disappeared. Air rushed into my lungs like a sob. I lay awake until dawn.

Despite my ragged nerves, I didn't do too badly in the meet that day, coming second in the 60-metres. BJ ran in the men's heats and injured himself in the final. It was inevitable. We all knew he'd been missing too much training. The celebrity circuit was taking its toll. There were too many nights out on the town and too many pretty girls vying for his attention. Larry had us locked into touring until February 18, however, and we had to keep going. The next stop was Genoa, Italy, with a ceremonial trip to the mayor's office and dinner at a villa with painted ceilings before the meet.

By the time we got home, I had decided against entering the National Indoor Championships. It would be the first time I'd missed them, except for the year I had Sasha, since the beginning of my career. I simply had no energy, no will. And I felt a nagging pull to get on with the other parts of my life. I went grocery shopping with Tosha and hired a housekeeper. The house was too big for Tony to handle on his own. I visited Tony's store – he called it Fashun 420 – and admired his renovations. He persuaded his father to let him expand the store into an adjoining space. They had remodeled it into an attractive boutique. His father had re-mortgaged the building to help pay for the renovations, and Tony began to buy from bigger suppliers with better-quality shoes. The bigger suppliers demanded payment for merchandise up front; you had to earn a credit rating with them. The business was doing well, though I worried about the heavier debtload.

My mind just wouldn't focus on track, even when I returned to York for workouts. One day, I slid down the banister at home for fun and cursed myself for bruising my hamstrings. I had never done anything so irresponsible.

I wasn't the only one goofing around. BJ and Desai took off for a week's holiday in St. Kitts. We were surprised to see Jamie pop up at York one day, while they were down there. He said that he had been over to the European Championships to see the Italian runner Pierfrancesco Pavoni. Pavoni had trained briefly with Charlie during the indoor season, and Charlie had introduced him to Jamie.

Jamie told us that BJ was getting treatment in St. Kitts for the hamstring he had injured in Germany. The treatment was something new and exotic with a machine called a biomatic. It was supposed to heal tissue painlessly, something like a portable laser. He told us the name of the physiotherapist who took the machine to St. Kitts: Jack Scott. I didn't think much about it at the time; Jamie was always bragging about the people he knew.

By Easter, the newspapers were full of headlines about the showdown between BJ and Carl Lewis. Larry had managed to pull off an arrangement unheard of in track and field. Lewis and BJ were squared off against one another in a 100-metre dash to be held in Tokyo. As the world's fastest human, Ben was allowed to choose the track he preferred. For this special, pre-Olympic duel, they each would be paid $90,000. The date was set for May 13, 1988. Little kids began to sneak into the training center at York, just to see Ben. He wowed them, stepping out of his Porsche in his sunglasses and gold chains. The kids all wanted his autograph. It was as though BJ and Lewis were world-champion boxers, not sprinters.

Jamie arrived, again unannounced, at York while Ben was in Japan. Charlie and Waldemar had both gone with BJ; they were getting paid $25,000 each for their services. I was getting a massage from one of the assistant coaches in a cubicle when I overheard Jamie talking. He said that he couldn't understand why BJ didn't see that Charlie and Larry were just after his money. Why, it was obvious, he said. They'd dragged him off to Tokyo for the money when he should be concentrating on preparing for the Olympics in Seoul.

I don't know who Jamie was talking to. Perhaps he was simply devious enough to make sure his remarks were heard by those of us behind the curtains in the cubicles. But I was enraged. To me, Jamie had finally shown his true colors. I knew that he, too, was getting $25,000 for the race in Tokyo. And no one had "dragged" Ben anywhere; he'd followed the $90,000 like a bloodhound. BJ lost the race in Tokyo. He stopped halfway down the track. His hamstring had given out again. This time he actually ripped the muscle.

Perhaps it was a mistake, but I told Charlie about Jamie's accusations when he got back from Tokyo. He was grim-faced, though he told me not to worry about it. BJ was satisfied with his money from Tokyo. Mazda had presented him with a car, as well as the cash. At the inquiry, Dubin was curious about the car, because BJ said that he gave it to Charlie, as a bonus. Dubin was after bigger fish – he wanted to know how Ben had managed to withdraw $100,000 from the Athlete Reserve Fund to buy a car – so he let BJ's generosity pass. I knew better.

This business of the Mazda was the first sign that BJ had become infected by greed, too. The truth is, he sold the car to Charlie, on the spot, in Tokyo. Charlie handed over $20,000 of his $25,000 fee, so BJ came home with not $90,000 but $110,000 in his shoulder bag. Later, when it came time to take delivery of the car, BJ haggled with Charlie and didn't want to sign over the papers.

Two days before we were to leave for the scheduled training camp and meets in Spain, BJ told Charlie and Larry that he didn't want to go. He said he wanted to go to St. Kitts instead. The only reason the Mazda club was going to Spain, BJ said, was because he, Ben Johnson, had been dangled in front of the meet organizers as the star attraction. Without BJ, the club would not get the deals for accommodation and facilities. Larry tried to mediate. He said the only reason Ben was getting such huge fees was because the Mazda club provided a strong package of performers – Mark and Desai held Canadian and world records, I was fourth fastest in the world.

Ben exploded. He was sick to death of supporting all the hangers-on, all the newcomers trying to make a name by their association with him. Charlie reminded him of the years the club had brought him along, when he was a newcomer. "Don't be down on the new kids," Charlie said quietly.

"Fuck 'em," BJ answered.

We didn't see BJ again until we arrived for a meet in Padua, Italy. We had been everywhere in Spain by then, fulfilling the agreements already negotiated by Larry – Malaga, Seville, Madrid. Mark and I both were suffering from bursitis, but there was no way we could back out of the meets, not with the stunt BJ had pulled. One day in June, I could barely walk, the pain was so bad. Somehow, Mark and I got to a drugstore, and over the next few days we each injected

3,000 milligrams of Butazolidin. "If this doesn't work, I'm finished," I wrote in my diary.

Tony brought Sasha over to Spain for a one-week holiday. My sweetie loved the beach. We couldn't get her out of the water; we had to tell her the beach closed at night to get her to sleep. Tony nearly had a heart attack one day when he and Sasha were at the hotel in Malaga. One second she was with him; the next she had disappeared. He searched the lobby, behind all the pillars and plants. Just as he had begun to panic, a friend who was traveling with them found her on the second floor. She had gone to play hide and seek.

The team arrived in Padua on June 12 for a meet the following day. Lo and behold, BJ showed up, with Jamie in tow. BJ was there for a one-day promotional shoot for Diadora, a fancy athletic-wear firm. BJ was apparently supposed to wear Diadora clothing at the meet, but he and Jamie strolled into the press conference wearing safari jackets and jeans – the favored outfit of islanders. They had a great time up there, laughing and joking for the cameras and the reporters, but Charlie told me that the Diadora representatives were upset that BJ hadn't worn their clothing. Ben's behavior appalled us. He seemed to be an entirely changed person. When Larry suggested that he accompany BJ and Jamie to Venice so he could talk about business, Jamie went into a sulk. Eventually, Larry went along.

This display of bad behavior was sickening, but the last straw for me happened when BJ made a remark about Charlie. Charlie came into our hotel with a shopping bag on his arm. He had recently started dating Angie Coon in Toronto. I could see that he'd fallen head over heels for her, and he wanted to look sharp. He must have thought, what better place to buy nice clothes than Italy? He walked through the lobby, and BJ turned to Desai and said, "You see those clothes he just bought? Those pants? They're mine. He bought them with my money."

When Desai told me this, I was speechless. How could he say that about Charlie, who had worked so hard to get him where he was today? Without Charlie, there would be no Famous Mr. Ben Johnson, the World's Fastest Human. I remembered when Charlie used to give BJ money to buy breakfast. I didn't speak to BJ until it became necessary during the preparations for Seoul.

One morning at breakfast, before the meet in Padua, we were at a table in the hotel restaurant when Jamie stopped by to deliver some pills. He passed them out by the handful, and most of the guys, including Ben, washed them down in a few gulps with their orange juice. Not one of us really knew what the hell we were taking anymore. Jamie gave Mark and me different pills. They were orange. Jamie told me later that it was Protensin, or something like that. Guaranteed to give a kick, just like that time my muscles fired me all the way to first place in the Maple Leaf indoor meet. I took it.

It gave me a kick, all right. I came first in the 100-metres, though with the unremarkable time of 11.41, and I felt like I could run a mile. Then my heart started pounding unnaturally, as though it would flap through my rib cage. It scared me badly; I couldn't get it under control. Mark told me he had the same problem. We suspected that Jamie was experimenting on us, giving us the pills before he tried them on Ben.

I suppose you might wonder why, with all the doubts I had about Jamie, I kept taking pills and injections from him. I was under enormous pressure to perform in the months leading up to Seoul and I knew I was running on empty. My motivation was confused. I was running to pay bills, and I had to keep running, no matter what my body told me. Our schedules were so tightly packed that I wouldn't have had time to try to sit down and assess my drug program or find a new doctor even if I had wanted to. And Jamie had been treating me since the fall of 1985, when I came back after having Sasha. I had made a successful comeback; surely his drug program had something to do with it.

I mistrusted Jamie for his greed, which seemed to be so obvious that it could easily be handled. I also mistrusted him for being two-faced with Charlie. One minute he'd be perfectly pleasant with Charlie, the next minute he'd be spreading rumors that Charlie was after Ben's money. But other people don't always follow the same code of conduct as I do with regard to friendships. I am an extraordinarily loyal person.

We continued on our tour and arrived home on June 30. Charlie had been told that Canada intended to implement random doping controls as of June 30, so we made an anxious re-entry. As usual, not much came of it. By the end of July, Charlie and Angie got engaged, and Tony and I gave a party for them. Our lives settled down and I got in some decent workouts at York. By August 6, I won the 100-metres with 11.01 at the National Outdoor Championships in Ottawa. I started to get excited about Seoul.

We left for a pre-Olympic tour of Europe on August 8. Every precaution was taken to ensure our best performance. We flew business class to Italy, so we wouldn't get cramps sitting in the narrower economy-class seats. I drank gallons of water, to avoid getting dehydrated on the trip. I canceled out of the first meet; it was scheduled too close to the big meet in Sestriere, a ski resort in the Italian Alps. All the runners from East Germany would be there, as well as Evelyn Ashford of the United States. It would be an excellent competitive field.

I was 45 metres into the 100-metre race when my hamstring gave out. Just as Ashford had done years before in Helsinki, I dropped to the track and had to lie very still while they applied ice. Ashford, who won the race with 10.94, came around later and shook my hand. And why not? We were forty-three days away from the Olympics. If my injury was serious, I might not make it. Ashford wouldn't mind one less competitor. I prayed that it was only a cramp and went to the swimming pool to kick behind a flutter board.

It was in Sestriere that the bombshell dropped on the subject of Jack Scott. Jack Scott and his magic biomatic machine. Jack Scott, in St. Kitts, treating BJ. We found out that Jack Scott had been Carl Lewis's physiotherapist for years. I chuckled to myself, figuring him to be one of those guys who attach themselves to the big names in track, like groupies. It fit my idea of the crowd Jamie liked to hang out with. Charlie, however, was ashen. We wondered if Jamie had told Scott about his method of treating BJ, about his customized drug and vitamin program. About BJ's use of steroids.

We went on to Zurich, and I threw everything in the book at my hamstring: anti-inflammatory cream, ultrasound, DMSO, Hepathromb, the muscle stimulator, interferential treatment, and a special visit to a private clinic for laser treatment. On August 17, I ran in the 100-metres. I came eighth, dead last, in a dismal time of 11.52. The hamstring would not heal. There was no point to going on, not if I had any hope of competing at Seoul. I got on a plane and flew home.

The rest of the team arrived back in Toronto a few days later. It was August 25 and the countdown to Seoul had begun; only thirty days to go. Jamie called to tell me that he had come up with a new program, something that would get me through the month and help to heal the hamstring. He told me to immediately go on a regime of a quarter cc injections of estragol and gave me a prescription for Moduret, a diuretic that would take the water out of my system. I was anxious not to gain too much because, at 138 pounds, I was close to my ideal running weight.

He also offered to sell me a bottled concoction of vitamin B-12 and the latest thing on the market, Protropin. I'd heard about Protropin. It was a synthetic human growth hormone. Jamie's reasoning was that the growth hormone would help to offset the muscle-building effect of estragol. He thought perhaps I'd hurt myself because my muscles had become so much stronger than my tendons and ligaments. The growth hormone would work to build up those tissues, in conjunction with the muscles. What's more, human growth hormone still couldn't be detected in doping tests. Jamie said he'd been treating BJ with the same mixture. I paid him $1,000 for ten cc and went on my way.

On the hot, muggy afternoon of August 31, I almost passed out on the track at York. I had never fainted in my life, so I didn't understand what was going on. In the blazing sun, a darkness began to push in at the corners of my eyes and my legs buckled. I had just run a 200-metre special endurance, and I had to lie down. I felt very, very ill.

The growth hormone had, again, given me an attack of low blood sugar, hypoglycemia. Jamie immediately gave me strict instructions to improve my diet. For the next month, I was to follow his menu religiously. Every day at breakfast, it was two boiled eggs, two slices of whole wheat toast, yogurt, and a small container of fruit. At midmorning, one apple, pear, or nectarine, or a quarter pound of grapes and more yogurt. For lunch, two slices of whole wheat bread, one or two boiled potatos, and the dreaded steak tartare. For dinner, steak tartare again, with the occasional substitution of broiled chicken or fish. Before bed, a protein shake of eight ounces of milk, one egg, and a tablespoon of honey. No deviations. I followed his orders.

Tony and I had a barbecue party at home for Sasha's third birthday the day before I left on the long trip that would take me to Vancouver, then Tokyo, and, finally, Seoul. It was a lovely day in the sun, under the dappled shade of the maple trees in our yard.

Sasha basked in the attention, and I adored her for it. I had just enrolled her in preschool, to start September 22, and I knew she did not have many baby days left. We took some silly pictures that day, of Tosha in an apron at the grill, Sasha wearing a paper hat. Even Olive got in on the act, clowning around, and all of Tony's family was there. There is no more pleasant sight in the world than a happy three-year-old, with birthday cake crumbs spilling down the front of her dress.

By September 16, we were in Seoul.

The next day Ben was supposed to carry the Canadian flag in the opening parade, but he didn't even march in it. Charlie's orders. Charlie didn't want his sprinters doing any useless marching in the opening ceremonies. "I'm here to win the gold medal," Ben said. "We'll look at it after next Saturday and decide who's the better man, who made the right decision."

The athletes' village was a sterile, godforsaken place. The developers had chopped down every tree and thrown up concrete boxes that were sure to become slum housing afterward. Someone had the bright idea they might turn a profit and sell the units as condominium apartments, but it would surely be a dreary place to live.

We always ate at the cafeteria in the compound, because we were nauseated by the prospect of eating in a restaurant. The Koreans eat dog meat, and you can't be sure what you're getting. One day, I saw a man walking into the compound with a German shepherd on a leash, and I wondered whether the dog was a pet or the man's take-out lunch. We made some jokes about that.

Joking aside, the business of what to eat was a serious problem for me. I certainly couldn't get the steak tartare that Jamie had been forcing me to eat, and I wouldn't have trusted any kind of raw meat anyway. I did my best with the cafeteria food. Desai tried to help. He walked up to the little Korean fellow serving food at the cafeteria and pointed to the stew behind the glass. "Woof-woof or moo-moo?" said Desai. The Korean flashed a broad smile. "Moo-moo," he said. This had us on the ground, laughing, but I was relieved.

Ben had taken one look at the athletes' village and hightailed off to a nearby hotel. He had his mother with him and a few other family members, and he moved them all into the Hilton. Ben decided against moving Waldemar to the hotel, and he stayed behind in an apartment-like unit at the compound. Ben raged against Waldemar when he went to massage Ben and asked to be reimbursed for the eight-dollar cab fare. "Don't come back, then!" Ben shouted. Interestingly, Ben ran into Charlie at the Hilton and remarked to him that he was sick and tired of complaints. Ben told Charlie that he planned to fire everyone – Jamie, Larry, and Waldemar – after Seoul.

Perhaps Ben had begun to come to his senses; perhaps he simply thought he didn't need anyone anymore. At the Dubin Inquiry Ben talked about the annoyance he felt at being a meal ticket to some of the people around him. His credit card bill at the Seoul Hilton Hotel amounted to $27,000.

Ben had his problems, I had mine. I was in serious physical trouble. The change in my diet was disastrous. I was getting dizzy spells. And the hamstring injury was flaring during workouts. Strangely, Jamie gave us all another diuretic to take. We had stopped taking drugs of any kind on September 5, in order to leave plenty of clearance time. In my case, with my first competition, in the 100-metres, on Sunday, September 25, I had allowed for nineteen days as I had been instructed, including the half-day I lost between Seoul time and Toronto's Eastern Daylight Time. I couldn't understand why Jamie thought we needed a diuretic, but I was glad to take it because for some mysterious reason my weight was creeping up. Every morning, I went to the scales in the weightlifters' compound and weighed myself. Every morning, I weighed another pound or two. I was getting bigger and bigger and my sciatic nerve was hurting again. By September 21, I weighed 151 pounds. This was terrifying. I couldn't understand why this was happening – all my experience told me I should be dropping weight, not gaining it.

Ben was scheduled to race the men's 100-metre final at 12:30 P.M. on Saturday, September 24 (11:30 P.M. Friday, September 23, EDT). He won, as we knew he would, in 9.79 seconds – a world record, and the Olympic Gold Medal. Carl Lewis came second, with 9.92. As BJ crossed the finish line he raised his arm and defiantly pointed a finger to the sky, a gesture that Charlie later said might have added a hundredth of a second to his world-record performance.

Ben's mother, who watched the race from the stands, jumped up and shouted, "He's a good boy! He's a good boy!" That evening, I wrote in my diary: "Ben is outrageous, now he is set for life." Ben's run made front-page headlines around the world. In Canada, *The Globe and Mail* report began: "It is Ben Johnson's Olympics." Years later, it probably will still ring true, but for all the wrong reasons. I went to bed early that night, in preparation for my own race the next day.

The first round of the women's 100-metre race was scheduled for 11.35 A.M. on Sunday, September 25, Seoul-time. I came third, in 11.44. To stay in competition, I had to come in the top four of the next round, scheduled for 1:40 P.M. (The difference in time meant Tony had to turn on the television back in Toronto at 12:40 in the morning.) By 1:41, it was all over. I finished fifth, down the track, in 11.27. My muscles had died on me. Part of me felt like a corpse. My old friend Flo-Jo went on to win the gold in the final in a spectacular time of 10.54 seconds. But I was out, finished. I went looking for Charlie's shoulder, as I had so many times before when my grief was more than I could handle alone.

I couldn't find Charlie, which was odd. And then I heard an ominous rumor. After Ben's race the day before, BJ had to pee in a bottle in front of an examiner for his routine urine test; a perfectly normal procedure. But the story was that just before the test, Jamie had hurriedly sent Ben a mixture of honey and vinegar to drink. Why would he do that? None of us could come up with an answer. Perhaps Jamie was just being extra careful. I set out again to find Charlie.

I never found Charlie. On my way to the athletes' complex, I saw Waldemar walking quickly along with Diane Clement, the manager of the Canadian team. I called out, asked them if they had seen Charlie. Waldemar shouted that he'd heard that Charlie had gone to the local hospital. They didn't stop.

I thought maybe Charlie had taken ill and gone to the hospital with a case of food poisoning or something. Or, maybe he was having trouble with his teeth again, which had happened before when we were on the road. No one seemed to think it was serious and I was too depressed after my disqualification to pursue it. I went to bed.

The next morning, I hopped onto the elevator to go downstairs for breakfast at the cafeteria. Jillian Richardson, another member of the team, was on the elevator, and she also told me she heard that Charlie had taken ill and gone to the local hospital. We drifted on toward the cafeteria, chatting, when Jillian said that she had heard another rumor that there might be a problem with Ben's urine sample.

"Where did you hear this?" I said.

Jillian shrugged and said she had heard it from her coach, who heard it from Diane Clement. Suddenly, I couldn't breathe; I knew the rumor must be true. Diane is the wife of Dr. Doug Clement, the team physician. Dr. Clement would know if there was a problem with Ben's urine sample. I tried to appear calm to Jillian, but inside I was screaming. Somehow, I had to finish breakfast, then shake Jillian and get to Mark and Desai with the news.

When at last I finished whatever was on my plate, I raced back to Mark and Desai's room and pounded on the door. Mark was there, alone, sitting on the end of his bed. He'd been up all night.

I told Mark what Jillian had said. Mark's shoulders slumped. He told me that he had left the compound Saturday night to go over to the Hilton. He wanted a half-decent meal for a change and Ben was in an expansive mood after his victory. Mark figured he'd stay over at the Hilton and leave straight for his semis in the hurdles at the stadium on Sunday. Mark said he was in Ben's room in the morning when there was a loud knock at the door.

Jamie was standing there. "Charlie wants to talk to you," he said.

Ben waved him away, "Yeah, yeah, later."

"Now," Jamie said fiercely. "Right *now*."

Ben got up and followed Jamie out of the room. Five minutes later, he was back and, without a word of explanation, he packed up every bottle and pill he had in the room, every vitamin, mineral — everything. He stuffed them into a paper bag and then he and Mark left for the track.

Mark hadn't seen Ben since. He was having a terrible time getting ready for the final of his own race, the 110-metre hurdle. (Later that day, he made the finals but finished seventh. Mark was one of the best hurdlers in the world; he should have won at least a bronze medal.)

I was uneasy but somewhat comforted by Mark's description of events. After all, if Ben had packed up all his pills and, presumably, handed them over to someone for analysis, it would quickly be determined that there were no banned substances among them.

And I knew that none of us had been on steroids since September 5. There was still no sign of Charlie, but, surely, if there had been a problem, he would have been there to deal with it. I went to the track after a short workout and spent a quiet evening with a few teammates, but it was the calm before the storm.

The next morning we were lounging around the unit – Tracey Smith, Molly Killingbeck, Angela Phipps, Katie Anderson, Rosie Eadie, and me – some of us upstairs, some of us in the living room downstairs, when Jillian Richardson burst through the door.

"Guess what! Ben tested positive!"

We were shocked. Stunned. Molly and I started to cry. The impossible had happened. My mind was reeling; there could be no rational explanation. Molly and I raced upstairs to Desai and Mark's apartment.

Mark didn't seem surprised. Desai said nothing. The four of us tried to figure out what had happened. I found myself repeating over and over that we *knew* the clearance times, we *knew* them, so how could it have happened? Finally, Desai said, "I think Jamie and Ben pushed it too far."

It was my turn to be silent.

When at last I found Charlie, he looked haggard. Carol Anne Letheren, the *chef de mission*, had gone to Ben's hotel room at three-thirty in the morning, while we slept, to personally retrieve Ben's gold medal. The International Amateur Athletic Federation had issued an automatic suspension barring Ben from all IAAF-sanctioned meets for two years. Jean Charest, the Canadian minister of sport, had already announced that Ben was banned from the national team for life. "Ben Johnson has embarrassed Canada and will never run again under our national banner," Charest said.

"How could this be?" I said to Charlie. "We knew our clearance times, Jamie gave us diuretics, Jamie gave us. . ."

"It was stanozolol," Charlie said.

"*What* was stanozolol?"

"Ben tested positive for stanozolol," he said.

"Winstrol!"

We had been taking estragol, not Winstrol. How could they have caught Ben for Winstrol? Charlie was certain, now, that sabotage was involved. Somehow, someone had tampered with Ben's test. Maybe someone had rubbed something into Ben's skin during the massage after the race. Something like spiked DMSO. Millions of dollars were at stake in endorsements, there would be millions of reasons to try to bring Ben down. Charlie and I discussed the possibilities.

Charlie said he wanted to go home. The mood at the athletes' village had turned ugly. Someone had strung up a banner in the courtyard that read, "From hero to zero in 24 hours." One of the Canadian distance runners had approached the Jamaican sprint team in the cafeteria and said, "You guys can have him back now." Everywhere we went, clusters of athletes would be talking in hushed voices about Ben and his teammates.

Molly and I helped Charlie get out of the village and on his way home. We went with him back to his unit, and the minute we opened the door, he was surrounded by coaches and other people from the Canadian team who had been waiting for him. Charlie was shaken; he pulled out a list of vitamins that Jamie had given him and tried to answer their questions. Molly and I slipped upstairs to pack his bags for him. We came back down and walked Charlie out of the room, then across the courtyard, three abreast, to the back gate of the village, away from the crowds of reporters.

A small group of Canadian runners watched us go. As we headed for the gate, Lynne Williams, one of the runners, shouted that Charlie had disgraced the Canadian team. I shouted back something obscene. I could feel tears of fury welling up; it was just like the old days in high school, when the cowards ganged up on someone, safe in their numbers and vicious in their taunts.

Later, I called Tony and found myself babbling, and weeping, on and on, about Ben, about the whole stinking situation, about sabotage, about how sick I felt. He listened patiently, then gently said, "Come home, Ange. It's over."

And it was.

Epilogue

In the summer of 1990, Ben Johnson was back in training, this time without Charlie Francis. He was still under suspension by the International Amateur Athletics Federation, though the suspension was to expire in September, 1990. As for whether BJ will ever run again under the national banner — Canadians were waiting for Sport Canada's reaction to the Dubin report, issued June 26, 1990.

As a result of his testimony at the Dubin Inquiry, Ben lost three world records. His 9.83-second 100-metre run at the World Championships in Rome was replaced by Carl Lewis's time of 9.92 seconds at the Seoul Olympics.

Dr. Jamie Astaphan was still practicing medicine in St. Kitts. On June 27, 1990, he was charged with professional misconduct by the College of Physicians and Surgeons of Ontario.

Larry Heidebrecht was working for a sports marketing firm in Phoenix, Arizona.

Charlie Francis married Angela Coon in the spring of 1989. By June 1990 he was working on a book of his own and coaching Angie in the hurdles. He remains a close friend of Angella and Tony Issajenko.

Angela Bailey, Desai Williams, and Mark McKoy all were back in training at the high-performance centre at York University. Mark's two-year suspension, for leaving Seoul without authorization, was to expire in January, 1991. His world record of 6.25 seconds in the 50-metre hurdles set in March 1986, stands.

Molly Killingbeck was employed as an assistant track coach at the University of Windsor. Tony Sharpe was employed as an automobile salesman.

Jean Charest had resigned as federal minister of fitness and amateur sport in January 1990. Gerard Mach had resigned in April 1989 as head coach and high-performance director for the Canadian Track and Field Association (now known as Athletics Canada).

In April 1990, Mr. Justice Charles Dubin was appointed Chief Justice of Ontario.

In the economic downturn of 1990, Tony Issajenko was forced to close the shoe store.

As a result of her testimony at the Dubin Inquiry, Angella Issajenko lost her 50-metre indoor world record of 6.06 seconds, set in January, 1987. It was replaced by East German Marita Koch's time of 6.11 seconds, set in 1980.

When Angella testified at the Dubin Inquiry, she was five weeks pregnant. On November 14, 1989, Angella gave birth to Natasha, her second child, a healthy baby girl.

Index

H

I

J

K

L

M

N